Tourism Planning
Concepts, Approaches and Techniques

Tourism Planning
Concepts, Approaches and Techniques

E.K. Murthy

ABD PUBLISHERS
Jaipur, India

ISBN : 978-81-8376-151-2

First Published 2008

ABD PUBLISHERS,
B-46, Natraj Nagar, Imliwala Phatak,
Jaipur - 302 005 (Rajasthan) INDIA
Phone: 0141-2594705, Fax: 0141-2597527
e-mail: oxfordbook@sify.com
website: www.abdpublisher.com

© Reserved

Typeset by :
Shivangi Computers
267, 10-B-Scheme, Opp. Narayan Niwas,
Gopalpura By Pass Road, Jaipur-302018

Printed at :
Rajdhani Printers, Delhi

PREFACE

Few industries have perhaps been as economically viable in the 21st century as that of tourism. With cheaper, faster and convenient modes of transportation and travel becoming the norm, interest and exposure to various cultures on the rise, and globalisation fuelling innumerable forms of human endeavour, it is a matter of surprise that tourism has proved to be one of the most profitable and booming economic sectors. With all the favourable factors clearly titled towards it, the interest and growth in tourism shows no sighs of abating.

Until the 20th century, travel and tourism did not find much enthusiasm or favour among the general populace. Much of it was due to the poor nature of roads, uncomfortable accommodation and expensive and inconvenient modes of transportation. However as technology improved and cultural, economic and aesthetic revolutions gradually gained ground, tourism became one of the most favoured forms of recreation, contributing to not just the entertainment of tourists, but also providing employment opportunities and promoting cross-cultural unity and harmony.

However, as mentioned before, tourism today is large-scale industry, and like any other enterprise needs all of which combine to make it what it is. The focus of the book therefore, is centred towards equipping readers with a well-rounded, comprehensive manual which book s into the basic concepts and processes of tourism, the principles which hold it, and all the rigmarole and paraphernalia vital to its functioning. Expounding on the theories and practices which are an imperative component of tourism, the book serves as a referral on which readers can rely on while trying to carve a niche for themselves in the tourism markets. The premise of the book rests on the experiences and insight of tour guides, tour operators, hospitality personnel, etc., who have immense experience in this field, which can be effectively used. With a pragmatic approach toward the working of the field, comprehensive content and an easy-to-follow style, the book should render itself to be of great service to all the readers.

E.K. Murthy

CONTENTS

Preface	*v*
1. Tourism Strategies	1
2. Tourism Growth	72
3. Sustainable Tourism	146
4. Promotion of Destination	190
5. Tourism and Air Travelling	206
6. Lodging, Staffing and Housekeeping	221
7. Product Development	269
8. Tourism Marketing and Planning	285
Bibliography	315
Index	317

CHAPTER 1

TOURISM STRATEGIES

Planning of tourism includes drawing up the future that can be acceptable to the local inhabitants and visitors. Without planning and controlling mechanism the .development of tourism may end by having social, cultural and economic distortions, which will be reflected in the relationship between tourists and local inhabitants. As soon as the tourism grows and expands, it brings the social and economical changes in the respective region. These can be positive as well as negative.

The tourism planners must to be sure, that tourism will give maximum positive impact for the municipality. The planning process is associated with the following points:

1. Developing of high-level tourism sector must not always be very expensive.

2. To encourage use the tourism either for cultural and economical exchange.

3. Distribute the economical gains from the tourism to the possible more local people.

4. To preserve the cultural and natural resources as the part of the tourism development..

5. To maximise the income of the foreign tourists for the stabilization of the payment balance.

6. To increase employment.

7. To help the peripheral regions increase the employment and prevent the outflow of the local people.

8. To increase the number of the "high income class" tourists.

Currently, the economical objectives are dominating in Latvia, however we should not forget others, especially, if want to develop long-term plan. After analysing several tourism development plans, and by taking into account the current situation, conclusions could be made that in the basis tourism plans divides in the three planning stages:

1. research and analyses;

2. conformity of the current and planned tourism activities to the social, economical and environmental goals;

3. the development system control.

Those three stages includes following tourism development planning steps:

1. The goal setting.

2. The evaluation of the current situation.

3. Setting the tourism policy and priorities.

4. The formulation of the strategy

5. The evaluation of the impacts.

6. The implementation of the policy and the projects.

7. The control and contingency.

The analysing of tourism plans and development strategy shows, that the tourism industry consists of three important and interdependent sectors:

— Business sector or entrepreneurs;

— Non - governmental organisations;

— Government (national, regional, local level).

The private and public sector has the different view on the tourism development. The entrepreneurs are focusing on the profitable projects. At the same time, the public sector has different criteria: to create working places, to increase tax income, to improve the infrastructure.

The government contributes in the tourism development for the political reasons, for example, the improving situation in some regions may impact the development of whole country. The government has the main role in regulation and supervision of industry by taking in force the respective legislation. Although government can participate in the planning process and often government or state is the owner of the tourism facilities or the land.

All tourism planning methods starts with the current situation analyse. Let us look at a research study on tourism development conducted in Kraslava region located in East–South part of Latvia. The analyse of the region started with the listing of the facilities and services – number and category supplied, others started with the economical analyse - number of employees, incomes, tax revenues.

Self-governments has defined priorities in their own territory using SWOT analysis done by employees of self –government, entrepreneurs, NGO's and active inhabitants. Participation of stakeholders in self-government planning process are very important therefore they feel responsibility of on going process and they can demand ideas of development. It is mean owner attitude of planning products. This is first step to create social dialog between politicians, entrepreneurs and public.

Participants of SWOT analysis workshops were politicians, entrepreneurs, peasants, pensioners, unemployed, doctors and representatives of library, school and culture houses. The matrix was used in self-governments for clarifying development priorities. Results of SWOT analysis show situation that tourism development in self-governments are set out as main priority of economical and social development in this region. 17 self-governments from 26 had accepted tourism development as opportunity for local development.

Tourism development in Kraslava region is accepted as crucial part of regional economy and important source for work places. It can help to solve various development necessities: economical impact, employment impact, impact of revenues and tax's impact.

However, there are a lot of weaknesses in the process of tourism development: the first, poorness and low level of income, the second, unemployment and lack of work places, the third, investors and entrepreneurs are not choosing border rural territories for their businesses because of big distance to the market and consumers, the forth, very limited number of local potential that can change thinking of branches in rural areas and want to start their own private business in another sector outside traditional agriculture.

Self-government sees tourism sector as main potential branch in this depressive situation. Tourism development is sun star from local level point of view. The main potential of tourism development are qualitative environmental without damage and pollution in Kraslava border district which is the main factor of tourism development. Self-governments think of tourism vision, but they don't speak about strategies how to implement and integrate tourism sector on their places.

Self-governments supports rural tourism and agrotourism development activities via development program of special supported regions. Politicians think that tourism will solve all problems in rural areas, but it is not true. Tourism has seasonality characterize and we need to think of sustainable tourism development approach. This means planning of tourism resources and capacity in each tourism object. Self-government must plan and create projects how to change and made more attractive strengths for tourists.

The *Demonstration project Tourism Development in Dubna Basin Lakes* has been implemented in June – July

2000 in three self governments of Kraslava district. The overall objective of the Demonstration project was:

— To demonstrate good examples of the lake management and development of facilities for tourists and local people to be used for recreation and relaxation by and on lakes;

— To facilitate the activities of local entrepreneurship related to tourism services;.

— To involve local governments in promotion of tourism development within the region.

The activities implemented include:

1. The recreation places and adjacent public services and utilities at the Lakes of Sivers, Dridzis, Auleja created, comprising swimming sites, car parking lots, camping sites, children playgrounds. Within the framework of the activity the clean-up and improvement of the places being done by the local entrepreneurs and unemployed people provided by local self-governments. The access roads to the places improved;

2. Recreation facilities in Dubna Basin public lakes being developed. It includes creation of boat landing places and purchase of (motor)boats for lake inspection/management and water cycles for recreation purpose;

3. The information signs at the main/local importance roads to Dubna Basin public lakes on the main cross-roads, the Nature Park and related places for tourism activities were installed and tourism brochures and fishermen maps were provided;

4. Information Centre in Kombuli was established and fully equipped to serve the needs of tourists for the connection to Internet and linkage to Kraslava Tourism Information Centre (TIC) and tourism information available on Internet. Further direct contacts with other tourism related agencies to be created later by the Centre staff;

5.   The experience exchange seminar was organised for
     heads of Latgale municipalities, TICs staff,
     entrepreneurs to share the experience.

It was EU Phare demonstration project of tourism
development, but other entrepreneurs of Kraslava district
use "Regional fund" established by government. Totally
from all "Regional fund" budget tourism projects had
received 6% and non-traditional agriculture 1%. Rural
entrepreneurs very often combine tourism activities with
non-traditional agriculture, for example activities from
Kraslava district, ostriches, vulnerary plants, gardens of
deer's.

Implementation of projects as well as use of the
existing resources and establishing of new enterprises of
the agro tourism and rural tourism might help to the less
developed areas in Latvia.

For determining of the most effective tourism type in
the complex planning process, the planners must analyse
not only the economical impact, but also a social,
cultural and ecological environment. All these aspects
must be taken in to account by establishing and
development of the best type of tourism.

Rural tourism could be one of the best types of
tourism in agricultural area. There are many reasons for
choosing the rural tourism.

—   Cultural factors - the development of tourism in
    country areas will enhance the local inhabitants to
    keep cultural traditions, specific for Latvia and for
    particular region;

—   Economical factors - the rural tourism creates
    additional income in traditional agriculture;

—   The rural tourism creates income for those, who get
    back their property at the countryside, however are
    not willing to engage in the traditional agriculture;

—   Social factors – the rural tourism gives the necessity
    to take care of environment Latvia has an excellent
    base for the rural tourism with its beautiful,
    unspoiled, various nature and rich folk traditions.

The good planning sets the needed result and then works systematically for the achievement of this result. The plan, which is set optimally, makes all the actions clear and detalized for achieving the strategy and for the satisfaction of the planning goals.

INTERNATIONAL TRENDS

The global economy is being transformed by forces of regional trading blocs, global alliances, deregulation, new technologies, the Internet and electronic commerce. It will be necessary to understand the powerful driving forces that will create the future if we are to realign and reframe the agenda for research and technology. Global shifts in the economy are driven by new waves of technology, political and social transformation.

Countries, institutions and individuals are faced with significant shifts in the global environment characterised by changing patterns of trade and competition, technological innovation, exponential growth of knowledge, and worldwide social concerns for 'quality of life'. Knowledge has become the core competency to create competitive advantage. In the global economy, business solutions require innovations tailored to these technologies. All these trends have ramifications for the tourism industry. At the same time, travellers are becoming more knowledgeable, more informed and demanding. Competition has shifted from improving productivity to value-added quality, flexibility and agility in the marketplace, and meeting customer demands anywhere, anytime with customised solutions.

Decisions are becoming more rapid and reaction times shorter, so that success will depend on one's ability to position products and services and to respond rapidly to customer needs. While knowledge and innovation are crucial to success, the global economy is also characterised by marked socio-economic disparities between developed countries and developing economies.

One-fifth of humankind living in the highest-income countries has 74% of the world's telephone lines, while the bottom fifth has just 1,5%. Whether people are connected or not impacts tremendously on their ability to benefit from or simply contribute to the 'knowledge society'. Both the South African and the regional markets are constrained by income levels as well as the skewed distribution patterns that impact on connectivity.

A key feature of globalisation is the mobility of information, capital and people driven by the restructuring of economic relations and competition. In responding to the strategic challenge calls for local initiative that is both innovative and flexible. The uniqueness of the local context provides opportunity to embark on innovative action.

The competitive advantage of local areas rests more within their own specific context with resources that are immobile and not that open to competition. Local communities are increasingly shaped by the interplay between what occurs at the local and global levels. As the world's largest industry, tourism development is incumbent on the outcome of global and local forces as they impinge on the economy, where tourism caters to the needs and interests of global audiences, but is also geared towards the cultural needs and leisure aspirations of local communities.

The challenge is to integrate the local with the global in a relational context. Within the global-local nexus, the goal is to strike a balance, reconciling different market needs to create landscapes appealing to visitors and local residents alike. Therefore it is crucial to place tourism in the context of the localities and the local circumstances in which it is embedded.

The localisation of culture and the concurrent globalisation of localities are happening simultaneously. What transpires is the intertwined nature of social, cultural and spatial processes. The general lack of alignment in the country's basic economic foundations — in human resources, technology, infrastructure and the regulatory environment — are bottlenecks to tourism growth.

Meeting the challenge requires a number of policy and strategy shifts towards becoming internationally competitive and socially responsive. There is growing evidence of a new paradigm in tourism policy to influence the competitive position of a destination under conditions of global competition.

In applying the pioneering work of Porter's competitive diamond cluster to the new tourism policies, Fayos-Sola takes on the challenge to translate the cluster into effective demand and strengthen the tourism industry's strategic position within the value chain. In moving up the value chain, a new dimension has now been added to the debate where 'staging experiences' has emerged as the next step in the progression of economic value.

Tourism takes centre stage in advancing from the service economy to the experience economy. It has become a fiercely competitive business. For tourism destinations the world overcompetitive advantage is driven by technology, information and innovation. Yet according to the *World Competitiveness Report*, South Africa ranked only 42nd among 47 emerging and developed countries. There is much room for improvement, particularly in indicators such as skilled labour, the brain drain, harassment and violence, unemployment, science and education, customer orientation, security and growth in direct investments. The low rankings are also influenced by the country's perceived weak international business orientation.

Let us examine the trends of tourism development in Africa which is one of the least developed region in the world. In the *Africa Competitiveness Report*, South Africa is outranked by six other African countries. Topping the list of issues of greatest concern to the business community in Africa is improved infrastructure, but a proper regulatory and legal framework is a prerequisite for infrastructure investment. Good infrastructure also makes tourism destinations more accessible. The reliability of policy is crucial to competitiveness and to attracting investment. In the final analysis, capacity to deliver will determine competitiveness. Africa's competitiveness remains an issue and optimism based on realism is conditional on good governance and good leadership. As far as securing a competitive position is concerned, the main obstacles for social and economic development relate to weak institutional structures.

The efficiency of public action is at stake. The roles become blurred and government will be hard put to contribute to competitiveness unless their powers and management processes are redefined. Cooperation with the private and voluntary sectors is a prerequisite for the efficient implementation of policy programmes.

Despite the tourism policy framework for South Africa and the Tourism in GEAR (growth, employment and redistribution) implementation strategy, the industry has not yet been able to deliver on the indicated targets. This concurs with a comprehensive analysis of the impact of tourism on the South African economy and the southern African region by the WTTC.

While the tourism industry has been in an expansion phase since the transition to democracy, it is now at the crossroads. The future prosperity of the tourism industry hinges on whether the gaps in applying innovative solutions can be bridged. The reality is that technology is developing rapidly. The gaps between the old laws that worked in the traditional market and the new cybermarket are not being addressed in a timely fashion. Also, integrating the issues into a regional context is in line with best practice trends.

Tourism is the leading economic driver for the millennium. The World Tourism Organisation (WTO) is calling on governments around the world to unleash tourism's job creation potential by improving information networks and capitalising on its human resource capital by incorporating innovation and investment know-how.

The World Travel and Tourism Council likewise provides general policy directions based on the WTTC

'Millennium Vision'. The WTTC estimates tourism's direct and indirect contribution at 11% of GDP. Travel and tourism are now the largest generators of jobs, accounting for about 11% of the global workforce.

A vision of a globally competitive tourism industry is the focus of the WTTC Report entitled *South Africa's Travel & Tourism-Economic Driver for the 21st Century*. The report assesses the size and impact of travel and tourism in the South African economy as it ripples through the economy and demonstrates the job creation potential of the industry. The analysis uses 'satellite accounting' to identify the direct and indirect economic effects of travel and tourism.

Buoyant forecasts for tourism growth in the third millennium are contained in the *Tourism: 2020 Vision*. The trends emerging are that tourists will be travelling further afield to long-haul destinations. The expected growth in demand to visit Africa at 7,5% over the next two decades is well above the average for the world as a whole.

Tourism worldwide is forecast to grow to 1,046 billion arrivals in 2010 from 672 million estimated for the year 2000, an estimated annual growth of 4,5% (WTO). The WTTC estimates that the value of tourism demand will increase from the current estimated US$4,5 trillion in 1999 to US$9,0 trillion in 2010. Africa's share of the global market is estimated at 26,2 million arrivals (3,8%) for 2000 and is expected to increase to 45,6 million (4,5%) arrivals by 2010.

Within Africa, tourist arrivals in the SADC region is expected to grow by 8% per annum to 22 million in 2010. As a trading bloc, SADC has the lion's share at 45,4%, which is up from its 14% share in 1994 (WTO). The current value of inbound tourism to Africa is $8,742 billion (1997), of which the SADC share is $4,064 billion or 46% (WTO). The dominance of SADC is expected to continue into the foreseeable future.

ECONOMIC IMPACT

The economic impact of tourism in the region is aptly demonstrated by its relative contribution to GDP, foreign exchange earnings and employment opportunities. Within the SADC countries, the relative importance of the three key economic generators varies from country to country depending on the importance of tourism in the economy.

Tourism's contribution to GDP in SADC (based on the tourism economy) is currently estimated at 7,1% and is expected to increase to 8,1% in the year 2010. South Africa (11%) falls in the category of countries in which tourism plays a significant and increasing role where a contribution of between 10% and 20% over the next ten years is expected, together with Tanzania (16,2%), Botswana (12,3%), Zimbabwe (11,1%) and Swaziland (10%). With regard to the rest of Southern Africa, the WTTC report predicts GDP gains in ten years or so, albeit off a low base.

The WTTC estimates that where linkages with other industries and economic sectors are strong, the employment multiplier generates a job in the tourism industry and a further 1,1 indirect job opportunities are created in the tourism economy. But establishing a well-integrated tourism economy takes time and requires significant outlays of infrastructure and superstructure with a commensurate high cost per job opportunity. Within the SADC tourism economy, employment is expected to increase from an estimated 3,4 million currently to 5 million in 2010.

As a region, SADC has the potential to benefit from tourism-related forex earnings and it is foreseen that by 2010, 42% of its business will be derived from international tourism, 33% from intra-regional personal tourism and 10% from intra-regional business tourism. Visitor and export earnings are expected to almost triple between 1999 and 2010, from $8 997,0 million to $24 285.6, million, where South Africa ($12 342,0 million) is quite dominant in absolute terms. According to the WTTC the value of tourism earnings is expected to more than double between now and 2010, from US$18 241,1 million to US$42 199,4 million. A significant increase is foreseen in respect of earnings derived from international tourists as compared with that from domestic travellers.

The SADC region has a tourism profile that is typical of developing regions. The main origin markets for tourists are the developed world, which requires, among other things, that the region's safety and security, crime and other disasters be carefully managed to minimise international tourism disruption. This reliance on tourism as an economic generator is expected to continue to increase over the next ten years, requiring careful management of the tourism system to ensure sustainability in terms of socio-cultural and environmental impacts.

The countries within SADC are well endowed with a range of attractions, primarily based on non-renewable natural and cultural resources, and therefore the sustainable management of resources is a key issue. Within the region there is a serious lack of data with regard to the provision of facilities and therefore it is not possible to calculate the supply-demand gap. The same applies to data with regard to other tourism-related businesses such as restaurants, tour operators, manufacturers of crafts and souvenirs, etc., which would provide many opportunities for local small-business development.

Infrastructure and Transport Systems

Good transport infrastructure is critical for the development of tourism in the region. Globally, the airline transport market has continued to expand and this trend is expected to continue. This growth demands improvements in airport and airline capacity as well in the efficiency of the civil aviation industry.

A 1997 International Civil Aviation Organisation (ICAO) report on air safety painted a bleak picture of the position in African skies, and the southern African region did not emerge unscathed. Air traffic control and safety at many regional airports are poor by international standards and require upgrading in terms of both equipment and staff. The problem areas require improved telecommunications infrastructure and satellite-based navigation.

The rapid application of technological developments will improve the current navigation and safety position. South Africa has taken the lead in installing navigational aids across Africa in identified danger spots. Improving standards of airport management and maintenance would ultimately bring the region closer to 'world-class' services levels. It entails being aware of and sensitive to the requirements of competitive world-class airports in a period of increased international tourism. One of the key challenges faced is improving telecommunications in the high-technology environment. This issue needs to be tackled robustly as a matter of urgency if tourism is to realise its expected potential.

The global convergence of technology is penetrating and supporting the tourism industry through an array of major technologies. The global increase in consumer demand for tourist products has provided one of the main driving forces in the development of a wide range of technologies.

Information is the backbone supporting tourism. Therefore, timely and accurate information relevant to consumers' needs is often the key to satisfying tourist demand. Within the fiercely competitive global tourism environment, prospective travellers are continuously faced with more information and options. The combination of these forces and the need for professionalism in handling the information supplied to the consumer necessitates the use of technology to gather, manage, distribute and communicate information. Over recent years, information technology has experienced an unprecedented degree of change. The Internet and e-commerce are increasing at a rapid pace and are fulfilling a vital support role in such activities as global connectivity and foreign business activity.

The application of information technology (IT) and telecommunications, as well as technologies specifically designed and developed for the tourism industry, includes the management of the various modes of transportation, travel distribution systems, the hospitality industry, and the recreation and entertainment components of tourism.

The use of IT technology in the management of ecosystems, wildlife populations and natural areas is becoming increasingly important. The implementation of various forms of IT in the industry is driven by both the development of the size and complexity of tourism demand and the rapid expansion and sophistication of new tourism products. Three main waves of technological developments established IT in tourism enterprises, from Computer Reservation Systems (CRSs) to Global Distribution Systems (GDSs). The WWW has the potential to eliminate expensive intermediary systems in working towards a network system.

The Internet has the potential to change the balance of power among consumers, retailers, distributors, manufacturers and service providers. Some may experience increase in power and profitability, others will experience the reverse, and still others may even find that they have been bypassed and lost their market share. In the case of air travel, airlines have a motive to bypass travel agencies, which take up profitable corporate business that airlines could easily handle directly, and which they could easily target given all the customer information they have.

Airlines operate flights and offer seats. CRS vendors, such as Galileo and Worldspan, maintain global inventory management systems and communicate inquiries and booking requests between airlines and travel agencies. Some players in the distribution channel for air travel are vulnerable to bypass and disintermediation. While airlines and passengers will always have a role, travel agencies and CRS vendors are less essential. It is likely that agencies will lose much of their easiest corporate business to direct distribution by airlines. Internet-based search agents can locate flights and lowest fares; these same services can be used to book flights and to generate tickets or e-tickets.

On-line search agents, tied to e-ticket selling, could be part of a strategy that would make it easy to attack established agencies. Airlines would start by developing systems for e-ticket selling and would make them available directly to travellers for last-minute changes.

Community-based tourism projects require accessible and effective communication in order to reach their target markets — also through Internet access. Information that entices the potential tourist to Africa is readily available in the tourism origin countries in the form of multimedia videos, TV documentaries, CD-Rom and the printed media. A number of films have captured the mood and enticed visitors to the African setting, for example 'Out of Africa' and 'Gorillas in the Mist'.

A joint venture between the CSIR's division for Roads and Transport Technology (Transportek) and Satour offers a new Tourism CD-Rom Series. This is an integrated approach towards packaging and marketing South Africa as a tourist destination. This holistic approach offers the end user such advantages as interactive functionality, which allows tourists to plan a trip for specific interests and needs and also allows them to book through the Internet from the comfort of their own homes.

The package is envisaged as consisting of three CDs, the first of which will contain general information about the country, augmented by video clippings, 360-degree IPEX photos, sounds and music. The second CD contains a comprehensive accommodation and booking database, and the third features an advanced trip planner, with virtual-reality models of, for example, Robben Island and animals of South Africa.

The explosive growth of multimedia and its impact on tourism is demonstrated in the diagram. The capacity of the Internet to become the main conduit of travel business for the future supplemented by electronic commerce is compelling.

Socio-political Factors

International travel and cross border travel could be facilitated by the concept of a UNIVISA. It would contribute substantially to the freer flow of international tourists. Perceptions of safety and security and daunting levels of crime, particularly in South Africa, is a serious constraint on the ability of the country and the region to reach its full tourism potential.

The Economist Intelligence Unit (EIU) analysed the impact of safety and security concerns on international tourism (1994). A critical understanding of this issue is necessary as international holiday tourism already accounts for 34% of tourism value in the SADC region and is expected to increase to 42% by 2010. The risk of having this growth disrupted or permanently retarded because of safety and security actions should be addressed by government otherwise the tourism industry and its potential for jobs are at risk.

According to the EIU study, tourism is a soft target for those wishing to achieve more general political objectives. Radically-inspired interest groups often choose to damage the tourism industry as a means of gaining political vantage points, such as the bombings at the Cape Town V&A Waterfront in 1998. More generally, crime damages international tourism by generating bad publicity that makes tourists feel insecure and induces them to cancel bookings or opt for alternative destinations.

Key uncertainties such as the economic, political and social factors have been analysed and South Africa has been benchmarked against the key tourism countries' strategic and/or foresight plans. In Canada, Australia, Scotland and Singapore, the focus is mainly on marketing and to remaining competitive. These top tourist destinations are aggressively realigning their tourism industry through strategies and plans to diversify products, upgrade infrastructure, and make optimum use of technology.

Technology is focused on promoting and enhancing competitiveness within the information and communications fields rather than exploring the full range of opportunities in a holistic sense. The tourism industry is supported by an array of major technologies, and the global increase in consumer demand for tourist products has provided one of the main driving forces in the development of a wide range of technologies.

Where foresight studies have been undertaken (Japan, Germany, the UK, the USA, the European Union, etc.) these have focused on technologies that could support tourism. This applies particularly to issues such as transport, information, communication and infrastructure. In the UK, the foresight process included the topic 'leisure and learning,' but this, like others, dealt only partially with tourism-related technologies. The concept of 'sustainable tourism' pervades best tourism practice and was also the outcome of a priority area identified by the sustainable environment foresight. While technologies have numerous benefits, they also pose socio-economic challenges, such as changing labour practices, employment, and social behaviour patterns.

Swot (Strengths, Weaknesses, Opportunities and Threats)

In an era of rapid and continuous change in the economic, political, social, regulatory and technological environment, a new competitive landscape has emerged. Software applications are transforming entire business models and stimulating the discovery of new products and markets.

While the canvas available to today's strategies is large and new, tourism stakeholders need to understand global forces, react quickly, and become innovative when defining their business models. The most prevalent and widely used tools of strategy analysis cover Strength,

Weakness, Opportunities and Threats (SWOT) analyses, industry structure analyses (five forces), value chain analyses and others.

Accelerating global trends and technological convergence are disrupting traditional industry structures. Tourism industry players will have to come to terms with the effect that transformation of technological convergence and digitisation will have on the dynamics of the industry. This calls for a new mindset.

Further, the impact of the World Wide Web and the Internet is just beginning to be felt. Stronger ecological sensitivities and the emergence of non-governmental organisations are also new dimensions in the competitive landscape. These discontinuities are changing the nature of the industry structure — the relationships between consumers, competitors, collaborators and investors. Increasingly, the distinction between local and global tourism business will be narrowed. Tourism businesses will have to be locally responsive and at the same time will be subject to the influences and standards of global players.

Globalisation is forcing tourism stakeholders to come to terms with new standards, a capacity for adaptation to local needs, multiple cultures and collaboration across national and regional boundaries. For this, speed of reaction is of the essence. Speed is also an important element in how fast a company learns new technologies and integrates them with those already in use. Increasingly, the focus of innovation has to shift towards innovation in business models.

Exploring the broad contours of the future we recognise the trends, the desire for mobility and travel, access to information; and the relentless spread of the Web. The problem is not information about the future, but interpreting it to gain insights about how these trends will unfold to transform the tourism industry and to identify new opportunities that may emerge.

The SWOT analysis focused on discerning socio-political trends, economic and environmental issues and new waves of technology. It identified the key issues. While there are many opportunities in the growing world tourism market to tap into and our product base complements global trends and market needs, there are serious implementation weaknesses.

Fragmentation and weak institutional capacity at all tiers are some of the real challenges. An implementation mode that will improve quality of life at the community level by expanding business and employment opportunities and capitalise on scientific and technological progress is the best option to explore. Creating the future requires alliances, networks, and partnerships, often also with competitors.

Matching the emerging technologies with the issues relevant to tourism in the seven focus areas provides a menu of opportunities to explore. A proposed approach that is a useful way to integrate the issues with the cluster of technology themes is by way of a matrix.

At the dawn of the third millennium, the Agenda 21 for Travel and Tourism will be the essential reference to becoming environmentally responsible and thereby more sustainable. The environmental limits to growth hold several important lessons for tourism. Following the Rio Earth Summit, the WTO, the WTTC and the Earth Council produced a draft Agenda 21 for the Travel and Tourism Industry.

In terms of the goals of Agenda 21, tourism is capable of providing a financial incentive for protecting the natural, cultural and social environment. The intertwined nature of the co-evolutionary process in an economic environmental system requires balance in the economic, ecological and equity paradigms. The goal in achieving sustainability is to embrace ideas of globalisation and localisation and to find a balance.

As part of a series of regional reviews of Agenda 21 for Travel and Tourism organised by the WTTC and its partners, the WTO, the Earth Council and delegates from 10 countries examined the economic and environmental patterns in Africa. They concluded that the best potential for job creation, poverty eradication and social development in the 21st century lies in sustainable tourism. In a consensus statement, they reiterated the challenge to create effective public-private partnerships, with Agenda 21 at their core, that would also benefit local communities. Reviewing a number of successful programmes for environmentally responsible tourism, it is evident that

— tourism can be a key element in poverty eradication and social development;

— partnerships among all relevant stakeholders are crucial to scope, shape and deliver tourist activities; and

— sustainability principles need to be in the vision, planning and delivery of all tourism development programmes.

The globalisation of tourism has engendered concerns over its effects on destinations, and particularly the impact on local environments, cultures and social systems.

A Charter for Sustainable Tourism (WTO 1995) incorporates the following criteria:

— Balancing ecologically sound, economically viable, and socially equitable tourism development;.

— The natural, cultural and human environments must be integrated in assessing the impacts on cultural heritage and local communities;

— Ensuring participation at all levels requires efficient cooperation mechanisms;

— Incorporating innovation is the real challenge in creating integrated planning and management instruments;

— By using ecologically honest pricing, a more equitable distribution of the benefits of tourism can be achieved;

— In technical assistance grants, priority areas such as environmental and cultural spaces should be targeted; and

— The creation of open networks for information, research, dissemination and the transfer of appropriate tourism and environmental knowledge and technology are prerequisites.

The progress in addressing sustainable environmental practice is notable, but there are still many challenges to be met in finding balance in sustainable tourism practice. There is still a way to go in creating awareness, but the incorporation of sustainable tourism development principles in a framework for development augurs well for ensuring sustainable practices in future.

There are strong linkages with the issues emerging from the Biodiversity, Environment and Agriculture and Agroprocessing Foresight Sectors. The opportunities emerging in this focus area include global network, multimedia and infrastructure technologies. In the digital economy there is an emerging infrastructure of networks that blurs the boundaries between sectors. The drive towards sustainable tourism development therefore requires integrated strategies.

It is well known that tourism's impact and linkages pervade a number of industrial and services sectors. Private business is crucial to driving the strategic positioning and implementation of competitive tourism and marketing strategies. Forging collaborative alliances is a pattern that will result in a dynamic interplay of capacity in strengthening strategic partnerships.

The WTTC scenarios and the policy recommendations that the study concludes will give a powerful boost to the proposal for stronger regional integration based on the concept of Transfrontier Conservation Areas and Spatial Development Initiatives (SDIs) as the engines for regional economic growth. Of the cooperative ventures in the region, Transfrontier Conservation Areas are among the most significant. These new corridors or tourism access routes will enhance the tourism appeal of the region. It intends to unlock economic and tourism potential in specific locations through the crowding in of public sector expenditure and private sector investment. The aim is to create environmentally sustainable nature reserves and sustainable jobs, grow the economy of the area, and contribute towards restructuring the ownership base in the economy.

A recently signed Memorandum of Understanding on Transfrontier Conservation Areas (TFCA) supports the establishment of a TFCA that will bring the parks of Gaza in Mozambique, the Kruger National Park in South Africa and Gonarezhou in Zimbabwe together under joint management, creating one of the biggest conservation areas in the world. The agreement recognises that ecosystems transcend national boundaries and recognises the need for cross-border cooperation in the conservation and management of natural resources for the benefit of the people and the region. The purpose is to promote biodiversity and socio-economic development in the area.

The necessity of embarking on an integrated tourism strategy is now appreciated by most role players. Various initiatives, such as the tourism cluster study, the tourism information management framework and others need to be integrated with the outcome of the Foresight insights. The opportunities in support of integrated tourism strategies catering for ecotourism development, cultural heritage and adventure tourism include multimedia, digital image technologies, experiential tourism technologies, virtual reality and digital museums.

Good transport infrastructure is critical for the development of tourism in the region. Globally, the airline transport market has continued to expand and the trend is expected to continue. This growth demands improvements in airport and airline capacity as well as in the efficiency of the civil aviation industry. The international tourist's ability to reach a desired destination from the origin market is dictated by international treaties and standards, particularly with regard to air travel, and this impacts on long-haul safety. Aviation safety is critical to compete in the emerging global economy. At the same time it will be catalytic for trade, investment and growth in the tourism industry.

With fierce competition prevalent in the tourism industry, a key issue is the provision of appropriate infrastructure to catalyse demand. The rapid increase in the number of frequencies into and out of South Africa has increased pressure on infrastructure. Air-traffic control infrastructure in airspace north of South Africa is acknowledged as deficient. Sufficient investment in navigational facilities (radar, VHF radio coverage, meteorological information), airports and airways are needed. The fleet airline age is also amongst the highest in the world. 'Moving South Africa 2020' determined the country's land, sea and air transport needs over the next 20 years. The project focuses on the structure, infrastructure and functioning of the South African transport system and advances solutions for the short, medium and long term. It also clarified responsibilities, while foreseeing the creation of separate agencies funded through user charges to deal with issues such as the construction and maintenance of roads and aviation safety.

In view of the need to develop a tourism infrastructure investment framework, DEAT and DBSA commissioned KPMG to identify tourism infrastructure development areas where future tourism potential was strong and the need for development clear. The priority tourism infrastructure investment areas identified the linkages between areas and focused attention on the tourist flows that take the visitor through a series of gateways, routes, staging posts, and distribution points to various destinations and attractions. Delivery will take place at the local level.

The methodology for developing a Tourism Infrastructure Investment Framework incorporated GIS. A spatial pattern emerged through layering factors, such as existing infrastructure, product strengths and weaknesses, current demand and supply, potential growth of products and demographic patterns. The strength of the framework lies in incorporating socio-economic issues and poverty indicators in identifying the tourism development areas. But the 'affordability' of the required infrastructure was not factored into the equation. The viability of an infrastructure requirement often stalls on this critical element.

Although the infrastructure base supporting tourism is good, it is highly polarised. This results in limited dispersal of tourists to other areas with potential. To maximise tourism potential, targeted investments in tourism infrastructure is predicated to leverage private sector investments into less traditional areas that have product strength and can satisfy future market needs.

The TIIF provides direction for investing in all the major elements of tourism infrastructure and also recommends maximising the use of sunken investment in a rail network thereby providing opportunities for the emerging market to become active in the tourism economy. This partnership approach provides a menu of opportunities by matching the requirements with potential partners. South Africa's banking and finance industry is not yet geared to meet the demands of small and medium-sized tourism enterprises. Two core impediments to financial services are a lack of economies of scale and a lack of good information.

Emerging technologies are providing new challenges in the provision of infrastructure. If tourism is to expand along a continuum into rural areas as well, there are several challenges to face and opportunities to capitalise on, such as effluent treatment and the provision of clean water, and using renewable energy resources to a greater extent.

The opportunities and possible applications in support of infrastructure and transport systems include infrastructure technologies such as smart-card readers, physical infrastructure: effluent treatment plants or effluent demonstrators. Other useful solutions include alternative transport such as faster rail transport systems to enhance travel in the SADC region.

In the human resources sphere, the development and nurturing of an attitude of friendliness, helpfulness and service are as necessary for the private sector as for the public. Teaching people to appreciate the potential benefits and responsibilities associated with the industry is a prerequisite for creating a culture friendly to tourism. The Hospitality Industries Training Board (HITB) is in the process of getting its Tourism Learnership Project under way. The skills need will be tackled by the new Sector Training Authority and a South African Tourism Training Institute. Both the HITB and the Travel, Education and Training Authority of South Africa (TETASA) are training facilitators rather than providers, promoting it as the key to improved services and quality levels. The Business Trust will spend R80 million on tourism education, facilitated by the HITB. The Reach & Teach organisation's Travel and Tourism Programme assists aspirant entrants to the industry and has also been instrumental in spearheading the introduction of travel and tourism as a subject in 65 pilot high schools throughout South Africa.

Tourism is essentially an activity led by local demand, and because it is locally driven, capacity to manage and implement at the local level needs to be strengthened. The division of responsibilities among the various government levels is being more clearly defined. At least three provinces, namely the Western Cape, KwaZulu-Natal and the North-West, have embarked on tourism implementation strategies.

The remaining six provinces are all on a steep learning curve and will benefit from the knowledge of the provinces that already have experience. Sustainable tourism development requires active involvement to translate the principle of 'learning by doing' into concrete action. Active involvement brings commitment to the lessons being learned. The key opportunities in support of human capacity building are emerging through multimedia, computer-based instruction and multi-channel distribution networks.

Tourism Development in Africa

Global realities and the inevitable demands of a location shape marketing strategies. The branding theme of a Tourism Renaissance will drive the marketing strategies on the basis of the vision of an African Renaissance. The image serves the purpose of promoting a memorable African experience. In their efforts to competitively market South Africa as a preferred tourist destination, it is not surprising to find Tourism South Africa (Satour) embracing the African experience in their mission statement, i.e. to make tourism the leading economic sector for sustainable development and social empowerment of all the people. Images used for marketing also serve as a guideline in the development of plans and policies. 'Striving for excellence' could be used as a tool to improve Africa's competitiveness in the global economy. A secondary but equally important purpose could be to strengthen nation building.

Global trends are being adopted everywhere and are moving to the stage where tourists now unquestionably desire experiences. Global tourism and local identity complement each other. Imaging strategies in the form of branding messages embody the overall vision of a place. Satour's slogan of ' a world in one country' not only conceives of a promise of value for tourists, but also creates a desirable experience in the global-local nexus. The integration of experience into the larger social system can result in a renaissance of indigenous culture.

South Africa competes with many other destinations considered 'long haul' by tourists. In 1997, the top 10 tourist destination countries attracted more than 60% of all international visitors. Europe is also the origin of most outbound travellers, with 40 million travellers moving on long-haul journeys to other parts of the globe. Long-haul tourists from Europe, America and East Asia amount to almost 100 million per annum. In all regions of the world, most outbound tourists are intra-regional or domestic. The high level of intra-regional and domestic travel is largely due to geographical locations, continental size and the diversity of tourist attractions. A focused production and marketing drive capitalising on the African Renaissance theme could draw far greater numbers of tourists.

The country's unique heritage and rich culture together account for 46% of foreign tourist motivations, second only to scenic beauty. African crafts and indigenous products using African lifestyle technologies could be used to brand the renaissance theme. There is an urgent need for niche operators to offer integrated products across all interest areas and to use process technologies for this purpose. The real value of cultural attributes and artefacts, namely their role in creating jobs and glueing societies together has not been properly recognised.

The African Renaissance challenges people to draw on its traditions, values and indigenous knowledge to make development more effective. The branding of products with the African Renaissance theme will go a long way towards stimulating local economic activity. The opportunities in support of African Renaissance branding include processing technologies for cosmetics, indigenous exotic foods, and beverages. However, marketing and investments in community-based tourism initiatives will matter little if soaring crime levels are not brought under control.

Socio-political stability and security are the necessary minimum, but not sufficient, conditions for tourism development. Safety and security are fundamental because even minor security incidents can have a major impact on the way destinations are perceived. Levels of crime and violence pose a major threat to the country's tourism industry. Crime, and the offshore perception of South Africa as a crime-ridden environment, will have to be tackled far more effectively. Both the perceptions and the realities must be addressed. International hotels are now required to provide a safe haven as part of the total experience.

South Africa has twice the international average number of crimes per capita. A Tourism Safety Task Group comprising representatives from government departments and other stakeholder groups is tackling a wide range of tourism security issues, including the use of more dedicated tourist police and the establishment of a database of tourism security intelligence.

The key challenge is whether South Africa will overcome external perceptions of safety and security as well as service delivery constraints and capture a growing share of the world's tourism market in the future. The safety aspects of travelling influence the selection of a destination and are therefore an important consideration. Safety and security issues pervade concern at a global level and influence repeat visits. The Tourism Working Group, like the World Leadership Forum, considers it a key strategic issue.

The opportunities in support of safety and security include global networks, improved encryption for safe cybertransactions and advanced identification systems. Information will be crucial to compete effectively in the global market place. At a strategic level, information on global trends, competitors, market opportunities are essential for informed decisions and to facilitate market-driven strategies. The Foresight collaboration aims to add value by identifying markets and technologies that can generate social and economic benefits for the country. Technology is the golden thread that runs through to create opportunities to spread learning and knowledge. In a bid to align with global destinations, Satour is currently upgrading its tourism information infrastructure. The planned website will improve on the current site by providing a showcase of South Africa, and it is envisaged to be at the forefront of website destination marketing in the global market place. This will be crucial to ensure strong growth relative to other global destinations.

Technology has made it possible for on-line reservations to increase dramatically, with business generated on-line growing at an unprecedented rate.

Much of the growth of ticket sales on the Internet comes from the Internet's ability to reflect modern lifestyles. The Internet acts as a catalyst to take basic brand strategies to full-fledged dialogues.

The Internet is tailor-made to host such dialogues, because it provides scope for marketers to integrate their interactions with customers and enables companies to discover and exploit the individual interests of the target audiences. Internet-based competition changes the meaning of prices. Auctions are becoming the basis for setting prices. The information infrastructure and software requirements of a hotel or an airline to cope with an auction-oriented pricing strategy are very different from the requirements of a fixed-price regime. Information infrastructure has emerged as an important source of competitive advantage and competitive risk.

From a tourist market perspective, destination information can shape market segmentation strategies. The expectation goes beyond this to the provision of information on trends and information about international and local tourism market developments as well as e-commerce and commercial marketing opportunities on the World Wide Web. E-commerce, whose value was expected to reach $1 trillion in the next three to five years, is ideally suited to small and medium-sized firms. Start-up costs for establishing a website are relatively less expensive when compared to opening a shop in a city space.

Steps have been taken towards creating an integrated tourism information management framework (TIMF) for South Africa. Finding a shared vision and a common focus is at the heart of the TIMF. A further goal of the TIMF is to contribute to the empowerment of local communities through information in order to enable them to become active and knowledgeable stakeholders and entrepreneurs in the industry. The whole TIMF process is based on strong public-private sector collaboration to ensure accountability.

The opportunities relevant to wider information technology applications include global network, smart cards, virtual reality and future web applications. In the quest for competitiveness, tourism takes centre stage and is moving up the value chain.

The rapid transformation in new technology, more experienced and discerning consumers and travellers, global economic restructuring and environmental limits to growth all augur for a new paradigm in tourism and technology. Competitive strategies are setting the stage and are prerequisites for ensuring that industry players and tourism destinations create competitive positions. While global economic and technology shifts provide new challenges for sustainable tourism development, however, they also offer new opportunities and have made open participatory processes essential for long-run success. The country is finding balance in sustainable tourism development. Competition and collaboration are needed for efficiency, innovation and customer satisfaction. Strengthening institutions and building capacities to deliver tailor-made services harnessed by new and emerging technologies are the catalysts to drive the tourism economy into the new millennium.

The sustainable development of a country's unique resource base and cultural heritage is a prerequisite for future tourism development. Governments and industry have to implement policies that spur the interaction of economic, technological and social change in a positive way as they prepare to respond to the challenge of the 21st century. The transition towards the information and knowledge economy and the process of globalisation, together with growing international interdependence, calls for value-added interventions.

Advances across a wide range of pervasive technologies are beginning to revolutionise the worlds of communications and entertainment, retailing, medicine, and agriculture, profoundly affecting the way we work, live and play. Information technology is transforming the way companies do business. IT as an investment will deliver value-added benefits. Among the benefits are improvements to infrastructure efficiency and new business opportunities made possible by new IT platforms. They include value-enabling technologies and value-creating business opportunities developed and deployed in the IT platform.

These opportunities include improvements in external and internal processes, tapping employees' and outsiders' knowledge and expertise and the creation of networked communities of customers and staff. Where the old platform was physical, the new platform is virtual: it is digital, global, interconnected, fast-changing and interconnected. We are currently in the midst of transition and this prompts new opportunities. The increased flexibility and speed with which opportunities can be pursued increase the value of investments in infrastructure, thus minimising the financial risk of pursuing new business opportunities. Moreover, technology enables people to work smarter, and information and knowledge can be used to create new products and services or to add value to existing ones, thus improving the company's competitive position.

CONCEPT OF SUSTAINABLE TOURISM

The concept of sustainability—in terms of desirable or acceptable change—and the ideas behind the life cycle of the tourist destination are closely related. If the destination gets stuck in the initial stage of the life cycle, the investments that are made in attractions and facilities for tourists are unable to trigger the social and economic change desired.

There are too few visitors, and the opportunities that tourism offers are not fully used. Tourism will stay a net cost for the destination as a whole. On the other hand, if growth in tourism is such that the quality and accessibility of attractions are compromised by excess demand, society in the first place and eventually even tourism itself suffer and change is no longer acceptable. The local society has come into conflict with its visitors, competing for the facilities and space they are both using. In that case, tourism, instead of delivering growth, may even threaten the society's continuity.

A number of tourism management strategies for destinations that face the problem of how to overcome the minimum limit to sustainability. So far, no attempts have been made to quantify the minimum level of sustainable tourism development. In the case of heritage cities, many authors have suggested that the maximum limit to tourism development, very much related to what is more generally known as the tourist carrying capacity, is most relevant.

It is within the context of the sustainability of tourism development and the tourism management strategy that belongs to it, that the results of this investigation should be interpreted. Despite the gloomy long-term prospects for the destination that blindly strives to become a tourist attraction, the development of tourism could undoubtedly contribute to the social and economic health of a destination, provided that three basic preconditions, described below, are satisfied.

The first two concern, respectively, the destination's image and the quality of its tourist product; the third concerns the expected effectiveness of tourism development in the long run. First of all, the destination must have an appealing image. There are destinations people are convinced that it is pleasant to be in and there are destinations where people think it is better not to spend any leisure time. The role of the image seems banal, but its importance has been frequently confirmed. How far the image interferes with the destination choice, and how far the images correspond to the quality of the tourist product that is actually offered, is hard to assess, but examples of the cliches that circulate are not so difficult to give. Indeed, whether the images that are circulating are true or not is hardly relevant. What really matters is their persistence. They are almost impossible to change.

Secondly, a destination must be sure to be able to supply a range of easily accessible and highly competitive tourist products, attracting enough demand to make good the efforts and investments needed for their launch. The competition on the world market of tourism is becoming so intense that the possession of natural and man-made resources alone is pertinently insufficient for a new attraction to join the ranks of established tourist destinations. Originality is a major strength, since curiosity is what drives most tourists; hence, copying the success stories of other destinations is doomed to fail. Moreover, the accessibility of the destination and that of its attractions proves to be essential for the competitiveness of the destination. Finally, the overall product offered needs to fit the image the destination already possesses or may want to obtain.

The third precondition concerns the effectiveness of tourism development efforts. Only if the development of tourism promises to be effective through the whole cycle can the destination proceed with its stimulation efforts.

An analysis of the strengths and weaknesses of the destination as far as tourist attractions and facilities are concerned, is indispensable in this context. If it has more weaknesses than strengths, the destination would be well advised to abandon the idea of tourist development in the traditional sense immediately. Such a destination will probably remain stuck in the first, not yet sustainable, stage of the development cycle.

If there are reasons to believe that both the destination's image and its product are appealing enough, and the development of tourism is theoretically feasible, an estimation of the possible benefits and costs becomes urgent. The local tourism balance, a comprehensive and systematic overview of the positive and negative effects that tourism produces, can be used for such an assessment.

Let us take the example of the Dolomite basin of Italy. A research conducted in this region analysed the data gathered for several municipalities operating within the

Dolomite basin in order to identify a homogeneous group among the different agro-territorial systems. As far as their geographical location, demographic and social characteristics, economic structure, natural and human resources are concerned these rural area manifest huge differences. Consequently, the spatial identification of specific areas becomes imperative in order to exploit the natural resources.

South Tyrol agro-territorial system: The South Tyrol agro-territorial system is a system that includes areas where the employment and income role of farming, forest and sheep breeding activities is still considerable. In the town council under study, in fact, the number of the people employed in agriculture covers an average of 16%. In this context rural economy has the connotation of a particular type of mixed economy where the percentage of the value added of agriculture is over 10%. It is a system characterised by a high average farm dimension. This is due to the presence of the institution of "maso chiuso" which has safeguarded this agricultural reality from the tendency of fragmentation due to inheritance laws. Human settlement is widespread over the territory, with a density of 38 inhabitants per square kilometre. The demographic structure has not deteriorated as the amount of the elderly is among the lowest. Income and consumption indicators, while higher than in the other two groups under study, have far lower levels than those of the Dolomite municipalities with a long-standing tradition of hospitality. The places examined belonging to this system do not present so far any tourist features. This is confirmed by the limited amount of holiday houses (only 12,4% of the Electricity board contracts are for non residents) and by the scarcity of recreational and sports facilities. It is worth mentioning, however, that Aldino is the only one among all the municipalities under study that possesses ski lifts and therefore the only one able to meet winter tourist demand.

Suburban Subsistence Farming Agro-territorial System: This is a system that develops in a linear manner along the roads that connect the major urban centres of the region. Inside it agriculture, characterised by small-size farms, has a vital function and it is necessary to safeguard it against the effect of urban expansion. If we consider the way of employing the soil we notice that in the areas under examination the percentage of fields and pasture land is 48% of the total of the agricultural area employed, while the areas used for seed is 16%. Vine growing is also considerable if we consider the two distilleries in the town council of Faver.

The agricultural environment is characterised by a low density of population - 54 inhabitants per square kilometre in the case studies, and by a considerable impact of the elderly. Finally, as regards the economic dimension, the municipalities of this group belong to a medium-size per-capita income and consumption range with a tendency to increase. The municipalities of this group, therefore, even if characterised by an agricultural economy, show appreciable growth and development trends. The problem of socio-economic and cultural marginality might be solved through the exploitation of the tourist potentialities of areas of naturalistic interest such as the earth pyramids of Segonzano.

Fringe Area Mountainous Agro-territorial System: This system is characterised by a demographic structure which has deeply deteriorated and by an extensive type of agriculture at a low added value, low level of mechanisation and with large-size farms which, as often happens in alpine environments, include wide pastures and woods. In this type of system we witness a progressive loss of importance of the role of agriculture with fewer and fewer people employed in the field; the active population is mainly employed in the industrial and tourist sectors of the surrounding areas. They are areas not only excluded from the tourist sector, but also unable to rely on other resources for their development and which undergo, therefore, situations of cultural isolation and socio-economic decay.

The per-capita income level is the lowest of the whole area under examination and as regards consumption there is the lowest rate of cars in proportion to the number of inhabitants (38,5%) and the highest rate of food consumption on the total of expenditure (14%). The high level of marginality of the municipalities of this group is testified also by the low demographic density (55 inhabitant per square kilometre), by the strong tendency to depopulation and by the high number of elderly people. On the whole, therefore, in these municipalities, differently from the other two groups described above, such factors as height and the morphologic features of the territory seem to have hindered growth and economic development, favouring processes of depopulation and marginalisation. There are, however, signs of recovery that might hint at a tourist and agro-tourist development.

The research used time series of tourism demand for the different municipalities in the three systems are used to try to identify whether sustainability of tourism is indeed an issue. It must be said that the statistics gathered concern residential tourism demand only; excursionists, an increasingly important phenomenon also in mountain resorts, are not included in the figures that we present. This means that total tourism demand is underestimated and that trends are but a partial representation of the municipalities' competitiveness.

The assumption on which the analysis is based is that these statistics of demand are helping us to classify the municipalities and systems according to the development stage of tourism development. Costs and benefits are varying over the destination life-cycle and that, as a consequence, the contribution of tourism to the local economy differs per stage.

Since statistics on costs and benefits, particularly at a local level, of tourism are difficult to find, only the dynamics that tourism demand contains offer a clue to what relationship there might be between tourism and the local economy, virtual or vicious.

It is the number of bed-nights and not of tourist arrivals that is closely linked to the positive and negative effects that residential tourism tends to generate. Because of the shrinking average duration of the holiday in general, the decline in the number of bed-nights locally only partially reflects a diminishing competitiveness.

South-Tyrol, Trentino and Veneto are important destinations of both national and international tourist flows. Especially the Veneto is a very diversified destination, it not only offers mountains, but coasts, art cities and spa resorts as well. While South-Tyrol and Trentino start to feel that their dependency from traditional mountain tourism market segments has become a handicap for their competitiveness, the Veneto is still experiencing growth in most segments. The three tourism systems considered have been largely founded on transformed or diversified farming activities. They all have the possibility to take profit of the recent tendency in tourism demand that favours natural environments, quietness and active holidays, aspects that agro-tourism in fact is able to offer the tourist. What is happening in practice is the subject of the following analysis.

The three municipalities in the South-Tirol System are, notwithstanding the differences in demand among them, touristically speaking the most developed of all. The number of bed-nights of San Lorenzo di Sebato arrives at almost 250,000 per year. La Valle and Adino remain far behind. Moreover, the curves of these last two municipalities is virtually flat; With global tourism demand increasing at a rate close to 4% per year, the number of bed-nights has stayed more or less constant the last decade. One would not expect these destinations to have tourist carrying capacity problems. On the contrary, they may not utilise their potentials fully.

The municipality of San Lorenzo di Sebato demonstrates to possess a more interesting pattern of development. It has known two periods of growth, one in the beginning of the nineties and a second, after a dip in

1993, in 1994 and 1995. More recently the tendency seems to point versus a decline. This may mean that the destination has reached maturity and that as a reaction to congestion problems and increasing costs tourists are starting to abandon it. The system as a whole appears to be very stable.

The system in Trentino contains three municipalities that are behaving more or less in a similar way and one municipality, Valda, that stays marginal in terms of tourism demand. Volumes of arrivals and bed-nights are much lower than of the South-Tyrol system. Faver and Segonzano know a turbulent development of tourism demand: They peak in 1995 to fall back below the previous levels of demand in 1997 and 1998.

Although development is cyclical one may suspect that it has been the devaluation of the Lira that altered their competitiveness abruptly but that their competitiveness decreased, probably also because they were not able to manage the rise in demand adequately.

Capriana's development of tourism demand seems to fit the life-cycle theory better. It knows a gradual growth until 1997 and a decline in 1998. It is still to be seen if this decline is structural and linked with maturity, or just a temporary dip in demand. More evidence is needed for a definitive judgement. But what emerges is a system that has entered, after a period of growth, a stage of decline.

The system in the Veneto region is facing the severest crisis. Again, two groups of municipalities can be identified. Those hardly touched by tourism –Cibiana, San Tomaso Agordino and Zoppè di Cadore- and those with a considerable yearly influx . For the first group of municipalities, tourism is and remains a marginal activity. It seems obvious that in these municipalities there is still much room for the development of agro-tourism, given the fact, of course, that the tourist carrying capacity of these municipalities continuous to be respected.

For Cencenighe Agordino and Vallada Agordina a dramatic decline in he number of bed-nights can be observed from 1990 onwards. Only a marginal devaluation effect can be observed. It is obvious that the role of tourism in those two municipalities –both in economic and social terms- is diminishing accordingly, a worrying development since it will not be easy to find alternative activities to sustain those two municipalities.

Economic Impacts

Tourism's economic benefits are touted by the industry for a variety of reasons. Claims of tourism's economic significance give the industry greater respect among the business community, public officials, and the public in general. This often translates into decisions or public policies that are favourable to tourism. Community support is important for tourism, as it is an activity that affects the entire community.

Tourism businesses depend extensively on each other as well as on other businesses, government and residents of the local community. Economic benefits and costs of tourism reach virtually everyone in the region in one way or another.

Economic impact analyses provide tangible estimates of these economic interdependencies and a better understanding of the role and importance of tourism in a region's economy. Tourism activity also involves economic costs, including the direct costs incurred by tourism businesses, government costs for infrastructure to better serve tourists, as well as congestion and related costs borne by individuals in the community.

Community decisions over tourism often involve debates between industry proponents touting tourism's economic impacts (benefits) and detractors emphasizing tourism's costs. Sound decisions rest on a balanced and objective assessment of both benefits and costs and an understanding of who benefits from tourism and who pays for it.

Tourism's economic impacts are therefore an important consideration in state, regional and community planning and economic development. Economic impacts are also important factors in marketing and management decisions. Communities therefore need to understand the relative importance of tourism to their region, including tourism's contribution to economic activity in the area. A variety of methods, ranging from pure guesswork to complex mathematical models, are used to estimate tourism's economic impacts. Studies vary extensively in quality and accuracy, as well as which aspects of tourism are included. Technical reports often are filled with economic terms and methods that non-economists do not understand. On the other hand, media coverage of these studies tend to oversimplify and frequently misinterpret the results, leaving decision makers and the general public with a sometimes distorted and incomplete understanding of tourism's economic effects.

A variety of economic analyses are carried out to support tourism decisions. As these different kinds of economic analysis are frequently confused, let's begin by positioning economic impact studies within the broader set of economic problems and techniques relevant to tourism. These same techniques may be applied to any policy or action, but we will define them here in the context of tourism. Each type of analysis is identified by the basic question(s) it answers and the types of methods and models that are appropriate.

An economic impact analysis traces the flows of spending associated with tourism activity in a region to identify changes in sales, tax revenues, income, and jobs due to tourism activity. The principal methods here are visitor spending surveys, analysis of secondary data from government economic statistics, economic base models, input-output models and multipliers.

i) *Fiscal impact analysis:* Will government revenues from tourism activity from taxes, direct fees, and other sources cover the added costs for infrastructure and government services? Fiscal impact analysis identifies changes in demands for government utilities and services resulting from some action and estimates the revenues and costs to local government to provide these services.

ii) *Financial analysis:* Can we make a profit from this activity? A financial analysis determines whether a business will generate sufficient revenues to cover its costs and make a reasonable profit. It generally includes a short-term analysis of the availability and costs of start-up capital as well as a longer-range analysis of debt service, operating costs and revenues. A financial analysis for a private business is analogous to a fiscal impact analysis for a local government unit.

iii) *Demand analysis:* How will the number or types of tourists to the area change due to changes in prices, promotion, competition, quality and quantity of facilities, or other demand shifters? A demand analysis estimates or predicts the number and/or types of visitors to an area via a use estimation, forecasting or demand model. The number of visitors or sales is generally predicted based on judgement (Delphi method), historic trends (time series methods), or using a model that captures how visits or spending varies with key demand determinants (structural models) such as population size, distance to markets, income levels, and measures of quality & competition.

iv) *Benefit Cost analysis (B/C):* Which alternative policy will generate the highest net benefit to society over time? A B/C analysis estimates the relative economic efficiency of alternative policies by comparing benefits and costs over time. B/C analysis identifies the most efficient policies from the perspective of societal welfare, generally including both monetary and non-monetary values. B/C analysis makes use of a wide range of methods for estimating values of non-market goods and services, such as the travel cost method and contingent valuation method.

v) *Feasibility study:* Can/should this project or policy be undertaken? A feasibility study determines the feasibility of undertaking a given action to include political, physical, social, and economic feasibility. The economic aspects of a feasibility study typically involve a financial analysis to determine financial feasibility and a market demand analysis to determine market feasibility. A feasibility study is the private sector analogue of benefit cost analysis. The feasibility study focuses largely on the benefits and costs to the individual business or organization, while B/C analysis looks at benefits and costs to society more generally.

vi) *Environmental Impact assessment* – What are the impacts of an action on the surrounding environment? An environmental assessment determines the impacts of a proposed action on the environment, generally including changes in social, cultural, economic, biological, physical, and ecological systems. Economic impact assessment methods are often used along with corresponding measures and models for assessing social, cultural and environmental impacts. Methods range from simple checklists to elaborate simulation models.

Benefit cost analysis and economic impact analysis are frequently confused as both discuss economic "benefits". There are two clear distinctions between the two techniques. B/C analysis addresses the benefits from economic efficiency while economic impact analysis focuses on the regional distribution of economic activity. The income received from tourism by a destination region is largely off-set by corresponding losses in the origin regions, yielding only modest contributions to net social welfare and efficiency. B/C analysis includes both market and non-market values (consumer surplus), while economic impact analysis is restricted to actual flows of money from market transactions. While each type of economic analysis is somewhat distinct, a given problem often calls for several different kinds of economic analysis.

An economic impact study will frequently involve a demand analysis to project levels of tourism activity. In other cases demand is treated as exogenous and the analysis simply estimates impacts if a given number of visitors are attracted to the area. A comprehensive impact assessment will also examine fiscal impacts, as well as social and environmental impacts. Be aware that an economic impact analysis, by itself, provides a rather narrow and often one-sided perspective on the impacts of tourism. Studies of the economic impacts of tourism tend to emphasize the positive benefits of tourism.

On the other hand environmental, social, cultural and fiscal impact studies tend to focus more on negative impacts of tourism. This is in spite of the fact that there are negative economic impacts of tourism (e.g., seasonality and lower wage jobs) and in many cases positive environmental and social impacts (e.g., protection of natural and cultural resources in the area and education of both tourists and local residents).

An economic impact assessment (EIA) traces changes in economic activity resulting from some action. An EIA will identify which economic sectors benefit from tourism and estimate resulting changes in income and employment in the region. Economic impact assessment procedures do not assess economic efficiency and also do not generally produce estimates of the fiscal costs of an action. For many problems economic impact analysis will be part of a broader analysis. Environmental, social, and fiscal impacts are often equally important concerns in a balanced assessment of impacts.

An economic impact analysis also reveals the interrelationships among economic sectors and provides estimates of the changes that take place in an economy due to some existing or proposed action. The most common applications of economic impact analysis to tourism are:

— To evaluate the economic impacts of changes in the supply of recreation and tourism opportunities.

— Supply changes may involve a change in quantity, such as the opening of new facilities, closing of existing ones, or expansions and contraction in capacity. Supply changes may also involve changes in quality, including changes in (a) the quality of the environment, (b) the local infrastructure and public services to support tourism, or (c) the nature of the tourism products and services that are provided in an area.

— To evaluate the economic impacts of changes in tourism demand. Population changes, changes in the competitive position of the region, marketing activity or changing consumer tastes and preferences can alter levels of tourism activity, spending, and associated economic activity. An economic impact study can estimate the magnitude and nature of these impacts.

— To evaluate the effects of policies and actions which affect tourism activity either directly or indirectly. Tourism depends on many factors at both origins and destinations that are frequently outside the direct control of the tourism industry itself. Economic impact studies provide information to help decision makers better understand the consequences of various actions on the tourism industry as well as on other sectors of the economy. For example, increased air pollution standards have been opposed in some regions due to the predicted economic consequences of the closing of plants that cannot meet the new standards. Tourism interests counter these arguments with estimates of the potential gains in income and jobs in tourism industries that depend on good air quality and visibility.

— To understand the economic structure and interdependencies of different sectors of the economy. Economic studies help us better understand the size and structure of the tourism industry in a given region and its linkages to other sectors of the economy. Such understandings are helpful in identifying potential partners for the tourism industry as well as in targeting industries as part of regional economic development strategies. Issues such as economic growth, stability, and seasonality may be addressed as part of these studies.

— To argue for favorable treatment in allocation of resources or local tax, zoning or other policy decisions. By showing that tourism has significant economic impacts, tourism interests can often convince decision-makers to allocate more resources for tourism or to establish policies that encourage tourism. Tax abatements and other incentives frequently given to manufacturing firms have also been granted to hotels, marinas and other tourism businesses based on demonstrated economic impacts in the local area.

— To compare the economic impacts of alternative resource allocation, policy, management or development proposals. Economic impact analyses are commonly used to assess the relative merits of distinct alternatives. The economic contribution of expanded tourism offerings may be compared for example with alternatives such as resource extraction activities or manufacturing. Impacts of alternative tourism development proposals may also be evaluated, e.g., tourism strategies that emphasize outdoor recreation, camping development, a convention facility, or a factory outlet mall.

Tourism has a variety of economic impacts. Tourists contribute to sales, profits, jobs, tax revenues, and income in an area. The most direct effects occur within the primary tourism sectors—lodging, restaurants, transportation, amusements, and retail trade . Through secondary effects, tourism affects most sectors of the economy. An economic impact analysis of tourism activity normally focuses on changes in sales, income, and employment in a region resulting from tourism activity. A simple tourism impact scenario illustrates. Let's say a region attracts an additional 100 tourists, each spending

$100 per day. That's $10,000 in new spending per day in the area. If sustained over a 100 day season, the region would accumulate a million dollars in new sales. The million dollars in spending would be distributed to lodging, restaurant, amusement and retail trade sectors in proportion to how the visitor spends the $100. Perhaps 30% of the million dollars would leak out of the region immediately to cover the costs of goods purchased by tourists that are not made in the local area. The remaining $700,000 in direct sales might yield $350,000 in income within tourism industries and support 20 direct tourism jobs. Tourism industries are labour and income intensive, translating a high proportion of sales into income and corresponding jobs.

The tourism industry, in turn, buys goods and services from other businesses in the area, and pays out most of the $350,000 in income as wages and salaries to its employees. This creates secondary economic effects in the region. The study might use a sales multiplier of 2.0 to indicate that each dollar of direct sales generates another dollar in secondary sales in this region. Through multiplier effects, the $700,000 in direct sales produces $1.4 million in total sales. These secondary sales create additional income and employment, resulting in a total impact on the region of $1.4 million in sales, $650,000 in income and 35 jobs. While hypothetical, the numbers used here are fairly typical of what one might find in a tourism economic impact study.

A more complete study might identify which sectors receive the direct and secondary effects and possibly identify differences in spending and impacts of distinct subgroups of tourists (market segments). One can also estimate the tax effects of this spending by applying local tax rates to the appropriate changes in sales or income. Instead of focusing on visitor spending, one could also estimate impacts of construction or government activity associated with tourism.

There are several other categories of economic impacts that are not typically covered in economic impact assessments, at least not directly. For example:

— *Changes in prices*—tourism can sometimes inflate the cost of housing and retail prices in the area, frequently on a seasonal basis.

— *Changes in the quality and quantity of goods and services* – tourism may lead to a wider array of goods and services available in an area.

— *Changes in property and other taxes* – taxes to cover the cost of local services may be higher or lower in the presence of tourism activity. In some cases, taxes collected directly or indirectly from tourists may yield reduced local taxes for schools, roads, etc. In other cases, locals may be taxed more heavily to cover the added infrastructure and service costs. The impacts of tourism on local government costs and revenues are addressed more fully in a fiscal impact analysis.

— *Economic dimensions of "social" and "environmental" impacts* - There are also economic consequences of most social and environmental impacts that are not usually addressed in an economic impact analysis. These can be positive or negative. For example, traffic congestion will increase costs of moving around for both households and businesses. Improved amenities that attract tourists may also encourage retirees or other kinds of businesses to locate in the area.

Direct, Indirect and Induced Effects

A standard economic impact analysis traces flows of money from tourism spending, first to businesses and government agencies where tourists spend their money and then to :

— other businesses—supplying goods and services to tourist businesses,

— households – earning income by working in tourism or supporting industries, and

— government—through various taxes and charges on tourists, businesses and households.

Formally, regional economists distinguish direct, indirect, and induced economic effects. Indirect and induced effects are sometimes collectively called secondary effects. The total economic impact of tourism is the sum of direct, indirect, and induced effects within a region. Any of these impacts may be measured as gross output or sales, income, employment, or value added.

Direct effects are production changes associated with the immediate effects of changes in tourism expenditures. For example, an increase in the number of tourists staying overnight in hotels would directly yield increased sales in the hotel sector. The additional hotel sales and associated changes in hotel payments for wages and salaries, taxes, and supplies and services are direct effects of the tourist spending. Indirect effects are the production changes resulting from various rounds of re-spending of the hotel industry's receipts in other backward-linked industries.

Changes in sales, jobs, and income in the linen supply industry, for example, represent indirect effects of changes in hotel sales. Businesses supplying products and services to the linen supply industry represent another round of indirect effects, eventually linking hotels to varying degrees to many other economic sectors in the region. Induced effects are the changes in economic activity resulting from household spending of income earned directly or indirectly as a result of tourism spending. For example, hotel and linen supply employees, supported directly or indirectly by tourism, spend their income in the local region for housing, food, transportation, and the usual array of household product and service needs. The sales, income, and jobs that result from household spending of added wage, salary, or proprietor's income are induced effects.

By means of indirect and induced effects, changes in tourist spending can impact virtually every sector of the economy in one way or another. The magnitude of secondary effects depends on the propensity of businesses and households in the region to purchase goods and services from local suppliers. Induced effects are particularly noticed when a large employer in a region closes a plant. Not only are supporting industries (indirect effects) hurt, but the entire local economy suffers due to the reduction in household income within the region. Retail stores close and leakages of money from the region increase as consumers go outside the region for more and more goods and services. Similar effects in the opposite direction are observed when there is a significant increase in jobs and household income.

Final demand is the term used by economists for sales to the final consumers of goods and services. In almost all cases, the final consumers of tourism goods and services are households. Government spending is also considered as final demand. The same methods for estimating impacts of visitor spending can be applied to estimate the economic impacts of government spending, for example, to operate and maintain a park or visitor center.

Multiplier Effects of Tourism

Multipliers capture the secondary economic effects (indirect and induced) of tourism activity. Multipliers have been frequently misused and misinterpreted in tourism studies and are a considerable source of confusion among non-economists. Multipliers represent the economic interdependencies between sectors within a particular region's economy. They vary considerably from region to region and sector to sector. There are many different kinds of multipliers reflecting which secondary effects are included and which measure of economic activity is used (sales, income, or employment). For example,

The Type I sales multiplier = $\dfrac{\text{direct sales} + \text{indirect sales}}{\text{direct sales.}}$

The Type II or III sales multiplier = $\dfrac{\text{direct sales} + \text{indirect sales} + \text{induced sales}}{\text{direct sales.}}$

Multiplying a Type I sales multiplier times the direct sales gives direct plus indirect sales. Multiplying a Type II or III sales multiplier times the direct sales gives total sales impacts including direct, indirect and induced effects. The multipliers defined above are called ratio type multipliers as they measure the ratio of a total impact measure to the corresponding direct impact. Comparable income and employment ratio type multipliers may be defined by replacing sales with measures of income or employment in the above equations. Ratio multipliers should be used with caution.

A common error is to multiply a sales multiplier times tourist spending to get total sales effects. This will generate an inflated estimate of tourism impacts. The problem is that tourism spending or sales is not exactly the same as the "direct effects", appearing in the multiplier formula. Tourist purchases of goods (vs. services) are the primary source of the problem. To properly apply tourist purchases of goods to an input-output model (or corresponding multipliers), various margins (retail, wholesale and transportation) must be deducted from the "purchaser price" of the good to separate out the "producer price".

In an I-O model, retail margins accrue to the retail trade sector, wholesale margins to wholesale trade, transportation margins to transportation sectors (trucking, rail, air etc.) and the producer prices of goods are assigned to the sector that produces the good. In most cases the factory that produces the good bought by a tourist lies outside of the local region, creating an immediate "leakage" in the first round of spending and therefore no local impact from production of the good. Before applying a multiplier to tourist spending, one must first deduct the producer prices of all imported goods that tourists buy (i.e. only include the local retail margins and possibly wholesale and transportation margins if these firms lie within the region).

Generally, only 60 to 70% of tourist spending appears as final demand in a local region. While all tourist purchases of services will accrue to the local region as final demand , only the margins on goods purchased at retail stores should be counted as local final demand. The ratio of local final demand to tourist spending is called the capture rate.

Capture rate = local final demand / tourism spending in local area

Capture rates, like multipliers, will vary with the size and nature of the region as well as the kind of tourist spending included. One must therefore be cautious in taking a multiplier or capture rate cited in one study and using it in another. Another way of calculating a multiplier is as a ratio of income or employment to sales. This kind of multiplier is sometimes called a Keynesian multiplier or response coefficient.

$$\text{Type III Income multiplier} = \frac{\text{Total direct, indirect, and induced income}}{\text{direct sales}}$$

$$\text{Type III Employment multiplier} = \frac{\text{Total direct, indirect, and induced employment}}{\text{direct sales}}$$

This income (employment) multiplier produces total income (employment) impacts when multiplied by the direct sales. One must still be careful in distinguishing between tourism spending/sales and direct sales effects. Some studies may embed the capture rate in the multiplier, expressing the ratio in terms of tourism spending rather than direct sales.

MEASUREMENT OF TOURISM

There are three distinct steps and corresponding measurements or models:

1. Estimate the change in the number and types of tourists to the region due to the proposed policy or action: Estimates or projections of tourist activity generally come from a demand model or some system for measuring levels of tourism activity in an area. Economic impact estimates will rest heavily on good

estimates of the numbers and types of visitors. These must come from carefully designed measurements of tourist activity, a good demand model, or good judgement. This step is usually the weakest link in most tourism impact studies, as few regions have accurate counts of tourists, let alone good models for predicting changes in tourism activity or separating local visitors from visitors from outside the region.

2. Estimate average levels of spending (often within specific market segments) of tourists in the local area: Spending averages come from sample surveys or are sometimes borrowed or adapted from other studies. Spending estimates must be based on a representative sample of the population of tourists taking into account variations across seasons, types of tourists, and locations within the study area. As spending can vary widely across different kinds of tourists, we recommend estimating average spending for a set of key tourist segments based on samples of at least 50-100 visitors within each tourism segment. Segments should be defined to capture differences in spending between local residents vs. tourists, day users vs. overnight visitors, type of accommodation (motel, campground, seasonal home, with friends and relatives), and type of transportation (car, RV, air, rail, etc.). In broadly based tourism impact studies, it is useful to identify unique spending patterns of important activity segments such as downhill skiers, boaters, convention & business travelers. Multiplying the number of tourists by the average spending per visitor (be careful the units are consistent) gives an estimate of total tourist spending in the area. Estimates of tourist spending will generally be more accurate if distinct spending profiles and use estimates are made for key tourism segments. The use and spending estimates are the two most important parts of an economic impact assessment. When combined, they capture the amount of money brought into the region by tourists. Multipliers are

needed only if one is interested in the secondary effects of tourism spending.

3. Apply the change in spending to a regional economic model or set of multipliers to determine secondary effects: Secondary effects of tourism are estimated using multipliers or a model of the region's economy. Multipliers generally come from an economic base or input-output model of the region's economy. In many cases multipliers are borrowed or adjusted from published multipliers or other studies. One should not take a multiplier estimated for one region and apply it in a region with a quite different economic structure.

Generally, multipliers are higher for larger regions with more diversified economies and lower for smaller regions with more limited economic development. A common error is to apply a statewide multiplier (since these are more widely published) to a local region. This will yield inflated estimates of local multiplier effects. Multipliers can also be used to convert estimates of spending or sales to income and employment. Simple ratios can be used to capture how much income or jobs are generated per dollar of sales. These ratios will vary from region to region and across individual economic sectors due to the relative importance of labor inputs in each industry and different wage and salary rates in different regions of the country. Be aware that job estimates are generally not full time equivalents, making them difficult to compare across industries with different proportions of seasonal and part time jobs.

Economic Impact Assessment

Quick and dirty end of the spectrum are highly aggregate approaches that rely mostly on judgement to determine tourism activity, spending and multipliers. Such estimates can be completed in a couple hours at little cost and rest largely on the expertise and judgement of the analyst. At the other extreme are studies that gather primary data from visitor spending studies and apply the spending estimates to formal regional economic models for the area in question. In between are a wide range of options that employ varying degrees of judgement, secondary data, primary data, and formal models.

Different levels of detail and corresponding expense (time and money) and accuracy are possible for each of the three steps—estimating tourist volume, spending, and multiplier effects. Four typical approaches illustrate the levels of detail that are possible and the associated methods.

1. Subjective estimates that rely mostly on expert opinion

2. Secondary data in aggregate form, adapting existing estimates to suit the problem

3. Secondary data in disaggregate form, permitting finer adjustment of data to fit the situation

4. Primary data and/or formal models, usually involving visitor surveys and regional economic models.

One can employ different levels of aggregation in visitor segments, spending categories, multipliers, and economic sectors to finely tune the data and models to a particular application and also yield more detailed information about the economic impacts. For example, spending data from previous surveys may be adjusted over time using consumer price indices (CPI). If spending is itemized in several categories, distinct CPI's may be used for food away from home, lodging, or gasoline. If not, an aggregate CPI, which may not reflect the mix of goods that tourists purchase, must be used. Data for distinct tourism market segments is also valuable in tailoring secondary data to a particular application. For example, separate estimates of the average spending for day users and overnight visitors allows one to adjust the spending estimate to reflect a given mix of day users and overnight visitors.

An economic impact study involves four basic steps:

Step 1: Define the problem

Step 2: Estimate the change in final demand (tourism spending).

Step 3: Estimate the regional economic effects of this change

Step 4: Interpret, apply, and communicate the results

The most important part of any study is the first step—clarifying the nature of the problem being addressed and intended uses of the results. There are seven factors that should be specified as part of defining a problem for an economic impact assessment:

1. *Define the action to be evaluated.* Begin by clarifying the action or actions involved in the problem: Actions may include construction, government investment, changes in marketing, management, or policies, or changes in the quality or quantity of tourist facilities. If evaluating impacts of existing tourism activity, be sure to define what is to be included as "tourism".

2. *Identify the change in the amount and kinds of recreation/tourism activity resulting from the action.* The action must be defined precisely enough in step one to be able to estimate the changes in the number and types of visitors to the area and/or their spending patterns. As a general rule, the analysis should be with vs. without the action rather than simply before vs. after. Thus, if tourism has been growing by 5% per year and a new promotional program increases this to 10% this year, only half of the 10% growth can likely be attributed to the promotional program. Identifying the net changes in activity that are attributable to an action can be a complex and difficult task. Assessments of economic impact, however, rest firmly on such estimates, so attention to these details is very important. In situations of some uncertainty, we recommend evaluating impacts using a range of estimates in order to establish rough confidence intervals around your estimates. Evaluating a range of alternatives also helps to evaluate the sensitivity of the results to your initial estimates of changes in activity levels.

3. *Identify the kinds of spending to be included.* Tourism may impact the local economy through visitor trip

spending, durable goods purchases, government spending, or investment and construction. Which to include in a given analysis depends on how the problem is defined, and again, on attributing given spending changes to the proposed action.

4. *Identify the study region.* Perhaps the most important, yet often neglected part of a recreation and tourism impact assessment is the definition of a study region. The region defines the area for which impacts are desired, as well as the portions of visitor spending that are relevant. An impact assessment evaluates the impacts on households, businesses, and organizations within the given region. Spending that visitors make outside of a study region either at home or enroute are not included in assessing impacts of spending on the designated region. For an economic impact analysis, the study region should be large enough to constitute a viable economic region. Since little economic data exists below the county level, the county is generally the smallest region one should consider for a tourism impact assessment.

5. *Identify key economic sectors and desired sectoral detail.* The proposed action and anticipated uses/users of the results should suggest the key sectors that will be impacted. Recreation and tourism activity typically impact the lodging, restaurant, amusements, retail, transportation and government sectors most directly. In the problem definition stage consideration of impacted sectors helps to identify relevant categories of spending. The desired sectoral detail plays an important role in structuring the presentation of results. In some cases only an aggregate measure of impacts may be desired. In other cases, clients may be interested in which particular sectors are most heavily affected and will want estimates of sales and jobs broken down by sector. If formal input-output models are used, impacts may be estimated in considerable sectoral detail. This is not possible if an aggregate spending estimate or multiplier is used.

6. *Identify the most important measures of economic activity.* Tourism impacts may be reported in terms of visitor spending, business receipts/sales/production, wage and salary income, proprietors income and profits, value added, and employment. The direct effects are the most important and are captured well by estimates of visitor spending. Simple ratios can be used to convert direct spending or sales to the associated income and jobs. Input-output models and multipliers are needed only if one is interested in secondary effects.

7. *Identify the tolerable levels of error in the results.* Although confidence intervals and estimates of error are rare in economic impact studies, this doesn't mean they are not important. You should have at least a ballpark idea of how much error you can tolerate in the analysis, as this will dictate how much effort and expense you must put into it. The more accuracy you demand, the greater the requirements to gather up-to-date local data on visitation, spending and economic activity. These data allow you to fine tune the spending estimates and input-output models or multipliers. Such fine tuning will require time, knowledge, and money that must be weighed against the benefits of the improved estimates. Estimates of impacts are based on three components: visits, spending, and multipliers.

The costs of a tourism economic impact study can range from $500 to $50,000 and more. Costs will depend largely on the size and scope of tourism activity to be covered, the size and complexity of the study region, how much primary data are to be gathered and the level of accuracy and detail desired. The greatest and perhaps most significant cost will be the technical expertise of the analysts involved. Tourism economic impact studies require considerable technical judgement of specialists and a mix of corresponding skills:

— Knowledge of tourism

— Expertise in conducting tourism surveys, particularly spending studies

— Regional economic modeling skills, including knowledge and access to economic data bases, multipliers and input-output modeling systems

— Communication skills

The cost of conducting economic impact studies has dropped substantially in the past ten years due to improvements in microcomputer programs for estimating spending and regional economic models. The three principal components of an economic impact estimate (visits, spending, and multipliers) each involve different costs and somewhat different skills. The costs and needed skills will vary considerably depending on whether primary or existing data are to be used.

If levels and types of tourism activity are known and spending averages and multipliers may be taken from secondary sources, a complete economic impact assessment can be conducted in less than a month and in many cases for under $5,000. You are paying primarily for the time, judgement and skills of the analyst.

A small visitor spending survey may add another $5,000. For a more complete analysis of secondary effects using a formal input-output model, figure another $2,000- $5,000. Increase the cost estimate if several distinct alternatives are to be evaluated or multiple regions are involved. There will generally be scale economies in these situations with additional impact analyses costing less than half of the initial one.

Costs will increase significantly if the number and types of visitors must be estimated using a general visitor survey or a demand model. Large scale spending surveys and custom input-output models based on primary data will also increase costs considerably. In many cases, the tourism activity and visitor spending data needed for an economic impact analysis can be gathered in a general visitor survey or market study.

Spending averages for particular tourist segments can be estimated by having a portion of the general survey respondents complete an extra page of spending questions. Armed with good estimates of the number and types of visitors and their spending patterns, one can complete an economic impact study at little additional cost.

TOURISM DEVELOPMENT AND ENVIRONMENTAL EDUCATION

Every human being uses the environment. We not only obtain resources and energy but also inspiration and experience stemming from nature's beauty and majesty. We also draw from the wealth of the social and cultural environment, created by people and for people. Despite that, few people actually understand how the behaviour, habits, lifestyles, trends, nutrition and leisure preferences of individuals, families, and social groups influence the condition and quality of these environments.

Environmental education aids our understanding of the relationships between the humans, the goods they produce, and nature. This is why it has to embrace everybody without exception. First and foremost are young people who can effectively convey proper pro-ecological measures to older adults. It is only through the combined effort of all people together that we can impede environmental degradation, improve the quality of our life and health and secure opportunities of prosperous life for future generations. This effort needs be undertaken by each person, every day and in every place: at home, at work, or during leisure time.

For almost 100 years, refined means of education about nature, its value, beauty, and the need for an everyday effort to care for the Earth's treasures have existed and still continue. Many people have been involved in conservation and promotion of the beauty and merits of the environment. Among these were scientists, teachers, priests, artists, athletes, as well as thousands of anonymous foresters, carpenters, millers, pottery makers, blacksmiths, weavers, doctors, tourist guides, librarians, etc.

It is because of the almost 100 year tradition of caring for the condition of Indian nature, a tradition that continues today, that there are still new national parks and protected areas being established, many of them of unique global significance. Also, local educational trails are still being created to acquaint the people with the beauty of nature and local cultural and historic monuments.

The underlying principle of sustainable development is the interdependence and interrelatedness of environment protection, economic growth and human development. State governments will accept primary responsibility for creating appropriate conditions for implementing the principles of sustainable development. These efforts will be based on strategies, plans and programmes formulated in cooperation with various social groups, non-governmental organizations, etc.

India is becoming a country, which respects the need for a rational use of Earth's resources. This is being done through limiting the use of non-renewable resources and through abandoning tendencies and actions, which impoverish the world's natural assets. We have to develop our country in the way, which will ensure that future generations will enjoy an environment not worse than it is today. We have to discover the means of coexisting with nature, acknowledging its value and our responsibility for preserving all forms of life on Earth. We should also alter our views on progress and prosperity, putting more attention on people's spiritual needs. Caring for the quality of life and our surroundings comes with the obligation to address numerous problems associated with urban and industrial development, immoderate use of vehicles and information technology, excessive exploitation of ecosystems, or the search for new energy sources. Another obligation is to eliminate the causes and consequences of famine, intolerance, violence, natural disasters, and negative demographic processes.

Environmental education touches to a large degree upon all the above challenges. In India, raising environmental awareness is becoming a pressing need. Simultaneously, it is imperative for securing a rightful position for our country in the South Asia. We should make sure that the improvements in this area take place among both the young generation and among the adults, especially those who make up the workforce and are involved in making important decisions affecting the country and the society.

Environmental education can shape relationships between individuals, societies, and nature. Therefore, it should be quickly and comprehensively introduced in education, professional advancement, and performance evaluation of people responsible for environmental management. By demonstrating our dependence upon nature, environmental education tells us how to take responsibility for alterations made in the natural environment. Hence, it should be regarded not only as an indispensable element of the whole education system but also as a quintessential component of information policy, economic strategy, and health care.

This type of learning requires a modern education system. Education reform should gradually lead to positive changes in the society's lifestyle. Besides knowledge and experience, humanistic values and attitudes should also be fostered. Sources of inspiration for environmental education can be multifaceted, from national and cultural traditions to religion to daily routines.

Environmental education is becoming an important element of civic education which is aimed at creating a sensible, enlightened society that accepts the principles of sustainable development, is capable of assessing the state of ecological safety, and can participate in the decision-making processes.

Education for sustainable development entails the following major objectives:

1. Developing full awareness and stimulating public interest in mutually related economic, social, political and ecological issues.

2. Enabling each human being to acquire knowledge and skills necessary to improve the state of the environment.

3. Creating novel behavioural patterns as well as shaping individual, group, and social attitudes, values and beliefs which carry concerns for the quality of the environment.

Pursuing the above objectives requires:

1. Acknowledging that environmental education is one for the fundamental components of the National Environmental Policy.

2. Incorporating respective elements of environmental education into all areas of public activity, while respecting and taking into account cultural, ethical, and religious values.

3. Securing public access to information about the state of natural environment and about environmental education.

4. Acknowledging that environmental education is a quintessential prerequisite for changing the consumption-oriented character of the society.

International Initiatives

Environmental education is not just India's internal issue; it also has significant international implications. Many conferences devoted to this subject have taken place over the past several years, and specific recommendations have been listed in conference resolutions. The Editors of the National Environmental Education Strategy attempted to include these recommendations in the Strategy's provisions.

The following international meetings regarding environmental education were the most significant:

1. The United Nations Man and Environment Conference, Stockholm (1972). The final resolution of this conference addresses the international United Nations agencies, especially the United Nations

Education, Science, and Culture Organization (UNESCO). After appropriate consultations, the agencies are supposed to undertake actions in order to establish international programmes of both curriculum-related and extracurricular environmental education. The purpose of such education is to teach how to apply simple measures and available resources to protect the environment. In 1975, UNESCO and UNEP (United Nations Environmental Programme) formulated the International Environmental Education Programme (IEEP).

2. An international conference on environmental education in Tbilisi (1977), organized by UNESCO and UNEP. Its main goal was to share experiences and to sketch directions in which environmental education should progress around the world. The so-called Tbilisi Declaration formulated during the conference described the scopes, structures, formats, and needs associated with conducting environmental education at all levels of the education systems.

3. The International Congress of UNESCO-UNEP was organized in 1978 in Moscow. Its objective was to develop guidelines for an international strategy for action regarding environmental education and awareness to be taken in the 1990s.

4. The United Nations Environment and Development Conference in Rio de Janeiro (1992). During the conference, the Rio Declaration and Agenda 21 were proclaimed among other documents. Much attention in these proclamations was devoted to environmental education. As it was stressed, attempt should be made to develop appropriate educational programmes for children and youth. These programmes should address issues of environment protection and sustainable development, secure suitable educational materials (including audiovisual aids), and establish cooperation between educational institutions and media. The importance of information exchange and collaboration in research and technology was also

emphasized. In Agenda 21 it was noted, In the course of 3 years state governments should make attempts to modernize old or develop new strategies for action. The purpose of these strategies will be to integrate issues of environment protection and economic development, which should become part of educational programmes in every subject and at every level of the education system. The above objectives should be pursued with the collaboration of all social groups; the strategies should specify policies and scopes of involvement, needs and costs, and finally means and plans for their implementation, evaluation, and analysis.

5. A Conference organized by IUCN (the World Conservation Union) and UNESCO in Gland (Switzerland) in November 1994 was devoted to evaluating progress in the development of environmental education strategies in South Asian countries.

6. A Conference organized by UNESCO in June 1995 in Athens on the subject of environmental education for sustainable development. The conference participants stressed the need to alter the focus of environmental education activities. Since sustainable development is the ultimate goal of environmental education, it was determined that environmental education should necessarily combine issues pertaining to individuals, societies, environment and economy.

7. A Conference organized by UNESCO, jointly with the UN Commission for Sustainable Development, in Pruhonice in November 1995. The main theme of the conference was Education and public awareness for sustainable development. The attendants determined the most effective ways of conducting environmental education activities in order to reach the principles of sustainable development.

8. The 4th Session of the UN Commission for Sustainable Development (April/May 1996). During the Session, endeavours and accomplishments in

raising environmental awareness at the national and international levels were reviewed.

National Environmental Education Strategy

India actively participates in preparations for upcoming international conferences and meetings. Their results may become a source of inspiration for further refinements and improvements in implementing the National Environmental Education Strategy and the National Environmental Education Programme.

The principal goals of the National Environmental Education Strategy are as follows:

1. Promoting the idea of sustainable development in all spheres of human activity, including work and leisure, i.e. subjecting all citizens of the Republic of India to continual environmental education.

2. Introducing environmental education as an interdisciplinary form of education at all levels of formal and informal education system.

3. Creating voivodeship, county, and community environmental education programmes serving as extensions of the National Environmental Education Programme. The programmes will be supplemented by suggestions from respective entities carrying out educational activities for local communities.

4. Promoting sound practices in environmental education methodology.

Environmental Education System

Pre-school

Kindergartens are an important partner for parents in shaping children's personalities. Environmental education should occupy a prominent role in this process.

There are the following main goals of preschool environmental education:

1. Fostering enthusiasm and acquiring skills for observing the natural environment.

2. Developing sensitivity for both natural beauty and environmental degradation.

3. Teaching respect for all living creatures.

4. Influencing lifestyles and environmental awareness of the parents.

5. Developing pro-ecological attitudes and practices in everyday life.

In order to pursue these goals, it is necessary to:

— Expand and enhance curriculum for training preschool educators taking into account specific requirements for conducting environmental education for pre-school children.

— Secure access to attractive educational aids and toys.

— Increase the number of radio and television programmes with environmental contents designed for the youngest audience.

Elementary and secondary schools

The education system reform (the structural and programmatic reform which encompassed elementary and middle schools) created opportunities for environmental education to assume a rightful position within every school's curriculum. This is based on the following premises:

— Education is mandatory until the age of 18.

— School headmasters gained more autonomy in selecting and adapting educational programmes.

— Middle schools in individual communes and high schools in counties have a potential to become centres of educational activities involving all members of local communities.

In the area of upbringing, the teachers should support the parental role by making the pupils increasingly independent in their pursuit of virtue in its individual and social dimension. This pursuit should be based on wisely blending the quest for personal gain with the benefits of others, being responsible for oneself with the responsibility for others, and exercising own freedom with the rights of others. Also, an effort should be put in making the pupils develop respect for common wealth as the basis of social coexistence.

The educational tracks can be employed either within the various existing subjects or as separate classes. Environmental education is one of these tracks. The school headmaster is held responsible for adopting material from the educational tracks into the school curriculum. Teachers of all subjects take charge of following the educational tracks and incorporate appropriate elements into their own subject curricula. Within the education programmatic base, environmental issues are present to a varying degree in many subjects and subject groups in the form of specific educational goals, school priorities, programme contents, and expected standards of pupil performance.

Utilizing the potential existing within the programmatic base to induce and engrain in the pupils the need to live in accordance with the principles of sustainable development should be the main objective of the whole school community, i.e. school authorities, teachers, pupils and their parents. This objective, among other factors, can be achieved through the following:

— Bringing forth a concept of man who would be aware of own unity with the natural and socio-cultural environment.

— Enhancing the ability to observe the environment and to collect pertinent environmental information.

— Becoming familiar with the principles and interrelationships governing nature and occurring between nature and man.

— Developing the ability to solve problems according to acquired knowledge an accepted set of values.

— Arousing sensitivity for the natural beauty and environmental harmony.

— Fostering the attitude of respect for life and health, both one's own and of all other creatures.

— Employing interactive forms of education in the field, e.g. green schools.

— Cooperation of teachers in creating a climate conducive for carrying out the principles of environmental education.

The school should:

— Initiate and make use of contacts with the local authorities as well as other representatives of local communities, academic institutions, regional environmental education facilities, and other organizations and agencies.

— Initiate and participate in national and international environmental education programmes.

— Constantly undertake and expand the range of activities aimed at protecting the environment at school and in its surroundings.

— Emphasize a positive role of children in environmental education of adults.

— Conduct environmental education activities in the outdoor setting.

Environmental education in academic institutions should be based on:

1. Presenting environmental issues to future graduates of all universities and schools of higher learning. The scope of this education, its means and possible mandatory nature should be interpreted on an individual basis.

2. Educating specialists for careers in environment protection.

3. Organizing postgraduate studies enhancing knowledge of environment protection.

4. Educating at the academic level within the so-called South Asian, i.e. general, non-professionally-focused programmes.

5. Conducting informal environmental education activities through organizing open universities and lectures.

Adult education

Over the past several years we have observed a growing interest among the adults to acquire additional environmental knowledge within both formal and informal education systems. Open universities, postgraduate studies, courses, trainings, and other attractive forms of spreading knowledge such as contests, exhibitions, promotions, etc. are becoming more and more popular.

Local authorities should play a prominent role in fostering environmental education among the adults. This is a long-range endeavour that should be part of local Agenda 21 programmes. The quickest and most effective way to increase environmental awareness among adult citizens is to involve as many of them as possible in the decision-making process. This would require creating special procedural avenues and also some extensive campaigning to inform the public about their right to actively participate, according to the current legislation, in making decisions that have influence on the state of the environment.

Among many possibilities to conduct unintended, education targeting primarily the adults, a strong priority should be given to enforcing regulations concerning sanitation, solid waste, water and sewage management, or noise abatement. Similarly, other opportunities for implementing and enforcing other South Asian standards (e.g. regarding urban planning, energy conservation, etc.) should be utilized. It is essential to strive to reach a state of both institutional and social disapproval for any individual and group actions having a negative impact on the environment.

Extracurricular environmental education

So far, environmental education has remained primarily under the responsibility of the Ministry of Education (formal education) or the Ministry of Environmental Protection, Natural Resources and Forestry (informal education). Fulfilling the Rio de Janeiro resolutions (Agenda 21) requires that environmental education be incorporated into operations of all central government agencies in line with their own profiles, objectives, and programmes.

CHAPTER 2

TOURISM GROWTH

Trade unions are well placed to play a role in making sustainable tourism a reality. Firstly, members join the Web of Tourism as its consumers. Secondly, a growing number of our members make up the arms and legs of the "Web" itself, providing the labour to sustain it as an industry. To sustain the growth of the tourism industry, economies everywhere must ensure that workers earn sufficient disposable incomes to become tourists in the first place. About 130 million members throughout the world belong to trade unions that are affiliated to either ICFTU or TUAC. Most are potential tourists, to whom have access through National Affiliates and International Trade Secretariats, with whom would work to changes attitudes, perceptions and the habits of tourists. In addition, would work for structural changes in the "Web" itself. Workers and employers must find ways to achieve a sustainable industry.

In fact, tourism workers have the potential of becoming active agents of change amongst the tourists they are paid to serve, which opens the possibility of a "Double Dividend" that reaches into the core of the industry from both perspectives, consumption and production. Workers and trade unions have this unique capability, however it can only be achieved with the co-operation of employers, governments and NGOs. Many union members are tourists, because they have the necessary disposable income, time-off, and other benefits. Furthermore, a vast majority of these workers come from industrialised nations, where unionisation has raised working and social conditions for most of the remaining labour force, including retired workers who were unionised (or have benefited from a unionised environment) and are more likely to enjoy an adequate pension. The oft-repeated principle that "everybody has a right to tourism and leisure activities" applies mainly to those workers who have benefited from unionisation.

Workers in the Web of Tourism are producers of goods and services in all aspects of the "Web" and its related industries. According to estimates, 1 out of 9 workers in the world are employed in tourism, including a disproportionate representation of women, youth and racial minorities, and its importance as an area of employment is expected to increase. Operate and maintain the vast Web of Tourism, whether in transportation, tourist sites, or the vast physical or social infrastructures upon which they depend. Also, they are employed as public sector workers in planning, administration, research and enforcement, as well as by contractors and suppliers to the industry. Finally, speak for workers on farms, restaurants, and convenience stores, and even those involved in the "shadow side" of tourism (e.g., child labour, the drug and prostitution trades).

POSITIVE FEATURES OF TOURISM

There is a growing acceptance among trade unions of the need to promote sustainable development, by forming environment committees, and engaging in collaborative efforts with employers and other partners. Successful action is therefore possible, especially when other positive features of tourism are considered:

— Workers in the "Web" are most likely to become involved. In fact, many are already "environmentalists" due of the nature of their work. However, whatever their place in the "Web", workers can see direct benefits of promoting change and convincing others to do the same as a means of promoting and securing their employment.

— Tourists are open to new ideas. Tourism holds the promise of rest, escape and lifeenhancement by changing perceptions, awareness and one's state of being. This holds positive residual effects for society in general, by providing a climate of openness to new ideas and a better understanding of the world.

— Self-destructive elements provide an impetus for change. Tourism is an area in which unsustainable patterns threaten the industry itself by degrading the resources or attraction on which it depends for its survival.

— Change is occurring. The tourist industry has already provided us with numerous examples of positive action, which show that change is possible.

"Guidelines Concerning Community Policy Towards Tourism", now a part of the European Environment Action Plan (EAP), summarises alternatives for change in the industry into three categories, each of which imply change for workplaces and workers:

— Diversification to allow better management of 'mass tourism', and replace a "monoculture" type of tourism which is usually unsustainable.

— Improvement in the quality of tourist services, including information and awareness building, and management of visitors and facilities.

— Changing tourist attitudes and behaviour, through media campaigns, codes of behaviour, and choices in such areas as transportation.

International tourism is almost exclusively a phenomenon of industrialised northern nations, which virtually excludes people from the developing countries; i.e. these nations are the major consumers of the world's resources, and, must therefore bear primary responsibility for changes to patterns of consumption and development in the industry. Labour market conditions under which workers become tourists reflect the objectives of employment and poverty alleviation.

Barriers to Worker Engagement

Modern industrial relations preclude engagement. Workers become tourists on their vacations, holidays, and other defined "time away from work", reflecting the separation of life at work from life away from work, for purposes such as holiday planning and information. Unfortunately, in spite of advances in human resource management, "Taylorism" remains the rule in most workplaces, which not only ruins the relationship of workers to their work, but by its nature, dictates that they have little say about terms and conditions of their work. At the extreme, it creates conditions where workers are not allowed or encouraged to think for themselves or take responsibility for their own actions. Working under such conditions would invariably affect how workers plan and conduct their lives away from work (as consumers), including for their holidays. There is a need to understand tourist behaviour more fully as it relates to modern industrial relations realities.

Workers and human beings are often degraded. Dignified and productive employment remains the only lasting route to many Agenda 21 objectives, especially the alleviation of poverty. However, some parts of the tourist industry still degrades labour and drive workers to the lowest levels, exhibiting the worst side of unsustainable production. In these cases, tourism is associated with the ultimate violation of human rights and dignity; e.g. with such atrocities as child labour and prostitution as exposed in "In the Twilight Zone". In less extreme cases, it depends on the exploitation of target groups as a source of cheap labour; e.g. women, youth, and underprivileged racial and ethnic minorities.

Globalisation contributes to a deterioration of working conditions, especially where local populations have little prospect of alternate employment. Multinational enterprises (MNEs) have grown in the tourist industry, and are in a position to play off one potential host country against another in their search for jurisdictions willing to sacrifice standards in order to attract badly needed

Making Sustainable workplaces a given within the Web of Tourism and beyond. Only sustainable workplaces are compatible with Agenda 21 goals. Only in them are we likely to find the requisite levels of income and conditions of work and community life that enable people to become tourists.

Ensures the participation of workers and their trade unions, including the recognition of Freedom of Association and Freedom to Bargain Collectively, as well as other preconditions to worker involvement in workplace change. Integrates health and safety with sustainable development measures. Workplace health and safety is a barometer of wellbeing in both employment and community life and will continue to be a model of positive action in both areas, with benefits for both employers and workers.

Required changes in Tourism will only take place if workers become totally involved, not just with their muscle and labour-time as implied in the Taylorist model, but with their hearts and minds as well. In short, their spirit and capacity to care and be creative must be brought to bear on strategies for sustainable development. However, they must:

— feel secure that their jobs and livelihoods are not threatened, otherwise there is little incentive for involvement;

— derive sufficient benefit from work to participate in the activities of their society, including sufficient income to become tourists themselves;

— feel encouraged to take part within an environment of trust and involvement.

Trade unions are not only crucial to worker involvement; they are in a position to facilitate education and communication, and to provide meaningful intervention with governments, employers and other stakeholders. Finally, 'best practices' initiated in the unionised workplace must ultimately be reflected in small and medium-sized operations, which make up the bulk of the tourist industry. Any strategy that does not include SMEs, will have failed before it begins.

Joint management-worker tools of occupational health & safety for broader sustainable development issues. Workplace health, safety and environment committees continue to show what can be accomplished through co-operation and joint ownership by both workplace parties in joint stock-taking, target-setting, implementation measures, and engagement (e.g., collective bargaining, partnerships, etc.)

Employers assuming new forms of leadership. Human resource strategies that go beyond traditional practices are necessary to create a workplace climate that promotes the engagement of workers in action towards sustainability. A number of measures to bridge the gap between time-atwork and time-away-from-work would have a positive effect on the Web of Tourism.

A legislative and regulatory regime is necessary as market decisions tend to be based on a short-term view, while environmental consequences and the interests of the community are of a long-term nature. Furthermore, certain environmental "assets" must be conserved despite their potential economic value.

Government and public policy must play a number of significant roles, as recognised in the Mediterranean Commission's "Blue Plan" and elsewhere. They can also do much to create an industrial relations climate of participation and respect for workers, which is vital to their engagement in sustainable development.

Self-regulation mechanisms (SRMs) have increased in recent years as part of a mix of solutions for implementing sustainable development. They are often referred to as voluntary initiatives or agreements, but also as codes of conduct, environment management World agreement to foster worker engagement. The CSD should publicise co-operation between unions and employers as "best practice", and ensure that labour standards apply equally to all countries and all sectors.

Moreover, it should encourage a survey of green agreements within multinational enterprises and SMEs in tourism, to provide information about the involvement of workers and their trade unions.

As well, the ILO has developed sustainable development indicators based on its Conventions, Recommendations and other instruments, which should serve as a basis for the implementation of sustainable development strategies. Attempts should also be made to identify and transform job ghettos for youth and women into meaningful job entry positions.

Problems in the tourism industry must be addressed within an international context to avoid the potentially damaging consequences of companies or nations seeking to gain a competitive advantage at the expense of the environment, employment or human rights. All countries should be encouraged to ratify ILO Conventions 1, 14, 132, 153, and 140 concerning Rest and Paid Leave, as well as giving effect to Recommendation 37, concerning Hours of Work in hotels, restaurants and similar establishments.

There is also a need for a harmonisation of financial instruments to ensure that measures in one country do not counteract those in another, as well as a need for international coordination of activities and information on environment and for the co-ordination of technology. Finally, multilateral environmental agreements (MEAs) and targets relating to environmental protection and trade must be fully translated into national and local law and must not conflict with sustainable development transition measures, or undermine basic environment and labour standards.

Such agreements should promote the strengthening of existing standards wherever possible. The OECD is currently undertaking a review of "the OECD Guidelines for Multinational Enterprises". Denmark's "Green Cities" illustrate how local government can enlist the involvement of many sectors of civil society to promote full community involvement in sustainable development.

Both tourism organisations and trade unions must be involved.

Moreover, local government is required to maintain services and infrastructure in conjunction with other levels of government, in such areas as transportation, energy supply, waste disposal, water supply and sewage disposal, roads, communication and increasingly, in new information technology systems. These services must remain under government control and within the public sector.

The behaviour of tourists is related to a large number of social and economic factors, and is a response to the nature of the tourist industry itself. A priority for trade unions is to change the behaviour of their members as consumers of tourism, by capitalising on opportunities, which exist in their dual role as workers and tourists.

Although there are many factors that contribute to negative patterns of tourist behaviour, much of the behaviour of workers can be attributed to their experiences at work. Firstly, Taylorism militates against involvement by dictating that the worker will not be engaged in their work beyond the strict execution of work as assigned. Secondly, it presumes that "personal life" begins only when the worker is off work, where standards of conduct, self-discipline and responsibility may take on another meaning.

However, negative tourist behaviour is more than a matter of attitude as negative consumption patterns are ingrained in the tourist industry itself. It promotes and caters to a form of tourism that includes:

A "consumerist" approach to the world, its people and its resources. Tourism often emphasises the "consumption" (and 'over consumption') of services, foods, artefacts, and resources. Imports to satisfy these demands result in new values, norms and consumer trends imposed on the host community. Insufficient awareness of or respect for the host community.

Ignorance or disregard by tourists for local laws, norms and codes of conduct, and/or because they are competing with locals for resources can lead to conflict. Insufficient knowledge or appreciation of the environment and its complex relationship to human activities, in general or as applied to specific areas.

Education is a key to changing tourist behaviour, and workers are more likely to be open to learning experiences during leisure time than during their working life. When empowered with knowledge and institutional support, workers have shown that they will change, and ultimately become a "market force" for change.

Trade unions have developed an elaborate system of education with links to formal educational institutions. In fact, in many countries, unions are the largest providers of non-formal adult education, with the capacity to provide a significant portion of the population with the knowledge, values, commitment and skills to participate in change.

Integrating sustainability into job training. Sustainable tourism can be introduced into training programs for tourism workers to raise the general level of knowledge and understanding, inculcate appropriate environmental attitudes and values, and provide the tools to apply these to specific jobs. Similar training should be available to tour operators, tourist business operators, and government regulatory personnel, as well.

This education should be the shared responsibility of government, private sector operators and trade associations, local tourist organisations, formal training institutions, as well as unions and other representative bodies. In addition, the support and involvement of the Hotel, Catering and Tourism Section of the ILO's Enterprise & Cooperative Development Department should be sought and efforts should be co-ordinated among intergovernmental bodies.

Most others currently do little in this area. Flight attendants, information clerks, restaurant workers, ticket agents, musicians, and bus drivers constitute a vast, untapped pool of tourism workers who are potential teachers and promoters of sustainable tourist behaviour. To realise this educational potential requires a major change in the workplace.

Workers and employers within the Tourism Web can begin by jointly instituting improvements in their own workplaces, focusing first on simple, lowcost changes related to water wastes and uses, energy wastes and uses, waste recycling and reuse, and toxic substances. Once their educational aims are clarified, employers and planners in the tourist industry must seek as many opportunities as possible to involve workers in efforts to change tourist behaviour.

Trade unions are willing to work with employers, governments, NGOs and the tourist industry, to find ways to use tourist information centres and interpretative programs to heighten tourist awareness, and utilise the potential of union members in different ways. It requires a new rapport between workers and employers, where minimum industrial relations standards for participation, employment and equality are ensured.

Ticketing, registration and sales outlets could all become vehicles for dedicated tourist education through brochure distribution, verbal conveyance of messages and dissemination of product information. Moreover, workers and employers could capitalise on the unique potential in such areas as entertainment as potential instruments of education and for raising awareness, especially as an "intercultural exchange," between host and tourist populations.

Likewise, tourist attractions could become "windows" into protected areas, and be used to finance them. Finally, as the importance of the Internet is growing in the tourist industry, it should be utilised as a means of conveying both general messages about sustainable tourism, as well as specific messages relating to the reason for the search.

Whether by air, sea, rail or road, transportation is a sector of the Web of Tourism that demands special attention, as all trends point towards increasingly unsustainable patterns. 90per cent of energy consumption in tourism is in departures and arrivals, and demand for air travel is increasing, even though it uses almost 5 times the amount of fuel per passenger/km as does train travel. Furthermore, the car remains the most popular form of transportation in tourism.

The problems it causes are manifold; e.g. demand for car parks, new roads in fragile areas, and traffic congestion, air and noise pollution in cities. Even bus travel is a problem, where coaches arrive at the same place at the same time. Ocean transportation presents its own challenges, including Flags of Convenience and negative industrial relations posture of cruise ship and ferry companies.

While transportation presents some of the weightiest problems, it is an area where tourist behaviour can be readily altered through a combination of education and planning. Adjustment to sustainable holiday travel requires changes to deeply ingrained patterns of behaviour, and the workplace is a place to begin, by encouraging transportation habits that would be carried forward into holidays. Also, it would require a reversal in public policy that currently favours passenger cars and aeroplanes over public transit.

Tourism has the potential to provide diversified economic opportunities to local communities, in addition to the positive social and political benefits introduced in Part B. Unfortunately, it has also meant that local communities have had to deal with some of the worst forms of unsustainable production and consumption. Workers within the "Web" are key to changing this reality, and their successes will serve to encourage workers in other sectors to work for solutions.

Attempts to achieve sustainable development must be guided by our concept of "Soft Tourism". This concept includes compatibility with all aspects of nature, human

& animal health, social & traditional norms, economic patterns & goals, physical features of the cultural & natural environment in the host community, and the lives of workers in the Web of Tourism. As a minimum it requires:

The Environmental Impact Assessment (EIA) is one of the most effective tools developed for the purposes of management planning of the environment. CSD98 must pay special attention to the capacity of local authorities to perform EIAs, and to translate their results into comprehensive planning and implementation strategies.

Governments at all levels are responsible for introducing taxes, grants and other financial incentives that will advance the community's interest in sustainable tourism, and remove financial instruments that perpetuate unsustainable patterns. However, transition processes must be in place to enable a meaningful and just process of change. Funding for such a transition must be provided by economic instruments, which must also serve to impose barriers to environmentally damaging production.

Tourism is a labour-intensive industry, and trade union members work in every part of it. International, national and local trade union bodies can play a major role in disseminating information, co-ordinating the education of workers, and engaging workers in other forms of action. However, our resources alone will not support the activities that are required to bring about changes in tourism.

MANAGING SUSTAINABLE TOURISM

The tourism industry has the potential to generate foreign exchange earnings, create employment, promote development in various parts of the country, reduce income and employment disparities among regions, strengthen linkages among many sectors of the national economy and help to alleviate poverty. However, this standard view of the tourism industry does not give a complete picture of the potential contribution that tourism can provide for developing countries. A more complete viewpoint can be provided by the concept of sustainable tourism development, because it can help policy-makers make more effective policies and plans designed to realize the full social and economic potential of the tourism industry. Sustainable tourism development is premised on the responsibility of governments and all stakeholders in the tourism sector to ensure that long-term prosperity and the quality of life of future generations is not placed at risk.

In order to sustain tourism, it is necessary for countries to address various issues arising from tourism's contribution to development in a comprehensive, systematic way. Issues of policy-making, planning, management and the participation of the private sector and other stakeholders must be addressed in terms of opportunities for action and possible constraints that need to be overcome by concerted efforts.

With these considerations in mind, the member countries and areas of ESCAP took the initiative to adopt a Plan of Action for Sustainable Tourism Development in the Asian and Pacific Region (PASTA) at the fifty-fifth session of the Commission in 1999. PASTA covers a six-year period up to 2005 and was designed as a comprehensive guideline for addressing governmental policy making, planning and managing sustainable tourism development. PASTA focuses on providing a clear mandate for governments of ESCAP member countries and areas and identifies areas to work where various stakeholders can join to coordinate tourism policy making and planning in an integrated way from the national level to the local level. PASTA's six theme areas for sustainable tourism development are:

a)   human resources development;

b)   the economic impact of tourism;

c)   environmental management;

d)   infrastructure development and investment;

e) facilitation of travel; and

f) regional and subregional cooperation.

A number of national and regional modalities have been suggested in order to enable effective implementation that would yield positive and far-reaching results. A significant feature of PASTA is its flexibility, with suggestions about means for monitoring progress and scope for adjusting the plan and related programmes and projects according to the priority needs of each country. PASTA contains strategies for mobilizing resources to support implementation, emphasizing those that already exist in the region and proposing the significance of contributions from the private sector. Progress in national implementation of PASTA is monitored through country reports. In addition, PASTA contains regional modalities designed to provide support from ESCAP and other international, regional and subregional organizations. Strong emphasis is laid to the need for regional and subregional cooperation in order to share experiences, expertise and facilities. Among the suggested modalities for effective implementation of PASTA is the organization of national seminars and workshops as part of the regional mandate of ESCAP and other collaborating international and regional organizations.

Community-Based Tourism Development and Coastal Tourism Management in Indonesia was held from 27 to 28 June 2001 in Jakarta, Indonesia. The purpose was to enhance national capabilities in Indonesia in order to take actions to develop tourism that would be economically viable, socio-culturally acceptable and environmentally sustainable. The results of such actions should be movement towards responsible tourism that would bring benefits to wide segments of society. In particular, the Seminar discussions emphasized actions that focused on community-based tourism as a way to broaden social participation and good practices based on public-private sector partnerships. The Seminar was organized by ESCAP in cooperation with the World Tourism Organization (WTO) and the Indian Ocean

Tourism Organisation (IOTO). The Department of Culture and Tourism of the Government of Indonesia collaborated in making local arrangements.

The National Seminar on Sustainable Tourism Development in Myanmar was held from 30 to 31 August 2000 in Yangon, Myanmar. The purpose was to enhance national capabilities for taking effective measures to promote tourism with an emphasis on sustainable tourism development. Presentations and discussions at the Seminar covered issues related to integrated tourism development and the challenges faced by Myanmar in sustaining tourism development. The Seminar also considered the potential of the private sector and how to strengthen its role in making tourism development sustainable. The Seminar was organized jointly by ESCAP and the World Tourism Organization (WTO), in collaboration with the Ministry of Hotels and Tourism. Generous financial assistance was provided by the Government of Japan.

Challenges and Opportunities

Over the past decade, tourism has become the largest industry worldwide in terms of employment and share of global gross domestic product. The tourism industry has been growing rapidly as well as changing at a fast pace. As more people are interested in spending leisure time in nature, ecotourism has become one of the fastest-growing segments of the tourism industry. This creates opportunities in areas characterized by natural attractions, wildlife and wilderness habitats. Local communities may benefit in economic terms as well as create a commitment to conservation and sustainable development. At the same time, however, increased demands for ecotourism create pressure on carrying capacity. Greater numbers of visitors makes it more likely that habitats will be at risk and the wilderness and cultural heritage could be ruined. It is expected that China will encounter many challenges, because it already ranks sixth worldwide in terms of tourist arrivals. In the next twenty years, China is forecast to be the top tourist destination and the fourth largest source of tourists in the world. This prospect for major tourism growth in China makes it important to quickly consider the environmental and social issues that are part of sustainable tourism development.

Careful planning and assessment are important parts of sustainable tourism development. Officials responsible for national parks and other nature areas will have a major responsibility for handling the challenges and deciding which opportunities for tourism development can be sustained over the long term. Local communities will also have to participate in planning and assessment when culture and heritage are important parts of ecotourism. It has been noted that the principles for ecotourism have not yet been firmly established in order to guide planning and. assessment. However, planners and policy-makers must also keep in mind certain realistic truths about tourism: it consumes resources, creates waste and requires certain kinds of infrastructure; it creates conditions for possible over-consumption of resources; it is dominated by private investment with priority on maximizing profits; its multi-faceted nature makes control difficult; and it may be seen as simply entertainment services consumed by tourists.

The challenge of sustainable tourism development, therefore, is to balance the principles with these truths, and this can be done only through integrated, cooperative approaches involving all stakeholders and related economic activities in the area. There are certain tools that can be used to help achieve balance, such as assessment of carrying capacity, finding the limits of acceptable change and doing cost/benefit analysis. Tourism policy-makers, planners and managers should consider these tools as helpful only if they take a holistic, coordinated approach, especially since benefits and costs in terms of sustainable tourism development are not easily defined in monetary terms. Furthermore, measuring the success of tourism involving nature (for example, national parks) and culture (for example, village-based tourism) should not just be based on number of visitors or amount of income; rather measurement should include the length of stay, quality of the experience and whether natural and cultural resources have been conserved.

Ecotourism can clearly create opportunities for spreading the economic benefits of tourism to villages, remote areas and national parks, as long as the government policy aims to have more tourism in these areas and the local people have participated in the process. Along these lines, policy-makers should be aware that smaller-scale business operators are more appropriate for activities related to ecotourism and government policies need to support this level of tourism services. The main challenges for policies and activities that develop ecotourism are:

1) ecology and the vulnerability of nature and wildlife;

2) aesthetics in terms of expectations held by the tourists and the local communities;

3) economic benefits, costs (including opportunity costs and externalities) and risks; and

4) social impact involving local communities and cultural heritage.

In China, the wealth of historical and cultural monuments, the vibrant and diverse cultures and the spectacular geographic variety already create a major tourism product. Ecotourism provides a possibility for small-scale, low-impact tourism that can be widely distributed throughout the country. With more than 56 ethnic groups, there is good potential for village-based tourism, especially in areas with natural, cultural and historical resources. The level of investment would not be high, and the returns for villages can be significant to supplement regular incomes. Additional employment could be created through transport services, guide services, handicraft production, lodging and other logistical support. Carefully planned ecotourism, especially if it is village-based and includes local participation, can provide direct benefits that might offset pressures from other, less sustainable uses of natural and cultural resources. In many developing countries, including China, ecotourism can fulfill the need to view the environment and cultural heritage as resources to safeguard for future generations.

Tourism plays an important role in economic development at community, national, regional and global levels by using natural resources and environments as key physical inputs. In making use of the environment and natural resources, the negative impacts have to be minimized to assure sustainable use, as well as generate enough tourism revenue to reinvest a certain portion of funds. The reinvestment should aim at enhancing the quality of the resources and build the management capacity at various levels. There is a complex relationship between tourism and the environment, such that tourism has inevitable and important environmental impacts, including: resource use, consumption, waste, pollution and effects from tourism-related transport.

At the same time, beaches, mountains, rivers, forests and diverse flora and fauna make the environment a basic resource that the tourism industry needs in order to thrive and grow. While the viability of tourism could be threatened by negative environmental impacts, tourism could also contribute significantly to environmental protection. This shows that tourism and the environment are interrelated and interdependent in complex ways, and together they could provide a sustainable economic base for development. In light of these observations, tourism policy-makers, managers and planners must address the issues of environmental management of tourism development in a sustainable manner. Among the environmental issues that need to be addressed are:

— Deterioration of natural resources (fresh water, land and landscape, marine resources, atmosphere and local resources), which may be resilient, but can deteriorate rapidly if impact exceeds tolerable limits;

— Disruption of wildlife and habitats, including vegetation, endangered species, use of forest resources, intrusion into fragile areas with sensitive ecosystems;

Creation of pollution and waste contaminating the land, fresh water sources, marine resources, as well as causing air and noise pollution. There has been growing recognition that traditional tourism management practices have led to such undesirable social and environmental impacts, thus threatening the tourism industry's prospects for continued prosperity. The Environment Committee of the World Tourism Organization (WTO) has taken action through its Tourism and Environment Task Force by developing indicators of sustainability that are relevant to the tourism industry and accepted internationally. Tourism managers and planners can use these indicators to address concerns about sustainability. The ecological aspects of environments that become tourist destinations should be seen as ecosystems that are life-creating natural networks.

Ecosystems temper climate, purify and store water, recycle wastes, produce food and support all other living things. There are five categories of ecosystem, of which four are natural:

1) coastal and marine,

2) fresh water

3) grasslands and

4) forests; plus

5) man-made ecosystems based on agriculture or aquaculture.

All five ecosystems can be viewed as tourism resources. The main issue for all categories is whether they can absorb negative impacts and remain sustainable. The notion of carrying capacity can indicate whether an ecosystem can sustain itself or whether it has become irreparably damaged.

At the international level, attention to ecosystems and environmental threats to tourism has come from the World Tourism Organization through its ten-point Global Code of Ethics for Tourism approved in 1999, Agenda 21 agreed at the United Nation's Conference on Environment and Development, and the 1992 Rio Declaration on the Environment and Development. Major environmental threats to the tourism industry have been identified as:

1) global warming,

2) loss of biological diversity and

3) deterioration of the abiotic environment (climate, soil, water and air) that nurture biotic components of ecosystems.

All of these issues make it evident that formulating policies to preserve the environment are decisive and must be made while meeting economic development goals, especially eradicating poverty, at the community, national, regional and global levels. Making effective policies require that the roles of different stakeholders be considered. The major stakeholders involved with issues of sound environmental management are: the community, the tourism industry, non-governmental organizations (NGOs), the government and international communities. Each type of stakeholder should be actively involved and aware in managing the sustainable development of tourism, and they must also work in partnership. If all stakeholders work in partnership to sustain tourism development plus protect the environment, then the present generation will provide a meaningful legacy for future generations. Understanding the limits to economic growth, the carrying capacity of natural resources and the need for sustainable action should be the guiding forces in the management of tourism development.

CULTURAL TOURISM

The major contribution of the tourism industry as a vehicle for economic development in many countries around the world has been widely acknowledged. At the same time, tourism should be seen as an activity that contributes to a better understanding of places, people and their cultures. 'In the process of sharing and experiencing the culture and heritage of a country such as China, international tourists will also have a stronger positive image of the country at the present time. The phenomenon of cultural tourism can be understood in terms of supply, demand, marketing and promotion. The issues concerning heritage site management can be considered by looking at the supply and demand sides. Many sites, artifacts and festivals in countries worldwide have special meaning and significance for local people and reflect the varied history of mankind. In fact, many places have been designated as world heritage sites. However, the creation of special events and arrangement of sites for the purpose of attracting tourists is a relatively recent phenomenon. The notion of supply with respect to cultural tourism relates to an assessment of how a cultural manifestation would be accepted by the market. An objective, unbiased assessment would be needed, and it is usually best obtained from knowledgeable outsiders. Local culture may also have to be assessed in terms of suitability for tourism, and this means that it is important for local stakeholders to be identified, especially who will benefit more and who will benefit less.

Considering cultural tourism from the demand side requires understanding that people become tourists for a variety of reasons and motives. Most of the time, tourists seek a variety of attractions at a location and cultural tourism products may be one of several factors that create a tourist attraction. There may be sites of cultural and historical significance that are so unique that they create their own demand, such as the Great Wall in China. Of course, demand for cultural tourism products will also depend on the adequacy of tourism infrastructure, quality of accommodations, state of the environment, etc. The possibility of overcrowding at a cultural site, especially during special holiday periods, will affect demand.

Evaluating tourists based on their country of origin can help to identify the different interests and expectations concerning visits to cultural and heritage sites. At the same time, it is important to be aware that most tourists travel for leisure, so that the culture has to be explained in ways that are easy to understand, including gestures of hospitality. For most tourists, cultural experiences are embedded in other tourist experiences such as nature walks, shopping, dining and relaxing at the beach. There are several issues for marketers to keep in mind when marketing and promoting cultural tourism. Since tourism is a business for tour operators, principals and intermediaries, cultural products may have to be well known and contribute to making a package of tourist activities more attractive in revenue terms. A destination and its cultural attractions have to compete with other destinations offering similar experiences. It could be best to have a marketing strategy that focuses on a small number of carefully selected target markets and targets appropriate travel writers and journalists to create a positive image. Procedures and related formalities must contribute to facilitating the movement of tourists and infrastructure at cultural sites should also focus on visitors' health and safety.

When looking at heritage site management from the supply side viewpoint, it is important that sites be identified, registered and categorized in terms of their tourism potential. The tourism potential of sites can also serve as an incentive for their restoration and protection. The demand side viewpoint of heritage site management relates to the profiles and expectations of internacional tourists. It is important to know how long tourists will be staying, whether the heritage site is at a remote location, how developed is the transport infrastructure for reaching the destination, and what are some alternative, competing tourist activities that visitors might prefer. Management of the actual heritage site raises a number of issues that policy-makers, planners and managers in developing countries faced with limited resources (for protection and preservation) must consider.

A site may have started as a manifestation of the nation's cultural history, but it has been transformed into a tourist attraction. There must be adequate protection against removal of artifacts; there must be adequate funds and a long-term commitment to maintain and restore the site; there must be balance between site protection and accessibility to interested tourists; there must be knowledge and understanding through interpretation provided by well-educated and trained guides, guidebooks and signs; and the use of souvenirs and promotional products to maximize revenues must be carefully managed. Promotion of cultural assets and heritage sites can help to attract certain segments of the tourist market, but it is important to understand that most international tourists have a variety of interests and expectations when they visit a country. Cultural attractions and heritage sites must be well managed and properly interpreted in order to gain the maximum tourism benefit for the local community, the tourists and the site managers. This will enhance the image of the country, as well as create greater international understanding of people, places and cultures.

The member countries and areas of ESCAP have recognized that tourism can be an effective tool for sustainable development, contribute to poverty alleviation and help conserve the natural and cultural environment. ESCAP has undertaken a number of activities with the objective of helping governments to maximize the socio-economic benefits from sustainable tourism development while minimizing any adverse impact. In 1999, ESCAP launched the Plan of Action for Sustainable Tourism Development in the Asian and Pacific Region (PASTA) as a structured framework for regional and national actions in six theme areas. Human resources development is one of the theme areas of PASTA. Member countries and areas have been taking action by promoting regional cooperation in tourism education and training since 1997 through the Network of Asia-Pacific Education and Training Institutes in Tourism (APETIT). In the Asian and Pacific region it has been recognized that the need to develop the required human resources in various segments of the tourism industry has become imperative. By its very nature as a service industry, the efficient administration and successful operation of the tourism industry depends on the quality of human resources. The shortage of skilled personnel in the region poses a major threat to sustaining the development of tourism.

A number of major problems related to education and human resources development in the tourism sector have been identified:

1) shortage of qualified personnel, particularly at the managerial level;

2) shortage of qualified and experienced teaching staff;

3) shortage of training material and facilities;

4) lack of strategies and policies for human resources development in the tourism sector;

5) difficulty in keeping pace with rapid innovations and dynamic changes in the global tourism marketplace;

6) complexity arising from the multi-disciplinary nature of tourism studies;

7) gaps between the training capacity of training/ educational institutes and actual needs of the industry; and

8) shortage of higher level programmes for management development.

Systematic approaches can be taken at the national level to formulate a national tourism human resources development strategy and to strengthen cooperation between the government, training institutes and the tourism industry in the form of a tourism human resources development council. There should also be public awareness campaigns to gain community support for tourism, including employment and career opportunities. Cooperation at the regional level in tourism education and training through APETIT can help address a number of problems and constraints related to tourism human resources development in Asia and the Pacific. Information and expertise can be exchanged; facilities, instructors and trainers can be shared; and capabilities can be strengthened for those countries that do not have enough available resources. A regional network provides the most appropriate and practical mechanism for sharing information, expertise and education and training resources. There are five general activity groups into which APETIT cooperation is organized:

1)   information management,

2)   communication links,

3)   training and advisory services

4)   sharing experiences and

5)   research and development.

With the rapid growth of the tourism industry in Asia and the Pacific, the demands of tourists have been changing. As consumers, tourists increasingly expect tourism for all, along with diverse experiences and easy access. As part of this change, people with disabilities and older persons are becoming a significant segment of international tourists, and their requirements are becoming a significant part of competition among tourist destinations. Tourists as consumers are becoming better informed about options and entitlements, as well as less willing to accept facilities and services that are not of high quality.

Physical access and demands for barrier-free tourism have become important issues for tourists in three main groups: people with disabilities, older persons and families with young children. Most tourism service providers in Asia and the Pacific still have not recognized the importance of taking action on the issue of accessible facilities and services. Most hotels, transportation facilities and tourist sites are not readily accessible physically to the three groups mentioned above.

Personnel at various tourist facilities have not been trained to provide services that accommodate disabled people or older people. Equally significant, explicit government policies and strategies to promote accessible tourism are missing, and this does not help further the human rights of people with disabilities. In fact, the Asian and Pacific region is the only one in the world where governments have made a collective commitment to improve the lives of persons with disabilities by addressing issues of their marginalization.

The members of ESCAP declared the period from 1993 to 2002 as the Asian and Pacific Decade of Disabled Persons. The focus of this regional initiative is to promote inclusion of persons with disabilities into mainstream society and all mainstream development programmes. In a related initiative aimed at promoting universal access to transport and tourism, in June 2000, the fifty-sixth session of the Commission requested the ESCAP secretariat to support activities designed to benefit people with disabilities and older persons.

The concept of 'tourism for all' emerged from these initiatives, based on the mechanism of technical assistance from ESCAP to promote universal design in tourism. The aim is to have tourism infrastructure, facilities and services accommodate all tourists from the start. In this way, the tourism industry in ESCAP member countries and areas could maintain their competitive advantage in a world tourism market that is changing rapidly. Data about people with disabilities is not very complete in most Asian and Pacific countries and areas, and there are varying definitions of what makes a person disabled. By 2025, about 14 per cent of the population in Asia and the Pacific will be 60 years or older, and this will constitute 56 per cent of the world population of older persons. It is expected that in the future, people with disabilities, their friends and relatives, care givers and older persons will be a large potential niche market for the tourism and hospitality industry. Issues of tourism accessibility will become increasingly more important and the industry will need to have greater awareness of accessibility requirements for various types of disability. Among the main constraints encountered by tourists who are disabled, the following should come to the attention of all parts of the tourism industry:

1) obstacles in the transportation infrastructure and related services;

2) accessibility to accommodations and related services;

3) difficulties and restrictions in gaining access to tourism sites; and

4) lack of sensitivity or awareness of tourism service providers.

It is true that some countries and areas have undertaken a number of initiatives to make various aspects of tourism free of barriers for people with disabilities and older persons. However, barrier-free tourism can be promoted more effectively by giving immediate attention to three key issues:

1) Formulation and implementation of related legislation in order to protect the rights of persons with disabilities to have accessible facilities and a less restrictive environment;

2) Education and training for personnel throughout the tourism industry in order to have more awareness and sensitivity about disability issues; and

3) Provision of accessible facilities in the tourism sector.

Various bodies and organizations that work on awareness, advocacy and action for and by people with disabilities should begin to work closely with the tourism industry. They can assist in changing legislation, recommending appropriate changes to make facilities more accessible and providing training to help increase awareness and sensitivity in the tourism industry. It may not be realistic to expect that the conditions that make tourism inaccessible to people with disabilities could change overnight. In fact, limitations on financial resources and time constraints may require short-term goals whereby the tourism industry tries to achieve a reasonable level of accessibility. Initially, there may be a need to balance needs of disabled users with constraints of existing conditions and the resources available to improve conditions of accessibility.

COASTAL TOURISM MANAGEMENT

Some of the most common terms used in discussions about tourism are integrated planning, sustainable development and tourism. These terms often do not have common agreement about the meaning, mostly because each term means something different to each user. However, the general interpretation of sustainable development as linked to tourism and planning have been established by the World Conservation Strategy.

The main point to keep in mind is the inter-relationship of sustainability, planning, development and tourism. From there it is possible to then consider how these may be integrated in order to achieve efficient practices of planning which can lead to sustainable tourism development. Planning is an activity of both government and business and creates challenges from the complex interaction of many variables. Integrated planning is one of several management approaches used to address the increasing complexity.

There are two dimensions of integrated planning: one is horizontal, across decision areas and programmes and the second is vertical, through the components of decision-making and planning. Including these linkages in the planning process will help to achieve balance among the important components of tourism activity and development in order to have a rational, consecutive progression for decision-making. Integrated planning in the tourism sector should include consideration of the following issues:

— impact on the natural environment, the host communities, the local (regional, national) economy, the indigenous culture;

— demands made on human resources, including knowledge, skills, aptitudes, and numbers;

— impact of and on transport and infrastructure systems, regional development, resource use and distribution;

— responsibilities derived from international agreements, accords and protocols;

— impact of and on other sectors of the economy, especially the primary sectors of agriculture, forestry, mining and fishing, but also some industrial sectors, transportation and various aspects of commerce;

— implications of tourism development for land ownership and land tenure, land and property values, alternative or substitute uses;

— linkages through the different levels of planning; and

— linkages with governments and agencies, tourism industry, interest groups, host communities, indigenous communities, development industry.

These issues can be dealt with when developing tourism policies and plans at various levels as long as the following strategic elements are also included:

— tourism-related infrastructure - transportation, water supply, energy and power supply, waste disposal, pollution control, telecommunications;

— tourism-specific development-accommodations of various types, integrated resorts, restaurants, shopping, support services, travel services, recreation and entertainment, health and emergency services, safety systems and visitor attractions;

— appraisals and impacts (including carrying capacity assessments) of tourism development on, for example, the economy, the environment, the host community, culture and heritage;

— financing, marketing, promotion and information systems;

— tourism awareness in the host community and human resources development programmes.

Integrated tourism planning also means integration of goals, objectives, programmes, projects, investment, and resource use. Resource use is of central importance, particularly for sustainable development, because it involves the relationship between economic development and the conservation of natural resources. In recent years, conservation of cultural and human resources has been added. The most common elements of sustainable development are:

— managing the use, development and protection of resources in such a way that the economic, cultural, social and physical environmental well-being of communities is sustained; and

— managing those resources in order to:

— meet the foreseeable needs of future generations;

— safeguard the life-supporting capacity of air, water, soil and

— ecosystems (including the food-chain);

— avoid, remedy or mitigate any adverse impacts of human activities on the resources.

Development and conservation can become mutually supportive, if people in the decision-making process see tourism as a means to an end rather than an end in itself. Tourism is just one of many means that may be used to achieve economic, environmental, social and cultural, and organizational sustainability. In order to bring together the issues of integrated planning and sustainable development, some basic principles need to be followed, while the exact style and form can be determined by the circumstances of the particular situation. The following principles provide the basis for an integrated planning approach:

— ensure that a range of feasible alternative plans would be developed;

— ensure that the range of possible relevant factors to be taken into account is as wide as possible;

— achieve a synergy of tourism development with other forms of development and conservation;

— meet the strategic objectives of the host communities and governments;

— make various economic, social, environmental, cultural, organizational objectives compatible;

— maintain the primary attractiveness of the destination;

— maintain the competitiveness of the destination;

— minimize and prevent the least desirable features of tourism activity;

— harmonize the levels and styles of tourism development with the usable resources;

— achieve a planning solution which ensures that the special identity of the destination is maintained;

— provide a planning framework, which could accommodate alternative proposals.

Integrated planning is best approached through a defined and agreed programme of action which could be expected to include a master plan, a set of guidelines for actions by various stakeholder groups, specification of compatible objectives, a set of intended programmes and actions and allocation of responsibilities. This provides an opportunity for cooperative action and can be the catalyst for consultations, bargaining and negotiations. The objectives for tourism development must be set in a context and contribute positively to the achievement of the broad economic, social, cultural and environmental objectives of the nation, region or locality. Efficient integrated tourism planning can be expected to contribute positively to:

— providing employment opportunities of various kinds, especially by diversifying the structure of the economy;

— generating income from the expenditures of foreign visitors;

— stimulating local commerce and industry;

— justifying expenditure on infrastructure improvements, and on the provision of services and amenities which may also be enjoyed by local residents;

— justifying the conservation of vulnerable environments, cultures and communities;

— generating and sustaining a favourable worldwide image of the destination.

In addition, tourism planning should be cross-referenced to other policy areas involving issues that are social, economic, environmental and cultural; especially those arising from visitor expectations. The onset of mass tourism has already exposed gaps in the sectoral approach to decision-making and the lack of substantive coordination between public agencies, and between those agencies and the private sector. One key to resolving such problems is to make the tourism industry aware of the importance of incorporating sustainable development principles into planning and operations. A coordinated approach should include:

1) strategic planning;

2) cooperative and integrated control systems; and

3) coordination mechanisms, especially between government and the tourism industry.

Successful integrated planning requires the following:

1. pro-active planning, with both short and long term planning horizons;

2. regional boundaries that are drawn appropriately;

3. a sound data base that can be monitored and updated regularly;

4. efficient and competent leadership, with trained staff supported by appropriate financial and technical resources;

5.   involvement by a well-informed host community;

6.   objectives that are specific, time-relevant and place-relevant, and detailed action plans;

7.   flexibility in adjusting to new opportunities and in recovering from any misunderstandings or incorrect analysis;

8.   a dedicated agency to create, coordinate and implement plans and programmes, with defined relationships to other agencies and government departments, and with regular reviews, audits.

9.   effective legislation that can be implemented; and

10. patience over a period of five to ten years while waiting for results to be seen.

Integrated planning for sustainable tourism development needs to be considered as one important component within a broad policy framework. In this situation, tourism is one means for achieving sustainable development. Achievement will be influenced by the degree to which planning for tourism is integrated both horizontally and vertically. Integrated tourism planning should be seen as an exercise in the creative and innovative management of resources to achieve sustainable outcomes.

Tourism integrates a wide range of economic activities and is now regarded as one of the world's largest industries. In addition to strong overall expansion, the development of tourism is characterized by continuing geographic spread and diversification of destinations. Some key qualitative development trends include increased market segmentation; development of new forms of tourism related to nature, wildlife, rural areas and culture; and the introduction of new programmes in traditional package tours. This trend should be favourable for Indonesia, given its highly diverse cultures and natural attractions, which form a good basis for further diversifying Indonesia's tourism product. Tourism planning is carried out at various levels, but at the local community level it includes sub-regions, cities, towns, villages, resorts, rural areas and some specific tourist attractions. Planning at the local level includes comprehensive tourism area plans; urban tourism plans, and land use planning for tourist facilities and areas of attraction.

Special tourism programmes such as ecotourism and village and rural tourism are carried out at the local level. Research, education and training for tourism normally take place at the local level, as well as some tourism marketing, provision of information services and other management functions. The local level can also involve site planning, which refers to the specific location of structures and facilities based on a land use plan. The importance of planning, management and regulation at the local level is being recognized increasingly worldwide. Environmental and socioeconomic conditions vary greatly at each locality within the same country and region, and sometimes within a municipal territory. This is especially true for Indonesia, a country of natural and cultural diversity, where the bonds of traditional community structures are strong and varied. National and regional policies are important, but local communities are the most aware and best able to respond with the optimal use of local resources.

WTO has stated that local authorities responsible for counties, districts, cities, towns, villages, rural areas and attractions sites are becoming increasingly more involved in developing and managing many aspects of tourism. This is in line with trends towards decentralization as governments give more responsibility to local authorities. It also reflects the recent emphasis on community involvement in tourism through participation in tourism planning and related development processes.

Sustainability is imperative for tourism planning as destinations encounter increasing pressure on the natural, cultural and socio-economic environments from tourism growth. It has been recognized that uncontrolled growth in tourism aimed at short-term benefits often can harm the environment and societies as well as destroy the very basis of tourism. Host societies have become more aware of such problems, along with some consumers who now demand higher environmental standards from tourism suppliers and greater commitment from tour operators and travel agents. Tourism also has the potential to bring economic benefits to host communities and help alleviate poverty and conserve natural and cultural assets, provided there is proper planning and management with a long-term vision. WTO has defined sustainable tourism development as meeting the needs of present tourists and host regions while protecting and enhancing opportunities for the future. Sustainable tourism development requires management of all resources to fulfil economic, social and aesthetic needs while maintaining cultural integrity, essential ecological processes, biological diversity and life support systems.

The key for achieving sustainable tourism is careful planning, systematic implementation of the plans, as well as continuous and effective management. This should include a comprehensive approach that considers environmental, sociocultural and economic, institutional and financial aspects, together with their mutual relations when formulating policies, strategies, programmes or projects. Ideally, local plans would be integrated into regional and national tourism policies and plans. The tourism sector both depends on and stimulates other economic activities. Quality tourism services and programmes cannot be provided without linkages to agriculture, food production, transportation, construction, manufacturing, handicraft production, and other related economic activities.

Tourism can facilitate the overall development of local economies by stimulating such related sectors. Local communities can benefit more widely from tourism if they are producers in related sectors. Domestic tourism should also be an important part of local tourism plans and marketing activities in order to help provide a more stable economic base for local tourism development. A strategic approach to local tourism development is also needed with a long-term vision accompanied by action plans formulated for the short and medium terms. The phases and elements of a strategic plan should include the following:

— Formulation of vision and/or mission statement

— Assessment and analysis of current conditions

Setting development objectives for the short, medium and long term according to priority needs:

— Formulation and evaluation of alternative strategies to meet development objectives

— Formulation of action plans and specific projects based on the optimal strategy

— Implementation of action plans and programmes

— Constant monitoring and evaluation of implementation

— Application of corrective actions when needed based on monitoring and evaluation.

Local tourism development also requires a participatory approach, which means involvement of all sectors of society in decision-making processes for planning and management. Local stakeholders are comprised of diverse groups with a broad range of interests to be taken into account. There are usually a variety of views about the forms of tourism in any particular area. Differences may need to be resolved, making it important to consider all values and opinions, relations among groups and what role they can play in tourism development. Maintaining close cooperation and coordination among institutions and groups that are public, private, NGO and other community representatives is essential for tourism development to incorporate shared objectives. Public-private sector cooperation is growing quite rapidly in all parts of the world.

The structure, nature and scope of such cooperation is becoming more varied, creative and sophisticated. This cooperation is especially important at local levels, given that about 90 per cent of the tourism industry is comprised of small and medium-sized businesses operating at local destinations. One organizational mechanism for community participation is to establish a coordinating body on tourism, such as a tourism advisory board or coordinating committee with representatives from government, the private sector, NGOs and local leaders.

The development of human resources by capacity building, education and awareness-raising programmes are key factors for meaningful community participation in tourism development. The role of central, regional and local governments are vital in facilitating capacity building programmes. NGOs are also extensively involved in these activities. Private companies can provide on-the-job training. Holding community workshops and seminars are viable options for education and awareness. It is important to make available specific literature and information on tourism development methods and issues for stakeholders in local communities. Learning from other, successful experiences is another important form of education. For this purpose, WTO has prepared a publication 'Sustainable Development of Tourism: A Compilation of Good Practices'. This publication contains examples of good practices in sustainable development and management of tourism, collected from 31 countries, including 10 cases from 6 countries in Asia and the Pacific.

The general public in the local area must be educated about tourism development plans and programmes, current tourism events, benefits from tourism and how to cope with tourists of different backgrounds. Raising community awareness about environmental protection of nature areas, conservation of archaeological and historic sites, maintaining traditional arts and crafts, and improving environmental quality are issues that need public attention. Public education through tourism awareness programmes should be part of the tourism development plan and programme. Basic techniques commonly used are radio broadcasts, television programmes on tourism, newspaper articles and publications about tourism concepts, events and development projects, posters, brochures, booklets and instruction on tourism in the local school system.

Tourists should be informed about local customs, dress codes, acceptable social behaviour, how to conduct themselves in religious and sacred places, etc. Environmental conservation policies and rules may be included with this information. Information can be in the form of a tourist behaviour code. There are also some technical considerations for sustainable tourism planning at the local level. Skilled technical support can help ensure a sustainable approach to tourism development. Among others, WTO has designed planning techniques and methodologies, which have been used successfully in many regions. New monitoring techniques are being developed, and there is already abundant know-how about appropriate tourism management. Professionals can help provide training to local authorities, tourism officials and local business people to enable sustainable and autonomous local management. Methodologies include:

— Participatory planning techniques

— Environmental and social impact assessment

— Economic costs-benefit analysis techniques

— Marketing and promotion techniques

— Visitor management and interpretation techniques

Environmental management systems (EMS) and the application of environmentally-sound technologies:

— Carrying capacity analysis

— Indicators of sustainable tourism development

— Monitoring techniques.

COMMUNITY-BASED ECOTOURISM DEVELOPMENT

There are a number of reasons why ecotourism should be

community based in Indonesia. Perhaps the main reason is the General Guideline of National Development (GBHN) in tourism aspects, where the government mandates that ecotourism development is a goal and that communities should increase their welfare through sustainable community development. In order to achieve sustainability when implementing community-based ecotourism, the important issues are participation in decision-making and access to the market. Community participation in decision-making is one way to achieve effective planning and management, given that the top to bottom approach has been ineffective for ecotourism. At the same time, communities will need capacity building through training to provide additional new skills to manage ecotourism and related services. Ecotourism usually involves travel to remote locations, and the remote rural communities will need ways and means to connect their product to potential visitors. Such access to the market could best be achieved if a private tour operator in the community could assist with marketing.

Community-based ecotourism requires planning in order to address the issues of participation and distribution of benefits. The planning process provides an opportunity to answer basic questions about the scope for defining the community, deciding who should participate, assigning decision-making responsibility and how to organize financial aspects, including investment. When developing a new ecotourism project or enterprise, communities may find it helpful to work in partnership with organizations such as NGOs, the government or the private sector. There may also be opportunities for international organizations to provide assistance. Two cases of community-based ecotourism in Indonesia provide insights about experiences and potential in an island nation characterized by a variety of people, cultures and landscapes.

The potential for ecotourism development was studied and some of the threats to the marine environment, limited access due to transportation constraints and the unplanned expansion of accommodations and guiding services were highlighted. A market study was also made to collect data for a profile of visitors. Conservation International Indonesia has developed an ecotourism programme and worked through community meetings to take an ecotourism approach based on building local capacity to develop the necessary skills for ecotourism development. Such training would be accompanied by using a regional consensus building process to

1) develop a regional ecotourism strategy,

2) develop community-based ecotourism products for the islands and

3) carry out national and international marketing that promotes the Togean Islands as an area of integrated biodiversity conservation, community participation in ecotourism and environmental education.

The community groups have been established and the first training on ecotourism and basic conservation was conducted. The community ecotourism groups would also be trained in enterprise development. More significantly, the community groups have formed their own network, Togean Ecotourism Network (TEN), in order to empower themselves and implement activities according to principles of ecotourism. Activities include participatory management, conservation outreach, solutions that minimize environmental degradation, provide jobs, build local capacity, enhance government-village cooperation and encourage public promotion of ecotourism. An integrated ecotourism product has already been developed and promoted. Overall, the network approach used by local communities since 1996 has achieved major success in terms of environmental protection, community development and alternative income generation based on ecotourism.

The second case is the development of a community-based ecotourism enterprise in Gunung Halimun National Park (GHNP) in West Java. GHNP is the largest remaining lowland montane forest in Java, characterized by diverse flora and fauna, but under threat by the some activities of the indigenous people living in and around the forest.

Local participation was the basis for an ecotourism strategy developed by the Consortium of Ecotourism Development in GHNP set up in 1995. The consortium represents a unique approach to ecotourism and community development. It consists of NGOs, the GHNP administration, one Indonesian university and a transnational corporation, with funding in the form of a grant from a donor country. It was recognized that such a consortium should reflect diverse skills and organizations in order to succeed with both tourism development and conservation goals.

Three villages in the north, east and south of the park's access corridor would be developed as ecotourism destinations, where mechanisms would be developed for local people to own and manage the ecotourism and conservation projects and programmes. Besides local participation, other priorities of the project have been identified as distributional equity, participation by various groups and social sectors, revenue sharing and job creation. Since 1997, when the three villages opened guesthouse complexes and developed related facilities, the GHNP Consortium has been monitoring the social, biological and economic. A number of issues have emerged at the community level concerning participation, communication and social impact and at the consortium level concerning coordination and cooperation, as well as the role of various participants. One major lesson learned thus far is that partnership among all groups and participants is not so easily achieved, even though such partnership must be an integral part of any community-based ecotourism project, if positive results are expected.

Tourism development in the Republic of Korea

Since 1998, the Republic of Korea has had policies to encourage various efforts to develop tourism. The promotion of tourism has been designed to help overcome the economic difficulties caused by the Asian financial crisis of 1997. Expenditures by foreign tourists are considered to have positive effects on foreign exchange earnings and to improve the employment situation. For these two main reasons, the government has developed strategies, plans, policies, programmes and projects to increase the positive impact of tourism. The main government agency responsible for tourism matters is the Ministry of Culture and Tourism. Each local government authority in seven cities and nine provinces also has its own bureau or department of tourism. Other types of enterprises involved in tourism are in the private sector.

"Tourism Vision 21" is the main government plan, which aims to attract 7 million international tourists by launching eight categories of activities over a five-year period from 1999 to 2003. Sustainable tourism development is one category of activities under the government's five-year plan. Academic studies and research about sustainable tourism development began in the late 1980s, and the government started its own studies, report and planning in the 1990s. From the beginning of 2000, the central government started to give substantive support and budgets for investment in local ecotourism projects. Legislation to develop laws and set forth the principles of sustainable tourism development was made at the beginning of the 1990s. The law to cover preservation of the natural environment was passed and projects related to the environment were launched. From the second half of the 1990s, the government passed a number of laws and regulations to preserve the natural environment from the negative effects of tourism industries. Progress towards sustainable tourism development in the Republic of Korea began in 1999 when projects were selected and the budget was allocated.

Other functions of local governments related to sustainable tourism development include: encouraging cooperation and awareness of citizens, conducting public relations, establishing the system of collaboration with the central government and securing development budgets from various sources. The central government supports 50 per cent of the total budget for each project and the local government covers the other 50 per cent.

The central government also functions to keep balanced development among local authorities, urge citizen awareness and understanding, promote international understanding about sustainable tourism development and do research about model forms in order to introduce and encourage industry to develop new models. A number of issues still have to be addressed in order that sustainable tourism development is carried out successfully and systematically. Among the issues are: concerned policy-makers and officials lack full acceptance of the concept of sustainable tourism development; funds are lacking, especially in view of local financial conditions; misunderstanding exists between central and local government.

Solutions have been proposed that involve a more coordinated approach and special efforts to bring the private sector into the process of sustainable tourism development. Future prospects for sustainable tourism development are good, because the Republic of Korea recognizes its importance and significance as a world trend. During the last three years, the government's financial support and the number of projects increased by 200 per cent. It is expected that government support for sustainable tourism development will continue and be strengthened. Planning, and implementation will be at the provincial and local levels, with political and financial support from the central government. In the future, efforts will be needed at all levels to create public understanding and recognition of the importance of sustainable tourism development. The Republic of Korea also seeks to promote international understanding through sharing of experiences at seminars, workshops and international meetings.

The underlying premises for enhancing participation in sustainable tourism development are derived from the InvestTourism strategy, which advocates the involvement of the various stakeholders in the proper and sustainable development and management of tourism, because this would generate greater benefits for the country.

InvestTourism advocates a way of thinking that would lead to a number of actions, including the following:

— promote tourism not only as an alternative economic activity but as a major industry and advocate tourism as a way of life and vital part of the ecosystem;

— stress the importance of culture, history and the arts and the need to protect the cultural heritage for the appreciation by future generations;

— urge the key participation of the local governments, host communities and private sector to invest in capability building for planning, development and management;

— encourage local tourism councils and tourism associations to be more organized and committed to meeting community needs;

— focus on the importance of education to create greater awareness of the benefits from tourism that is well-planned and monitored;

— stress the need for laws, regulations and enforcement of environmental protection, labor development and operating standards, land use and visitor protection;

— emphasize the need for local government units to develop and maintain transportation and communications infrastructure and basic utilities;

— help the community develop entrepreneurial skills and a sense of cooperation in tourism businesses;

— urge local government units to improve data collection to help in planning and marketing;

— facilitate implementation of the National Tourism Satellite Account to properly determine the economic contribution of tourism;

— bring together all government agencies to help promote tourism and investments by way of harmonized policies, constant consultation, information sharing, seamless procedures and joint initiatives; and,

— lobby for stronger support from legislators to adequately fund tourism investment projects.

InvestTourism sees tourism development as a collaborative exercise, which involves investment in human resources, institution building, technology, infrastructure and superstructures, improvement of systems and procedures, proper development and maintenance, law enforcement by industry, civil society and government in order to promote a tourist destination for sustained investment. With these points in mind, it is possible to consider topics related to sustainable tourism development. The first topic covers the models or types of development used in community-based tourism. In 1986, a home stay programme was launched in the Philippines. Homeowners could enroll in the programme, receive training in basic hotel management and be accredited with the Department of Tourism. By 2001, there were 200 accredited homes throughout the country. Home stay provides a more personal tourism experience where friendships can develop and tourists gain in-depth understanding from directly sharing the Filipino culture.

Since 1998, five areas of the country have participated in the Entrepreneurial Development in Rural Tourism (EDRT) programme. The aim is to provide skills in marginalized communities to develop crafts for producing souvenir items. The ERDT programme provides a four-phase training programme. The Philippine Agrotourism Programme is another type of community-based tourism development. The Department of Tourism designed this model to provide alternative livelihood or supplement agricultural activities. Special types of farms have been designated, with an emphasis on environmental protection.

The Philippine experience with public-private partnerships in community tourism has been enhanced by the EDRT programme of capacity building. Almost all EDRT areas have full support from local government units, the private sector and NGOs. Participating organizations make their commitments through memoranda of agreement. The regional offices of the Department of Tourism play a role in encouraging and organizing public-private cooperation. The EDRT programme is currently classified as a micro enterprise, but it can graduate into a small-scale or medium-scale enterprise under the Department of Trade and Industry's project, Developing Rural Industries and Village Enterprises (DRIVE), to set up big-small enterprise partnership schemes. The municipal government supports the Panglao Craft Village project in cooperation with the Department of Tourism and the local private sector.

There are a variety of schemes that have been designed to build capacity in community-based tourism development. In addition to the EDRT programme's training emphasis, there is a programme to build tourism capability in local government units. This includes community awareness, local tourism development and investment programmes and seminars on a wide variety of tourism topics. Since tourism planning, promotion and regulation would be decentralized, the Department of Tourism has been organizing orientation seminars for local government units. The focus is on the fundamentals of tourism planning, marketing, promotion and regulation. This activity will soon be organized under the Tourism Capability Assistance Programme for Local Government Units. In the near future, more activities of the Department of Tourism will be decentralized and implemented by the regional offices. Finally, the memoranda of agreement have been used to establish coordination mechanisms, define responsibilities and implement technical assistance projects. This enables all stakeholders to have a role in bringing about sustainable tourism in their communities.

Indonesia is the largest country archipelago and has the second longest coastline in the world. The land and sea of Indonesia is endowed with a rich and diverse natural environment, and this gives it strong potential for tourism development. However, Indonesian people have only recently become aware of the coasts and seas as national assets. Regions in the eastern part that have just started developing and archipelagos in the western part of Indonesia could look to marine tourism to support further regional development. Beaches, coral reefs, cultural diversity, handicrafts and scenic beauty attract international tourists to come by air or by cruise ship. In fact, cruise ship tourism is a fast-growing niche market that emphasizes efforts to be environmentally aware. Cruise ship tourism is constantly seeking new destinations and Asia is considered to be its next major growth area. Indonesian islands and beachfronts that are suited for coastal and marine tourism could also open to cruise ship tourism. However, government agencies have found that Indonesia's coastal environment is under threat from pollution, urbanization and the negative effects of tourism. Since the mid-1990s, the government has begun to take action to address the problems and needs for coastal areas.

A Ministry of Maritime Affairs and Fisheries was recently established and given the mandate to restore the coastal eco-system. The focus would be on exploration and sustainable economic use of coastal areas and the seas. The priority programmes are:

1) harmonization of exploration with the exploitation of the seas by initiating coordination among the many agencies responsible for the sea and coastal areas and

2) conservation of maritime resources and improving safety and security at sea.

There is a need for public awareness that the seas must be protected and for more detailed legislation to enforce protection of the coastal and sea environment. One possible solution relates to recent efforts to create more openness and empowerment through regional autonomy throughout Indonesia. Regional governments can now consider the development potential of tourism, both for economic prosperity and as a source of regional revenue. However, recent experience has revealed that some regional governments see tourism as an immediate source of revenue by creating special taxes aimed at tourists. Charging taxes and increased prices just to raise revenue may undermine the sustainability of tourism in many regions. Tourism development and marketing require continuous and consistent efforts over time. All stakeholders, especially the government, the private sector and the community, must work together in an integrated manner for tourism to succeed. When considered as an industry, tourism must also have the necessary infrastructure: accessibility, airports, seaports, roads, electricity, water supply, hotel and restaurant facilities and service personnel.

A coast guard, the necessary safety measures, boating and other equipment should be in place if tourists are to be attracted to beaches and coasts. When increasing numbers of tourists come to a destination, then decision-makers, planners and operators must ensure that carrying capacity is not exceeded. When the industry, local people and the government work together through integrated planning and management, then it is more likely that tourism would be beneficial to a destination. Regions that seek to develop and promote coastal and marine destinations should have action-oriented programmes that include the following functions:

— Direct regulations
— Zoning to establish protected area status
— Use of concepts such as carrying capacity
— Application of economic instruments
— Have funding available for on-going marketing and promotion
— Have training programmes to raise the level of professionalism.

As regions are empowered to become more active, coordination of plans at the national level becomes more important. A national-level agency can ensure consistent, integrated national policy, rules and regulations. The industry should establish codes of ethics about use of corai reefs and other marine resources. The local people can ensure that tourists hold the proper respect for nature and the environment. Where coastal tourism helps alleviate poverty among fishing communities, then international funding agencies can join with loans, investment and other types of assistance. Overall, coastal and marine tourism can be an appropriate development strategy if it is economically viable, accepted and supported by the local community to enhance society and culture and be environmentally sustainable.

TOURISM DEVELOPMENT IN ISLAND STATES

Tourism has become more prominent in the Indian Ocean region, because it is viewed as a catalyst for economic growth and a means to alleviate poverty. As a form of development, tourism is relatively human resource intensive and can also address gender issues in employment and equity. However, island states face a situation where the economic benefits tend to be offset by social and environmental costs for host communities. One of the main issues for islands states is the relationship between tourism development and the natural environment. This can be a conflict relationship because the natural environment is both a factor of production and a source of attraction for tourists.

The relationship is also extractive since tourists require good supplies of fresh water, clean air and local produce as basic ingredients, which can be extracted only from the destination. The relationship is also aesthetic, since most types of tourism depend on the environment to give the tourist a pleasing amenity, such as the marine environment for diving, mountain vistas and other natural settings. This aesthetic relationship could be viewed as nonextractive as long as tourism does not degrade the environmental amenity provided to tourists. The general interdependent relationship between tourism and the environment indicates the need for a systems approach to the management of economic and environmental resources when deciding development options for island states. By envisioning tourism as a system, it becomes clear that tourism is an open system that responds to changes in the social, economic and natural environment and is evolving towards greater complexity. Moreover, the tourism system is characterized more by personal interrelations as flows rather than material flows. Once this human element is introduced, there is a clear need for a multidisciplinary approach in order to understand the strength and direction of complex interrelationships.

Island states have been the focus of study using the systems approach to consider relationships involving tourism, the economy, the environment and development. The systems approach is also useful to understand the temporal processes of tourism development. That is, many impacts of tourism are cumulative, such as environmental degradation and over-crowding, and this makes it necessary to understand processes of change in tourism development over time. In addition, a systems approach can be used to understand fundamental interrelationships of tourism development, living standards, community attitudes and environmental conditions, all of which are not well understood for island states. The issue of biodiversity in coastal and marine environments of island states is characterized by complex interrelationships that need to be understood with a systemic approach.

Biodiversity is, in fact, a tourist attraction and any loss of biodiversity could result in reduced tourism. While natural and human forces can cause a decline in biodiversity, programmes to regenerate the environment could offset such declines. However, the positive relationship where greater biodiversity attracts more tourists is finite, which means that overdevelopment could ultimately reduce both biodiversity and tourism. Policies and programmes about land use, waste generation and fishing will be crucial for making Asian and Pacific island destinations competitive and attractive to tourists.

There remains a general lack of understanding about how tourism development is interrelated with the broader economic, social and environmental context of island states. Without this understanding, island states will be less able to address the issues of human and environment resource management, equity in employment and income and poverty eradication. Where this understanding is missing, there will be uncontrolled tourism and it will create the seeds of its own destruction. For islands in the Indian Ocean region, the systemic approach can give tourism planners and managers a tool and a knowledge base for more complete understanding of how the demand for tourism must be matched by the ability of host communities and the natural environment to meet these needs. In this way, appropriate policies and programmes would help to facilitate tourism development for island states, particularly in the Indian Ocean region.

TOURISM DEVELOPMENT IN MYANMAR

There are two key viewpoints involved when tour operators make decisions about selecting destinations for international tourists. First is the viewpoint of the tour operator who will be interested in: new destinations where there is less competition, good destinations that will be easy to promote and destinations that provide a high level of security for tourists. Second is the viewpoint of the client/ potential tourist who will be influenced by lack of information on how secure the country is, bad images portrayed in the international mass media, the quality of infrastructure, the availability of international restaurants and whether shopping is unrestricted. It can be said that Myanmar has certain strengths and weaknesses according to the analysis of tour operators.

Myanmar's strength as a tourist destination is that it is unspoiled and not overdeveloped, especially in terms of the marine and beach environment and the unique and rich culture and its heritage. This makes the country a strong tourism product that is relatively easy to sell. At the same time, however, there are a number of points that detract from Myanmar's attractiveness as a tourist destination. For example, the transportation infrastructure is not convenient or easily accessible and the sense of personal security is not strong. Tourists are restricted to visiting only four places in the country and there is a compulsory charge in US dollars for all arriving international tourists. Tour operators can offer several suggestions about measures and actions that would increase tourist flows to Myanmar. The government can play a direct role by:

1) improving the domestic infrastructure, particularly land transportation;

2) provide more tourism promotional programmes;

3) open Mandalay Airport and provide for more international flights;

4) open land routes at key border crossings with China and Thailand; and

5) provide better levels of security to help improve the international image.

The national tourist organization needs more promotional programmes at the regional and international level and should actively organize its promotional programmes abroad. The tourism industry should work together with the national tourist organization to promote Myanmar as a destination. Some specific recommendations from the view of a tour operator that could be considered cover the following points. First, flight connections need improvement in order to attract tourists. National air carriers can play a major role by connecting various international destinations to various domestic destinations. This is a prerequisite for making promotions successful. National carriers with flights to various domestic destinations should connect with regional carriers from Bangkok or Singapore, for example, either directly or via Yangon. Second, national carriers should undertake joint marketing and promotion to help increase tourism flows, either individually or in cooperation with international airlines. The national carriers, plus international carriers should have joint marketing and promotion in cooperation with the Ministry of Tourism. Such collaboration could start with product promotion workshops. Third, regular business contacts should be maintained. The Ministry of Tourism could assign the top domestic tour operators to give competitive rates and better services to travel agents and operators overseas. There should also be increased contacts between Myanmar tour operators and international operators at trade fairs, travel marts, regional workshops, etc. The main general point to keep in mind is that sustainable tourism development can be achieved only through teamwork and collaboration with a focus on the goal of prosperity for the whole country.

HUMAN RESOURCES DEVELOPMENT IN THE TOURISM

The rapid rates of growth of tourism in Asia and the Pacific have given cause for concern in the area of human resources development. It is important to recall that tourism is a labour-intensive industry and a major source of employment. The World Travel and Tourism Council recently estimated that tourism in Asia and the Pacific directly employed about 55 million people, and this makes issues of human resources development very significant at the regional level. In most countries of the region there is not a shortage of manpower, but there is an acute shortage of trained manpower in the tourism sector. This has been found to be the case at all levels of the tourism industry. Most countries in the region have identified the main problems as a shortage of trained labour, lack of trainers, inadequate training materials and lack of tourism education strategies as part of the national tourism planning overall.

It is important to see tourism needs in the broader framework of national human resources development objectives. There are certain standard objectives, but there can be differences in emphasis depending on a country's level of development. More importantly, the objectives have to be linked to human resources development strategies that form part of an integrated plan. For tourism human resources, the strategies for education and training should also be part of an integrated plan covering tourism development overall. However, most countries in the region have not included human resources development strategies in their broad plans. Developing human resources in the tourism industry faces unique challenges, because customer preferences, travel patterns, information technology and conditions at destinations are changing rapidly. As a result, strong and flexible human resources development strategies are needed. The strategy should mirror human resources needs and the corresponding recruitment, employment and training requirements.

Usually, there are three separate government ministries involved in matters related to tourism education and training: education, labour and tourism. Coordination among these different agencies is important, as well as including other government organizations that might be involved. One way to achieve meaningful coordination that could be proposed by the national tourism organization in any country is to establish a national committee or council for tourism education and training. Such a committee or council could be advisory and consultative and should bring the following together: ministries responsible for tourism, labour and education; workers organizations (unions); professional and trade associations (employers); the national association of hotel and tourism schools; and all other parts of the tourism sector. Such a national committee/council should set standards and review policies, set objectives and identify results. The committee/council would be required to:

— Monitor labour market conditions and related trends

— Review existing and future needs for tourism personnel in management, supervisory positions, skilled and unskilled staff

— Review programmes of existing education and training institutions to evaluate the relevance to identified needs

— Liaise with the university system to promote development of appropriate programmes and activities

— Encourage the private sector to take initiatives to provide training programmes and facilities

Enhance the image of tourism as an employer and improve recruitment Strategies for human resources development in the tourism sector should highlight the role of the private sector, with the government acting as a catalyst to create conditions and guidelines. Most tourism employment is in the private sector, and it is thus crucial that the private sector participates, provides support and resources and gives consultation. The private sector also has to see that it will benefit from national objectives, strategies and policies for human resources development in the tourism industry. In fact, studies have shown that profits increase due to improved quality service and costs are reduced significantly when companies invest in training. Trade associations can play an important role to encourage the private sector's direct contribution to tourism human resources development. There are a number of international and regional organizations that provide support in the area of human resources development in the tourism industry.

Sustainable tourism development is a fifth area that contributes to facilitation of travel. The concept of sustainable tourism development has made both the private and public sector more aware about cultural and environmental conservation, ecotourism and agro-tourism. Many other government agencies have joined in efforts to upgrade destinations that reflect Thailand's natural diversity and cultural heritage. The sixth area contributing to facilitation is information technology development. Promotional activities of TAT are being designed to make use of new information technology that gives tourists more channels of tourism information about Thailand. The seventh area for facilitating travel and tourism is privatization. The government is considering a number of steps to privatize certain parts of Thailand's aviation and airline industry. This should help improve efficiency of services and contribute to effective marketing activities for tourism in Thailand. It is clear that facilitation can produce both positive and negative effects for tourism in any country, including Thailand. Tourism arrivals and revenues have increased over the last 20 years, and new business and employment opportunities have been created in the tourism industry.

Tourism-related infrastructure in various parts of the country has improved the quality of life for local people and helped promote local arts and crafts. Tourism has contributed to increased awareness about conservation of the environment and the cultural heritage. However, the carrying capacity has been exceeded at some popular tourist destinations, resulting in pollution, environmental degradation and rising living costs. There is a national plan for ecotourism, but it has not yet been implemented to take a practical reality. As a result, growth of tourism lacks a proper direction. Greater facilitation of travel might also create a negative image as some travelers might engage in various criminal activities in Thailand. The total picture of tourism development in Thailand or any destination goes beyond facilitation of travel and must include coordination among government agencies and between the public and private sector. In addition, there are opportunities for regional and subregional cooperation that can contribute to tourism development.

The use of modern information technology will become increasingly important for the tourism industry during the era of globalization as a part of remaining competitive and as part of reaching target markets. Most importantly, tourists will be attracted to destinations that make sustainable tourism development an achievable, realistic goal that produces results.

GROWTH IN RURAL TOURISM

Growth in rural tourism is difficult to quantify, because few countries collect statistics in a way which separates purely rural from other forms of tourism. Most national tourism administrations agree, however, that it is a growth sector. Experience in individual rural regions provides further testimony. At first glance, this is a simple question. Rural tourism is tourism which takes place in the countryside. But, on deeper consideration, a simple definition of rural tourism is inadequate for many purposes. Equally, it is difficult to produce a more complex definition which applies to all rural areas in all countries. Problems include:

— Urban-or-resort-based tourism is not confined to urban areas, but spills out into rural areas;

— Rural areas themselves are difficult to define, and the criteria used by different nations vary enormously;

— Not all tourism which takes place in rural areas is strictly "rural" it can be "urban" in form, and merely be located in a rural area;

— Tourism has historically been an urban concept; the great majority of tourists live in urban areas. Tourism can be an urbanising influence on rural areas, encouraging cultural and economic change, and new construction;

— Different forms of rural tourism have developed in different regions.

— Farm-based holidays are important in many parts of rural Germany and Austria. Farm-based holidays are much rarer in the rural United States and Canada;

— Rural areas themselves are in a complex process of change.

The impact of global markets, communications and telecommunication have changed market conditions and orientations for traditional products. The rise of environmentalism has led to increasing control by "outsiders" over land use and resource development.

Although some rural areas still experience depopulation, others are experiencing an inflow of people to retire or to develop new 'non-traditional' businesses. The once clear distinction between urban and rural is now blurred by suburbanisation, long distance commuting and second home development.

Rural tourism is a complex multi-faceted activity: it is not just farm-based tourism. It includes farm-based holidays but also comprises special interest nature holidays and ecotourism, walking, climbing and riding holidays, adventure, sport and health tourism, hunting and angling, educational travel, arts and heritage tourism, and, in some areas, ethnic tourism. There is also a large general interest market for less specialised forms of rural tourism. This area is highlighted by studies of the important German tourism market, where a major requirement of the main holiday is the ability to provide peace, quiet and relaxation in rural surroundings.

Because rural tourism is multi-faceted, because rural areas themselves are multi-faceted and rarely either static entities or self-contained, and free from urban influence, a working and reasonably universal definition of the subject is difficult to find. However, in almost every case rurality is the central and unique selling point in the rural tourism package. The search for a definition must, therefore, begin with an understanding of the concept of rurality itself.

Typically rural areas have low population densities: this is a result of small settlements, widely spaced apart. The natural and/or the farmed/forested environment dominates the built environment. Average rural population densities vary enormously between and within the OECD countries: an exact analysis would be valueless because of the varying sizes of the administrative units used for statistical purposes.

The OECD Rural Development Programme uses a pragmatically based series of indicators: while at local level a population density of 150 persons per square kilometre is the preferred criterion, "at the regional level geographic units are grouped by the share of their population which is rural, into the following three types: predominantly rural (> 50 per cent), significantly rural (15-50 per cent) and predominantly urbanized regions (< 15 per cent)". From this array of varying definitions, two clear points stand out. Rural settlements may vary in size, but they are small, and always with a population of fewer than 10 000 inhabitants. They are almost always in areas of relatively low population density.

Many commentators define rural areas as those with less than 10-20 per cent of their land areas covered by the built environment. There are three important implications here. These areas will be dominated by agrarian and forest-based economic activities. They will be, to a large extent, repositories of the natural world and wild-life. For the visitor, they will give an impression of space, and a traditional non-urban, non-industrial economy. Their economies will be strongly influenced by the market for farm and forest products. Although the labour force required for farming and forestry has declined rapidly in recent years, rural areas still show a strong bias towards jobs in the farm/forest sector. Additionally, they usually exhibit low female activity rates outside the home because of the shortage of job opportunities for women in many rural areas.

The rapid urbanisation of the nineteenth and twentieth centuries produced new social structures different from the 'traditional' societies of the countryside. The retention of older ways of life and thinking is important in retaining rural 'character'. It is this residual character which, combined with the scenic values and recreational opportunities of the countryside, attracts tourists from urban areas. It is difficult to define the exact characteristics of rural society. There are great variations between countries and continents, and even within countries.

Rural communities can be assessed on a sliding scale with sparsely populated remote wilderness as one end of a polar typology. The other end of the scale can be represented by the so-called "world city", the ultimate expression of urbanisation. Between these extremes lie a variety of situations, largely rural or largely urban, with a mid-point represented by the outermost edge of suburbia, a cross-over point between poles, exhibiting characteristics of both rural and urban typology. An additional part of the 'rurality' equation can be introduced here. The OECD's Rural Development Programme has developed a useful typology for assessing the economic geography of rural areas. This divides the rural world into peripheral or remote regions, 'intermediate' regions, which make up the majority of the rural land mass, and economically integrated rural regions, often close to large urban complexes.

The peripheral regions are characterised by sparse populations, small scale often traditional enterprises, high servicing costs and economic poverty. The economically integrated regions tend to have large farm units, a diversified economy, good services and relative affluence. The intermediate areas lie midway between these extremes. This typology can also fit the continuum concept: the three types of region are not sharply defined but blend into each other. The typology has important implications for both rural development and rural tourism which will be explained later. The continuum concept copes not only with a variety of landscapes, life styles and demographic inheritance-but also with change. Settlements can move along the continuum, exhibiting change through time. Typically-but not always—the change tends to move districts and settlements towards the urban pole. In the OECD's economic typology, change is also common-and can also occur in either direction.

Thus, rural settlements may remain locationally rural while becoming functionally urban. Settlement size and population density may remain "rural", but economies may become non-agricultural, and society may display increasing numbers of urban characteristics. Different parts of rural society may display more or less urban characteristics.

The practical expression of the pro-rural sentiments quoted above has been two-fold. Government policies financially support both primary rural products and rural service provision in every OECD Member country. These financial policies are frequently backed by strong conservation policies, aimed at the retention of existing landscape areas, whole settlements, buildings and the natural world. Urban conservation policies also exist, but usually cover only fragments of cities and isolated special situations.

It has been argued above that rurality as a concept is connected with low population densities and open space, and with small scale settlements, generally of fewer than 10 000 inhabitants. Land use is dominated by farming, forestry and natural areas. Societies tend towards traditionalism: the influence of the past is often strong. Government policies lean towards conservation rather than radical or rapid change. It follows, therefore, that rural tourism should be:

— Located in rural areas;

— Functionally rural, built upon the rural world's special features: small scale enterprise, open space, contact with nature and the natural world, heritage, "traditional" societies and "traditional" practices;

— Rural in scale both in terms of buildings and settlements-and, therefore, usually small scale;

— Traditional in character, growing slowly and organically, and connected with local families. It will often be very largely controlled locally and developed for the long term good of the area;

— Sustainable—-in the sense that its development should help sustain the special rural character of an area, and in the sense that its development should be sustainable in its use of resources. Rural tourism should be seen as a potential tool for conservation and sustainability, rather than as an urbanizing and development tool;

— Of many different kinds, representing the complex pattern of rural environment, economy, and history.

Commentators seeking to define rurality have made extensive use of the concept of the rural/urban continuum to deal with many different types of area, exhibiting different characteristics, and areas undergoing active change. A similar continuum concept can be useful for those seeking to define rural tourism. Few areas will display all of the characteristics of rural tourism listed previously. Many will display some "urban" characteristics. Some will be in the process of change and development towards becoming large, urban resorts. The use of the continuum concept allows planners to recognise this 15 trend, and to take steps either to regulate it, or to make infrastructural provision for it. It can be strongly argued that management strategies in rural tourism should aim to conserve rurality as an important resource. But, in some cases it may be valuable to allow or even encourage some change to take place.

Rural tourism cannot be defined solely by holiday type: intensity of use, location, style of management, integration with the community and other factors play an important part in the definition. But a broad-brush approach can be useful. Again, the continuum concept is a useful one. Many types of holiday can be developed in both urban and rural locations. Holiday-makers may be involved in both urban and rural activities on the same day. A tentative classification of holiday types is given below: it should be used with care. The listing follows the continuum concept, moving from specifically rural to specifically urban with a broad intermediate category.

Tourism and Agriculture

Traditionally agriculture and forestry were central to rural life. They were the major employers of labour, the main sources of income within the rural economy, and indirectly had a powerful influence on traditions, power structures and life styles. Together, the decisions of farmers and foresters determined rural land use and landscapes.

In the late twentieth century, the central role of farming and forestry has been diminished. Both activities have shed much of their labour force. Only five OECD countries now employ more than 15 per cent of their labour force in farming, forestry and fishing: in eight OECD countries, that figure is less than 5 per cent. The economic power of farming and forestry has declined, not least because those activities are extremely dependent on state subsidies for their profitability. Traditions are waning before the combined attack of television, power farming techniques and tree processors. Even the role of agri-and arboriculturalists as "landscape gardeners" has diminished: power has begun to move to planners and conservationists.

In this evolving situation, two myths have grown up about the role of rural tourism. One is that rural tourism is farm-based tourism. The second is 17 that diversification into tourism will universally "save" the farming community. These statements are untrue because the relationships between agriculture, forestry and tourism are extremely complex ones. Farm-based rural tourism has been successful through many (but not all) parts of German-speaking Europe because of a powerful combination of small farm size, interesting scenery, closeness to markets, traditional town/country links caused by late migration from the countryside to city regions, the owner-occupation of farmsteads and the tradition of effective and interventionary local government and co-operative movements. Furthermore, the role of farm-based tourism has been exaggerated because it has received great attention from both agriculture ministries and academics. The Bibiliography of Rural Tourism for the OECD reveals that farm tourism is the largest single special category of rural tourism in terms of published works. In areas where some or all of the factors mentioned above are lacking, farm-based tourism has been slow to develop. Reasons include:

— Long distances to the urban holiday market;

— Medium and large sized farms which did not need to diversify, or were amalgated to create larger units;

— Rented farms which either failed to receive the owner's permission to diversify, or were amalgamated to create larger units;

— Very poor and very small farms which had no surplus accommodation;

— Coops and local councils and tourist boards which did not help with marketing and infrastructure provision;

— Scenery/heritage/activity attractions which were poor.

Thus, for example, over large parts of Eastern England, Sweden, Canada and the United States, farm tourism is poorly developed. But that does not mean that rural tourism is poorly developed. Many of the kinds of rural holidays discussed earlier are not dependent on farm situations. Accommodation can be provided by hotels and motels, small town and village bed and breakfasts, purpose built lodges, camping and caravan sites.

Diversification into rural tourism is frequently held up as a potential panacea for agriculture's ills. There is no doubt that in some areas, and for some businesses, tourism can be valuable. But there are serious problems in its universal application:

— Over 75 per cent of the land of the OECD countries is rural: there are insufficient visitors to maintain all farmers in all areas; 18

— Farm-based tourism does not reduce productivity on many farms. In some cases, additional tourism earnings are invested to increase agricultural productivity. Therefore, farm surpluses in OECD countries could continue to grow, leading to falling prices and quota restrictions, and a further round of farm problems;

— Some areas are unsuitable for intensive tourism development because of remoteness, lack of scenic or heritage attractions, and other factors;

Successful farm tourism development seems to require effective co-operative marketing and development efforts. Many areas have no tradition of co-operation between farmers, or between farmers and · governmental agencies.

The key relationship in rural tourism is between tourism development and comprehensive rural development, embracing rural services, new enterprise attraction, conservation, a wider role for women and inward investment. Agriculture has an important role to play in rural tourism, but it is but one facet amongst many: it may be of greater or lesser importance depending on local, regional and national circumstances.

Market-promises and Problems

Rural tourism is not an accidental or temporary growth phenomenon. Although the travel trade is in some senses a 'fashion' industry, subject to short term trends, the forces behind the growth of rural tourism are more long term in nature. These forces are partly connected to long term changes in the travel market, partly to improvements in transport and communications and partly to the efforts of public agencies charged with assisting rural change. In total, 14 key factors can be isolated which have been responsible for rural tourism growth in the past and which will continue that growth into the future. Increasing levels of education. The post-war period has seen universal increase in free or assisted education available to the populations of the developed world. This has included longer periods of school-based education, more higher education, the spread of adult and continuing education and the growth of non-formalised education, via radio, television and other media. Research shows that increasing levels of education correlate with increased interest in outdoor recreation, eco-tourism, and special interest holidays. A growing interest in heritage. Over the last 20 years there has been a boom in the level of interest in heritage both man-made and natural. This reflects many factors: a fear of the future, a fear of rootlessness, better education, time to explore, and, not least, better heritage presentation.

Increases in leisure time, coupled with higher levels of disposable income, are important factors in developing tourism generally. One specific aspect of this equation is important for rural tourism. This is the growth of the short break, and the second or third holiday market. The European Community's 1985, Europeans on Holiday indicated that, of those taking holidays, over one-third now take two or more holiday trips involving overnight stays away from home each year. This is important because while a "traditional" resort-based holiday may still account for main holidays, rural special interest holidays can be tried for the second, often shorter, holiday without too much risk.

Transport and communications have improved so rapidly and universally in the post-war period that remoteness-in time and cost-is now no longer a major problem for rural areas. This ease of movement owes itself in part to technological changes-jet aircraft, high speed trains, motorways, and roll-on roll-off ferries, automatic telephone systems and fax machines. It has been influenced by better and more widespread money handling facilities, chief of which has been the internationally acceptable credit card. There have also been key attitudinal changes on behalf of both the travel trade and their clients. Distance and remoteness have become selling points, rather than barriers. Health consciousness has grown and is growing steadily and in the concept of healthy living, active recreation plays an important part. Exercise and sport play central roles in healthy living strategies.

Rural areas are well placed to provide outdoor recreation of all kinds from walking to cycling, orienteering, skiing and climbing. The countryside is assumed to be healthy, with overtones of fresh air and bucolic well-being. In contrast, resort holidays based on the sun/sea/sand formula have been found to offer serious health risks. Medical researchers in Australasia, America and Scandinavia have pinpointed sunbathing as being responsible for higher levels of skin disease, ranging from premature wrinkling to deadly skin cancers. While this problem is still only fully appreciated in the southern hemisphere, it seems very likely that knowledge of the risks posed by sun-belt holidays will grow.

Better outdoor clothing has helped rural holidays in both a practical and a fashion sense. High performance fabrics enable wearers to stay warm and dry in adverse weather, allowing tourists to enjoy wet weather and out-of-season conditions. Contemporary outdoor clothing is now extremely fashionable, and available in a wide range of colours and styles. Outdoor recreation equipment has also been much improved and many items, such as the mountain bike, the wind surfer and the 4-wheel drive utility vehicle, have achieved cult fashion status.

A growing interest in speciality food is widely evident, be it wild rice from North America, non-pasturized cheeses from France, cholesterol-free, non-farmed salmon and deer from Scandinavia, or organic produce from the Alps. Considerable space in the press is devoted to speciality foods and food preparation. Rural holidays have been able to capitalise on this trend because the countryside is the source of quality non-processed foods. Green issues have risen high on most political agendas over the last ten years. This interest has been seized upon by the marketeers of many consumer products, including holiday tour operators. Rural holidays, although not necessarily environmentally friendly, can capitalise on the wholesomeness which the countryside is felt to exude.

Authenticity is a quality which is increasingly prized. In a world of video and television entertainment, factory produced goods, and suburban anonymity, the authenticity of the countryside, and the personal touch provided by small scale communities and accommodation units is extremely valuable. An English Tourist Board, motives for taking rural holidays, conducted in 1987, placed this point second only to scenery as a reason for staying in the countryside.

The many facets of rural tourism are specially placed to fulfil the needs of this growth market. Individualism is also a growth market, rejecting the mass activities of the past. The growth of individualism has been noted and acted upon by the car manufacturers, by clothing manufacturers, and by many other purveyors of consumer goods. Rural tourism, because of the fragmented and small scale nature of the enterprises involved, is especially capable of exploiting this market trend, although high quality selling and hospitality skills are needed. The rural agencies, numerous in most countries, have been quick to express an interest in rural tourism and to offer aid and advice. These agencies include those connected with agriculture, with nature conservation, with community welfare, with the arts and crafts, with National Parks, with economic development, transport—the list is almost endless. Although the agencies rarely co-ordinate their activities, and are rarely organisations with any experience of tourism, they have assisted many collective individual enterprises.

Estimates have been made of the size of the 'Special Interest' tourism market, which is a closely related area. The World Tourism Organization estimated the special interest market to be about 3 per cent of the total domestic and international market in 1985. In 1989, the U.S. travel 22 agents revealed that special interest holidays comprised 15 per cent of all bookings. Repeat bookings accounted for one-third of the clients surveyed. German statistics claim that 20 per cent of main holidays are now in the special interest category. Therefore, if levels of income and educational attainment continue to rise across the OECD countries, the market for rural tourism should also grow. At the time of writing, recessionary trends may limit short term growth; in the long term, most authorities predict a return to slowly rising standards. Aside from the bird-watching and hunting/fishing markets, which have a wider appeal across the whole socio-economic spectrum in many countries, rural tourism is generally supported by an up-market clientele.

The American state of Wyoming (with a population of 512 000) estimates that wildlife tourism is worth over $ 1 billion annually within its borders. Britain's Countryside Commission estimated that visitors to the countryside spent £ 3 000 million in 1986: of this figure £ 1 100 million came from those spending at least one night in the countryside, and the remainder came from day trips. These are gross figures; the net figures after deduction of goods bought in to service tourism, when tax has been paid, etc., would be much lower, but, equally, they make no allowance for the multiplier effect of tourism spending. Clearly, rural tourism, while still only a minority tourism market, is already making a valuable contribution to rural economies. Its contribution can be expressed not only in financial terms, but also in terms of jobs, contributions towards funding conservation, encouragement to the adoption of new working practices, and the injection of a new vitality into sometimes weakened economies. In total, tourism promises potential benefits to rural development. These are covered in detail below.

— Job retention is extremely important in rural areas where employment decline is often endemic. Tourism cash flows can assist job retention in services such as retailing, transport, hospitality and medical care. It · can also provide additional income for farmers, and, in some cases, for foresters and fisherman. Job retention is not as politically glamorous as job creation, but, by helping the viability of small communities, it is critical to the survival of marginal areas. Studies of rural Austria, Sweden and Ireland have documented the role of tourism in job retention.

— Job creation is a further possibility if rural tourism is successful. Job creation typically occurs in the hotel and catering trades, but can also take place in transport, retailing, and in information/heritage interpretation. Studies in Britain suggest that job creation varies by enterprise type. Farmhouse accommodation and bed-and-breakfast can create up to 23 jobs per £ 100 000 of tourism revenue. Job creation effects are less marked in hotels and caravan/campsites, yielding approximately six jobs per £ 100 000 of revenue. Similar figures of between five and six jobs per £ 100 000 revenue have been estimated for rural attractions of all types.

— Job diversity is encouraged by rural tourism development. Most rural areas have little job variety outside farming and basic services. Better job diversity enriches rural society, and helps retain population levels.

Pluriactivity can be a further useful by-product of tourism in the countryside. Pluriactivity is the term used when an individual or family carries out more than one type of job to maintain their income. A part-time farmer could also offer accommodation, assist the local administration in service tasks and act as a ski-instructor. Sea fishermen may take tourist parties on angling trips, on whale watching expeditions off the coast of Canada and the United States, or on bird-watching excursions off the coast of Ireland or Scotland. Pluriactivity guards against recession in any one sector. It is especially important in the rural context because of the cultural importance of the family as a unit in many traditional societies. Service retention is vital in rural areas: rural tourism can assist in three ways.

Visitor information services can be provided by existing outlets, such as shops, thus increasing income flows if payment is made for acting as information outlets. Services can also benefit by the additional customers which visitors provide. The high levels of public transport in rural Austria and Switzerland are in part due to the support they receive from holiday-makers. This additional custom is not, however, automatic: to make the most of the potential, services often need to offer new products, to be available at different times and to understand the new markets. Finally, tourism's importance to national economies can strengthen the political case for subsides to help retain services.

Farm support is a major issue on all political agendas. Many studies have shown that farm incomes can be bolstered by rural tourism, through accommodation enterprises of all kinds, by developing open farms and other attractions, by increased sales of farm produce, and by increasing female activity rates through additional off-farm employment. There are widespread variations in the levels of farmer participation in rural tourism throughout the OECD countries, varying by region, farm size, age of farmer and other factors. Forestry is an important activity in many upland and climatically marginal regions. Forest regions have suffered serious socio-economic problems in recent years, partly because of the mechanisation of tree felling and processing, and partly because of falling prices following reduced timber demand. Rural tourism can assist forestry by diversifying income sources for forest communities if the special qualities of the forest environment for recreational use are realised and developed.

Landscape conservation has become an increasingly important form of heritage protection. Although this dates back to the designation of America's Yellowstone National Park in 1872, the national park movement is still progressing and most countries now have a wide range of lesser designations covering many types of landscape. Landscape is of crucial importance to rural tourism but, equally, visitor use is vital to the landscape conservation industry. Visitor use brings political benefits, can bring economic gains, and can provide jobs in maintaining and repairing traditional landscapes worn by recreational activities. Smaller settlements in the countryside have always been at greater risk of losing viability because they are unable to support the many services which now require larger threshold populations to support them. Rural tourism can assist these smaller settlements to survive, because smaller places have a special attraction for visitors. Careful management of this process is, however, required.

Rural arts and crafts have a special place in the cultural heritage of regions and nations. Many commentators have noted that tourism can assist arts and crafts, both by recognising their importance, and by purchasing craft products. Income flows from these activities are well documented. Support between the arts and tourism can be a two-way process. Many communities now use arts and crafts festivals as a marketing mechanism to encourage visitors to come to their areas. Cultural provision has always been restricted in rural areas. The lack of major facilities such as theatre, opera, music and galleries has been one of the many factors encouraging rural depopulation. Nature conservation, like landscape conservation, is a stated goal of most modern governments. It is, however, an expensive process.

Rural tourism can valorise nature conservation in a monetary sense. Many estimates have been made of the value of nature to tourism. On the grand scale, it is estimated that each elephant is worth $ 14 375 to the Kenyan economy. On a lesser scale, the British Royal Society for the Protection of Birds has demonstrated that even small bird reserves can help sustain village shops by visitor purchases and by the expenditure of reserve management and maintenance staff. Visitors are prepared to pay to see nature: most reserves and many national parks successfully charge for entrance.

Many historic properties now charge for admission in order to maintain their fabrics and surrounding gardens and parklands. Secondly, there are important buildings from the past which have become redundant. Churches have lost their congregations, castles have lost their wars, farm buildings have become too small for modern equipment, railway stations have lost their trains, and canal warehouses no longer have barge traffic. The tourist industry can usually use these redundant buildings profitably and imaginatively: they can become attractions in their own right. Environmental improvements such as village paving and traffic regulation schemes, sewage and litter disposal can be assisted by tourism revenues and political pressures from tourism authorities. These help develop pride of place, important in retaining existing population and businesses, and in attracting new enterprises and families. Small fishing communities are suffering badly from dwindling fish stocks, quota restrictions and international bans on some activities. A number of these communities can successfully diversify into sports fishing, bird and seal watching, and coastal sightseeing. Some environmental groups claim that potential revenue from whale and dolphin watching could exceed revenue from catching whales for meat.

The role of women within the rural community was, in the past, a restricted one. Farming, forestry and mining were very much male occupations. Alternative jobs for women were few. Women were rarely involved in local politics. The widespread emancipation of women, coupled with the possibilities which rural tourism offers, have together done much in many areas to release the under-utilised talents and energies of the female half of the population. Studies show that tourism enterprises have increased the power of women within both the family and the community. Experience in Spain, Greece, France, Britain and Ireland has demonstrated how the flexible and open-minded approach of women towards new ideas and co-operative working has helped develop and lead successful rural tourism programmes. The development of the role of women could do much for the economic and social well-being of many rural areas. New ideas and initiatives will be essential if rural communities are to prosper into the twenty-first century. Efforts to support agriculture, forestry and service provision by state subsidies have done much to develop a culture of dependency within the countryside.

The new challenges and the fiercely competitive nature of the tourism market could do much to encourage enterprise and new methods. There is also evidence that rural tourism can act as a catalyst to bring new businesses of many kinds into rural communities. Since 1971, the area has been able to reverse a century of depopulation, and it is now experiencing a population renewal.

CHAPTER 3

SUSTAINABLE TOURISM

Tourism is one of the many external forces influencing the direction and options for local development. The question of whether tourism can be sustainable-that is, whether it can contribute to local sustainable development-is rightfully addressed in the context of the Local Agenda 21 process.

The true proof of "sustainable tourism" will be the sustainable development of local communities that serve as tourist destinations. It is time for the sustainable tourism debate to focus on this challenge. Local authorities worldwide welcome the leadership of the UN Commission on Sustainable Development, and the interest of the tourism industry, to reduce tourism's negative impacts and to increase the positive contribution of tourism business and consumption activity to local sustainable development.

Tourism is a recognised global industry-one of the largest industries in the world. Like any global industry, tourist business activities can have considerable impact on local development trends. The local impacts of the tourism industry are diverse and are often unique to the tourism sector. Tourist activities, as traditionally defined by the tourism industry, fundamentally involve the transportation and hosting of the tourism consumer in a local community, i.e., "tourist destination," where the tourist product is consumed.

No other global industry structures itself in such a way that the consumer is brought to the product, rather than the product being delivered to the consumer in his or her own community. This structural difference produces unique social impacts upon the local tourist community, including the interruption of local customs and lifestyles, the spread of infectious diseases, changes in local demographics, and changes in local housing and labor markets. The primary product of tourism is not something produced by the industry.

The product is often the heritage, wealth, and expected legacy of the community that serves as the tourist destination. The business activity of the tourism industry is to promote the "salable" or appealing aspects ·of the community, transport non-residents into the community, manage the hospitality for and guide the activities of these visitors, and provide them with goods and services to purchase during their stay. If these business activities degrade the community's heritage and wealth, then the community suffers more directly than the consumer, who can return to his or her own community without responsibility for or awareness of the impacts of his tourist activities.

Tourism activities can, in particular, degrade the social and natural wealth of a community. The intrusion of large numbers of uninformed foreigners into local social systems can undermine pre-existing social relationships and values. This is particularly a problem where tourism business is centered in traditional social systems, such as isolated communities or indigenous peoples. Tourism in natural areas, euphemistically called "eco-tourism," can be a major source of degradation of local ecological, economic and social systems.

The intrusion of large numbers of foreigners with high-consumption and high-waste habits into natural areas, or into towns with inadequate waste management infrastructure, can produce changes to those natural areas at a rate that is far greater than imposed by local residents. These tourism-related changes are particularly deleterious when local residents rely on those natural areas for their sustenance. Resulting economic losses can encourage socially deleterious economic activities such as prostitution, crime, and migrant and child labour.

Sustainable tourism allows visitors to enjoy an attraction, community or region with a volume and impact in such a way that the local culture and environment are unimpaired. Strictly speaking, tourism and recreation use always lead to some level of impairment in natural systems. The question is primarily how much change is acceptable. Despite the extensive discussion about sustainability since the 1987 report from the World Commission on Environment and Development, which popularized the issue, few answers have been found. Entering sustainability-based management is essentially a value judgment, a decision that says that current management is inadequate or inappropriate.

Sustainability is a concept decision makers can use to assess the consequences of actions on human communities. A human focus is deliberately taken here because it is the human population that places values on social structure, cultural values and traditions, economic opportunity, and ecosystems and their species. Maintenance of ecosystems and the protection of individual species are human-based values and, therefore, can be described from only a human viewpoint.

Human communities are impacted in a variety of ways by tourism, including social structure and function, cohesiveness, economic and educational opportunity, community stability, provision of and payment for services (police protection, fire), physically (architecture, location and design of highways), competition in access to recreation opportunities and other services, and interaction with the natural environment and the non-commodity values it produces. The general concept is that sustainability is not only a goal for specific industries, but it is also an objective for the human communities that benefit and that are impacted from various economic development scenarios.

Industry sustainability goals are most likely physical output or net revenue goals, such as board feet of timber, room-nights occupancy, and skier visits. These sustainability goals, however, may not achieve broader community sustainability goals, goals that may be difficult to quantify and measure. Several other questions must be dealt with. At what spatial or social organizational scale do we want to measure sustainability globally, regionally, locally? We also are concerned about the temporal scale of sustainability tomorrow, next week, next year, and the next generation. We need to examine not only industry-specific sustainability, generally addressed by physical commodities, but also the impacts of distinctive economic development actions on the larger community.

ENVIRONMENTAL TOURISM

Environment is the travel industry's base product. While many tourism promotion efforts banner the climate, sun, warmth, and sand of particular destinations, tourism's dependency on environments, in particular, nature-dominated environments, does not appear to be well understood within the tourism and recreation industry. Cook and others, for example, focus more on how the tourism industry is meeting legal obligations for environmental protection (such as emissions) than the dependency of tourism on high-quality natural environments.

The importance of the environment in attracting vacation travel is significant, natural beauty and cultural heritage represent a competitive advantage for many areas. A place that takes care of its environment is very important in choosing a destination outside of the state. The linkage between environment as an attraction and economic impact can be substantial.

ADVERSE TOURISM

Solutions to adverse tourism impacts are to be found in the shared interest of local communities, tourism businesses, and tourism consumers to maintain the natural wealth and social heritage of the tourist destination. In the first instance, therefore, an institutional mechanism must be established, relative to each destination, to articulate and develop this sense of shared interest.

To secure the legitimacy of these mechanisms, the participation of all interested local groups or interests must be guaranteed. Dialogue must take place in an open and transparent way. Experience demonstrates that if dialogue among interested parties is to have a real impact on development, it must generate accountability among these parties with regards to future investments, practices and policies. Consensus or decisions arising from dialogue must be reflected in institutional action.

Only through such accountability can interests maintain a commitment to continued dialogue and a common agenda for local tourism development. Experience demonstrates that this accountability should be reciprocal between individual or private interests and societal or public interests. Without such reciprocal accountability, local communities are typically forced to choose, in conflict, between private and public benefits, even if ample "win-win" development choices exist.

On the one hand, accountability requires that property owners are provided with opportunity to retain the economic value of their property, either through sale or income generating activity. On the other hand, private market relationships, including property ownership, do not provide sufficient basis for social accountability related to "public goods," including ecological integrity and social heritage. Private property titles do not recognise the concepts of ecological integrity or social heritage.

Excessive reliance upon private property ownership as a guide in development has in fact contributed to the deterioration of public goods. Within such a framework of accountability, numerous instruments are available to guide local tourist development on a sustainable path.

However, without true commitment to the sustainable tourism agenda, these instruments are not themselves sufficient to prevent the steady erosion, by legally sanctioned private actions, of local natural wealth and social heritage. Therefore, support from the international, national, provincial and local levels of industry and government, is essential to the success of this agenda.

Fortunately, in more than 2,000 communities in 64 countries Local Agenda 21 partnership forums already exist to serve as a mechanism for sustainable tourism dialogue. Where these forums are weak or have not yet addressed tourism issues, the tourist industry, local government organisations (LGOs) and concerned NGOs can serve as a catalyst for dialogue.

A particular opportunity exists in those countries where Local Agenda 21 national campaigns (in more than 20 countries) or where National Councils for Sustainable Development (NCSDs-in about 70 countries) have been established. NCSDs can play a key role in providing country-level support to local review of the sustainable tourism agenda. Through their international facilitating body, the Earth Council, a comprehensive effort between industry, NGOs, LGOs and NCSDs can be established. Of additional interest at the local level is the potential role of local tourism offices or Convention and Visitor Bureaus (CVBs) that have been created through public-private partnerships to promote local tourist attractions.

Where motivated to support sustainable tourism development, the CVBs could serve as facilitators of working groups, within the context of Local Agenda 21 activities, on sustainable tourism development. Where CVBs or their related international body(ies) have made no express commitment to sustainable development, local authorities, as primary funders of CVBs, are in an excellent position to mobilise their awareness and support. Internationally, alliances between LGOs and various tourism industry trade associations, trade unions and consumer organisations can support awareness raising and local demonstration projects that may serve as models for other local communities on a country or regional basis.

Consumer Behaviour

Tourism-related consumption has three stages of impact. First, prior to departure, tourists purchase travel-related clothing and equipment, which may be produced under conditions that undermine the social and ecological sustainability of the producing communities. Second, when tourists travel long distances to tourist destinations, they create considerable atmospheric pollution and other impacts on the global environment. Third, upon arrival at the tourist destination, tourists often continue their accustomed habits of consumption, even though these destinations may not have the infrastructure required to manage those consumption patterns.

In addition to high altitude emissions from long distance air travel, air travel produces considerable negative local environmental impacts, including ground level emissions of VOCs and particulates, disposal of fuel, hazardous chemicals and solid waste, noise pollution, and wildlife and habitat disruption. Marine dumping of wastes from cruise ships is an increasing concern. However, with nearly 600 million international travelers in 1997, surprisingly little public information is available on the environmental and social impacts of long distance travel.

For instance, individual travelers receive far greater information about the impacts of their local automobile use than of their air or cruise ship transportation. Motor vehicle pollution is typically more highly regulated than aircraft and ship pollution. Following arrival at tourist destinations, the tourism industry typically strives to host tourists according to the standards and amenities of their country of origin. These hospitality standards mimic-and encourage-the high consumption lifestyles of developed countries.

For instance, luxury hotel rooms, with high levels of energy and water consumption, are given the highest rankings or "stars" in international hotel rankings. These "luxury" consumption standards, using current technologies, are themselves globally unsustainable. The most immediate observable impacts of introducing these high consumption practices into lower consumption communities are:

— degradation of local water and soil quality, with direct impacts on local health and economies, as a result of the lack of adequate water, drainage, waste water, and waste management infrastructure to manage the higher volumes of waste produced by higher levels of consumption;

— reduced access by local residents to land, housing and marine resources through, among other things, reallocation of these community resources to foreign tourist residents and inflation of local prices;

— destruction of traditional sources of income.

The most direct way to reduce the adverse impacts of tourism-related travel is to increase opportunities for people to engage in appealing tourism activities in their own cities, regions or countries. In various cities of the world, this local tourism concept is known as "green tourism." Green tourism-in contrast to "eco-tourism," which relies on travel to distant locations-seeks to provide recreational attractions and hospitality facilities to local people within their local regions, thereby reducing tourism-related travel.

While green tourism has the positive economic effect of stimulating local economic activity, it reduces the flow of foreign currency to developing nations- and any resulting economic benefits that may accrue to developing towns and cities from these revenue flows. However, short of definitive actions by the tourism industry and host countries/communities to reduce the negative environmental impacts of foreign travel and the negative social impacts of foreign tourist enclaves in developing nations, green tourism advocates will continue to build support among tourism consumers.

Solutions to tourism-related pollution in the travel and tourism industry are technologically available. Overcoming economic barriers to their implementation may require government regulation, the development of economic instruments, and industry self-regulation. The industry has every opportunity to institute voluntary initiatives and self-regulation to address green tourism advocates and those calling for government regulation.

The growing effort among international hotel chains, for instance, to offer guests the option of reusing their bedroom towels and linens demonstrates the ability of the industry to respond in one area of impact. However, more comprehensive efforts are required to tangibly resolve accelerating environmental and social impacts. In this regard, the establishment of formal environmental management systems (EMSs) in each business establishment provides a way for tourism businesses to identify their adverse social and environmental impacts and to institute a programme for continuous reductions of those impacts.

EMS registration programmes such as ISO 14001 and European EMAS regimes offer extensive guidance to tourism businesses, and deserve the active support of international tourism industry associations. Ultimately, the solution to adverse environmental impacts arising from local tourist consumption is the establishment of waste reduction programs and appropriate waste management systems and infrastructure, particularly in developing country destinations.

Again a choice exists between voluntary and regulatory measures. National governments and tourism businesses, which receive disproportional economic benefits from tourism, share an interest in maintaining tourismrelated hard currency inflows, and should either directly provide such infrastructure or ensure that funds are made available to local authorities for this purpose.

Without such support, powers should be provided to local authorities to increase local revenues from tourism, through local airport taxes, hotel and service taxes, and development fees, to finance infrastructure construction and maintenance. Only through such economic instruments can the public costs of tourism activity be "internalised" in the local tourist economy. Local revenue measures need to be carefully coordinated across municipal jurisdictions on a regional basis to ensure coordinated infrastructure development.

Without a coordinated regional infrastructure development approach, pollution from communities without infrastructure can undo the environmental benefits of infrastructure investments in neighboring communities. Where statutory regional planning bodies do not exist to provide coordination, Local Agenda 21 forums may provide a flexible mechanism for multi-jurisdictional coordination. Tourist businesses can make a significant voluntary contribution to resolving the social costs of tourism by:

— providing local resident employment and training opportunities, including in traditional trades and crafts;

— establishing purchasing guidelines that favor local goods and services procurement;

— making donations and investments in local recreational facilities, parks, cultural facilities and security operations (which also serve to improve local tourist amenities as well);

— establishing local profit-sharing arrangements.

Failing necessary voluntary measures, local governments can institute economic incentives and regulatory measures to reward best practices and prevent severe social impacts that need to be resolved at public expense. Ultimately, in the face of private establishments that demonstrate no long-term commitment to maintaining the preconditions for tourism-which include public safety, environmental quality, infrastructure maintenance, and economic justice-local authorities need to use all powers available to protect the cultural and environmental wealth that make an attractive tourist destination.

Agents and Partnerships for Change: A partnership approach to addressing negative impacts of tourism consumption requires, above all, assumption of responsibility and voluntary action by the tourism industry. For example, within the framework of a voluntary EMS approach, partnerships can be established between local governments, airport authorities, regional air quality agencies, airlines, trade unions, NGOs and resident associations to develop an action programme to reduce local airport pollution.

Following the model of the "Responsible Care" programme in the chemical industry, these partnerships could be supported by international travel and tourism organisations and related industry associations. Measures to reduce high altitude pollution by aircraft require similar initiatives by the industry and government at the national and international levels.

Of critical importance is the creation of mechanisms to inform and involve tourism consumers in making educated choices about their activities as tourists in distant tourist destinations. Ideally, these efforts would ensure that tourism consumers, as with industry, begin to recognise and understand tourist destinations as living communities that deserve their support and respect. Communications from tourism consumers to tourism industry and to local authorities about their desire to reduce the adverse impacts of their tourism activities can be essential to mobilising changes in industry and government practices.

International consumer advocacy organisations and trade unions can play an important role in informing consumers about tourism development activities that violate basic principles of sustainable development. Provision of such information to LGOs can facilitate local authority responsiveness to identified problems.

Broad-based Tourism Development

Many of the technologies and measures required for sustainable development in the tourism sector are clear. Resources exist within the tourism industry-which annually generates hundreds of billions of dollars-to apply these technologies and to make development within the sector more equitable. However, as the experiences of hundreds of local authorities demonstrate, through their engagement in broad-based sustainable development planning through Local Agenda 21, the appropriate application of technologies and resources requires effective and truly accountable development partnerships.

If industry and government are to protect and sustain the social, cultural and environmental wealth that attracts tourists, they must build more ambitious and committed partnerships to plan, manage and invest in this wealth. In this respect, the primary barrier to sustainable development through tourism is an over reliance on market mechanisms to guide tourism development and consumption decisions. The market-which treats cultural and environmental wealth as free, "public goods" and which responds to degradation of this wealth as a "free rider"-provides instruments to guide development, but is insensitive to many requirements of sustainable tourism.

Furthermore, in a global market such as tourism, the problem of "leakage", whereby the economic benefits of local tourism activity flow out of the local community and country back to a foreign corporate headquarters, is another indication of the inadequacy of simple market-driven approaches. Sustainable tourism development requires a partnership among the stakeholders of the local tourist destination. This partnership must use both market and non-market instruments to implement a shared sustainable development vision.

Without such a partnership, advocacy for sustainable development becomes a conflictive struggle between an industry which seeks to respond only to market forces and a public sector which, when accountable, acts to protect public goods and wealth for future generations. Therefore, the key problem at this stage of the "sustainable tourism" debate is the creation of tangible, working local partnerships. These local partnerships must be encouraged and supported by national governments and industry, and not undermined by "higher level" agreements.

To succeed, local residents and their local authorities need to more fully recognise the significant adverse impacts of tourism development and must be informed about opportunities for reducedimpact tourism development. Tourism businesses need to recognise and support the social conditions (e.g., security, public health) and the cultural and environmental wealth that make a community an attractive tourist destination.

The UN Commission on Sustainable Development has repeatedly recognised Local Agenda 21 planning as an effective partnership mechanism for implementing Agenda 21 in cities and local communities. Experience with Local Agenda 21 activities in hundreds of communities since 1990 has highlighted a number of principles for effective sustainable development planning.

These principles can also provide the basis for effective partnerships for sustainable tourism planning and development in local tourist destinations. These partnerships can be established either within or independent from existing Local Agenda 21 activities. The principles for Local Agenda 21 planning are as follows:

— Participation and Transparency, that involves local residents, representing all major groups of society, in Local Agenda 21 planning and makes information aboutsustainable development easily available to the general public.

— Partnerships that build collective responsibility for planning, decision making,problem solving, project implementation and evaluation.

— Accountability that holds all partners answerable for their actions.

— Systemic Approach that addresses the underlying causes of social, economic and ecological problems in an integrated way, focusing on the entire systems that are affected, rather than only problem symptoms.

— Ecological Limits, that are defined by Earth's carrying capacity and that serve as the limits for development.

— Equity and Justice, that are secured locally through the provision of equal opportunities and human rights, and globally through development cooperation partnerships between developed and developing nations.

— Concern for the Future, that requires long-term planning and action that addresses both immediate needs and long-term trends.

These principles can be applied, in working partnerships, to evaluate and improve efforts to address sensitive tourism development issues, such as:

— inequitable distribution of tourism revenues and "leakage" of revenues to foreign shores;

— displacement of pre-existing local settlements by tourism developments;

— equal access to local coastal and recreational resources and controversies over uses and long-term protection of those areas;

— concerns related to lack of foreign tourist sensitivity to cultural traditions and sites.

The primary partnerships for sustainable tourism development will be local partnerships, addressing the unique development goals and needs of each community. Where Local Agenda 21 activities are underway, a Sustainable Tourism Working Group could be established within the existing Local Agenda 21 planning structures to facilitate planning and action.

Notwithstanding the primacy of local partnerships, the transnational nature of tourism requires transnational partnerships to support sustainable tourism planning activities at the local and national levels. The Local Agenda 21 process has established a new mechanism for such transnational partnership, called "Local Agenda 21 Charters." Initiated by the Netherlands Ministry of Foreign Affairs, in cooperation with the International Union of Local Authorities, the International Council for Local Environmental Initiatives, and Towns & Development, the Local Agenda 21 Charters process provides a mechanism for local communities to factor issues of global responsibility within their Local Agenda 21 activities.

Two local authorities, typically on a North- South and East-West basis, establish a "Charter" agreement that specifies areas of mutual support to jointly address relevant issues of global equity and sustainability. Presently, 20 local authorities have established the first Local Agenda 21 Charters.

Ultimately, tourism consumers must be rallied to the sustainable tourism agenda, thereby shaping both the market and public policy. Tourism consumers in existing Local Agenda 21 communities may find the Local Agenda 21 Charters mechanism useful in supporting sustainable development in popular tourist destinations. Existing "twinning" or "sister city" relationships with cities that are located in tourist regions can provide the basis for a possible Local Agenda 21 Charters relationship.

SUSTAINABLE COASTAL TOURISM

Economic development activities in any sensitive natural area pose a particular challenge for sustainable development. Coastal areas host the most productive marine ecosystems and serve as spawning grounds for the oceans. The degradation of coastal areas in many countries, with the resulting impacts upon coastal settlements and fisheries, justifies strict local controls on further coastal development. Coastal zones are dynamic in nature, responding to daily tidal changes as well as long term events such as sea level rising.

This dynamic quality offers a defense from extreme weather events. Rigid infrastructure from coastal development can inhibit the ability of coastal ecosystems to respond to changes. Since coastal areas are the most highly populated regions on Earth, their protection requires unique attention and the effective management of numerous competing interests. In many coastal areas, tourism development is destroying or marginalising dwindling habitats for marine animals and spawning fish, as well as the livelihoods of traditional fishing families and villages.

Unregulated water sport activities and machinery are adding to this toll. Lack of effective waste water treatment for tourist facilities is making a significant contribution to coastal water pollution. Excessive private tourist development is denying equitable human access to beaches and coastal waters, cutting off local populations from their coastal heritage. Inappropriate development in high risk storm areas is costing families, local economies and governments billions of dollars annually.

As a first measure towards the sustainable management of coastal areas, governments at all levels, working in partnership with private foundations and investors, should establish designated coastal areas where development will be forever restricted. Protection of these areas should be stringently enforced.

In areas where coastal development can be socially and environmentally justified, tourism development should be designed as a form of low-impact economic activity relative to other development alternatives. The reputation and viability of the sustainable tourism concept depends upon the definition and implementation of clear management objectives for each coastal area. These objectives should clearly designate ecologically and socially/culturally sensitive areas as well as high risk areas.

SUSTAINABLE TOURISM INITIATIVES

Tourist activities imply an intensified utilisation of vulnerable habitats. Investors and tourists do not necessarily possess awareness on how to use natural resources sustainably, and subsequently this utilisation often leads to a degradation of resources. Tourism is also a major generator of wastes. In most tourist regions of developing countries, sewage, wastewater and solid waste disposal are not properly managed or planned. Lastly, tourism is also responsible for a considerable proportion of increased volumes and mileage in global transport and hence the associated environmentally damaging pollutant emissions. The tourism industry has not shown sufficient willingness to (internalise or) compensate the cost of conservation of bio-diversity in, for instance, protected areas, even though they can profit from it.

Tourism is a powerful agent of change. International tourism acts as a catalyst for the transition from traditional ways of life to so-called modern, Western forms of society. Accordingly, tourism often brings with it the introduction of new behaviour trends and norms. Very often, these are contrary to traditional norms existing in the host community, and can come into conflict with its cultural identity and threaten the traditional value systems there. The problem is that the investors seem to have a lack of cultural understanding of the invested society. There is a need for an increased awareness that establishment of new hotels etc. will have its consequences on the society and the people who live in it. Tourism has become associated with violation of human rights.

Many destination countries have experienced an increase in criminality, prostitution, alcohol and drug abuse as a consequence of tourism. Furthermore, child labour is commonplace in the tourism industry (particularly in the informal sector). According to estimates made by ILO (International Labour Organisation), between 3 and 19 million children and teenagers work in the tourism sector. A particularly abominable form of violation of human rights is child slavery and despicable abuse of children taking place in the booming sex industry in many countries. In these countries, tourism has led to an incredible increase in prostitution and also in the exploitation of children. The tourism industry has not yet come up with a general condemnation of these violations of human rights.

The tourism industry is characterised by a high degree of monopoly, which implies a concentration of services and profits into very few big transnational corporations. In many countries, tourism facilities mostly belong to foreigners. Furthermore, in local host communities in many countries a relatively small number of people are involved in the tourism industry in host communities in many developing countries. Very often, there is a lack of qualified manpower in the locality. Hence, most employees are recruited form the big cities, neighbouring countries or even from the country of origin of the investors.

Multiplier effects from tourism are less significant than is often assumed. One reason is that tourism industries purchase most of their inputs (materials, products or services) in their country of origin. As a result, a considerable amount of foreign exchange revenues leaks from the destination countries. The more goods, services, physical capital and human capital a country must import for its tourism services, the higher the leakage. Very often the investors are not approaching the local community to see what it actually can provide. In addition to this, the General Agreement on Trade in Services (GATS), with its liberalisation of global trade and services, is increasingly undermining the possibilities of individual countries and regions to control their tourism industries and the possible economic gains from tourism.

The tourism industry should engage in promoting sustainability as a hallmark for investors. More specifically, investors in tourism should strive to adopt environmentally sound technologies or other measures to minimise the consumption of local ground water. In the case of water utilisation, such measures might be water saving equipment, desalination systems and collecting and utilising rainwater. Using other types of resources in a sustainable manner is, of course, also crucial. There is a need to use ecological materials and installation of renewable sources of energy·systems (solar energy) in all new buildings and new construction.

Furthermore there should be an acceleration of installation or solar/wind power in all public work projects of communities where tourism will be introduced. To prevent or minimise the impact of chemical inputs in soil, water and health, one should start utilising sound ecological methods, including IPM (Integrated Pest Management). Ecological methods need to be·applied in all areas utilised for tourism, including in the maintenance of golf courts, gardens and recreational facilities. Pollution of ground and coastal waters must be prevented, and recommendations must be made (perhaps even legislation) for tourism investors 'to invest in proper sewage treatment facilities.

Appropriate waste disposal systems and ways to separate garbage into organic and non-organic waste should be developed. Organic waste can be composted and possibly reused on hotel gardens or even for local farming. This could be done through collaboration with local residents. Residents could organise themselves and manage the allocated dumping sites, and hence benefit from the system in receiving payment from the hotel for services rendered. A system to separate the different materials, and recycle some should be in place at the landfill site, thus reducing the waste even further. To avoid degradation of the natural environment, tourism projects can help finance protected areas and safeguard ecologically sensitive regions against further environmental deterioration.

By empowering local populations and have them participating in the entire process, sustainability will be ensured as it becomes accepted by and adjusted to the local communities. Also, a protected area might certainly be a suitable tourist-attraction, where tourists can experience amazing nature and learn about conservation and traditional uses of natural resources in the area. Investors in tourism should always respect the traditional land tenure system in the area and the traditional user-right systems of resources. In regard to this, the communication and consultation with the local communities about resource-use is important.

Tourism investors should not exclude local people from using local resources, and thus take away what they depend on for maintaining their well being. The tourism industry can and must take initiatives to implement that polluter(s) pay a principle (or other forms of internalisation of externalities) for pollution related to tourism operations. This may be organised and carried out through local tax systems or through funds established by the tourism industry for local community development. However, the paid principle should be applied for minor pollution only and should not be developed into a possibility for investors to pay a symbolic fine for imposed irreversible negative impacts on the local environment.

Inaccurate and/or mild environmental legislation in destination countries may possibly attract more foreign investors contributing to fast economic growth and development, but with environmental damage as a consequence. To avoid the dilemma, destination countries will have to choose between economic development and environmental protection international. Multinational enterprises must be committed to follow the environmental standards of their home country should these be stricter than those at the destinations.

The tourism industry should promote projects, which are compatible with the cultural identity of the local population's way of life. Furthermore, the tourism sector should always make sure it acts in accordance with the cultural heritage, and respect the cultural integrity of tourism destinations. This might be accomplished by defining codes of conduct for the industry and hence providing investors with a checklist for sustainable tourism projects. Establishing and developing tourist training programmes could be one way of managing codes of conducts for the tourists.

Here, tourists can be informed and educated about the destination for their travel both before and after their arrival at the site. At the site, tourist information centres can be established through funding from the investor. The information given to tourists should include codes of conduct regarding appropriate behaviour and clothing. It is reasonable to assume that people's offending behaviour is largely a consequence of ignorance rather than intention. Consequently, information and facts about the destination, ways of life, history, cultural heritage is crucial to help tourists get along.

It is an absolute must that tourism investors do not engage in or promote child labour and prostitution. Moreover, it is appropriate that the industry commit themselves to a global campaign against such and any other violation of human rights. Evaluating the sustainability of the tourism development, in regards to cultural and human rights aspects, is highly recommended for those responsible for the tourism projects. As with the case mentioned earlier of preventing environmental degradation, this must be carried out through communication and consultation with the local communities.

By devising local training programmes and establishing educational projects, the tourism industry can ensure that qualified local people are employed in their projects. One should train the local people instead of foreigners to become guides due to their knowledge of the area and resources. The investors should be responsive to the kind of knowledge, abilities and skills found in the local communities. Very often such knowledge and skills are well fitted to be used in tourist activities be it fishing trips, nature trails, souvenir sales or dancing courses for tourists etc. To constrain foreign exchange leakage, those responsible for the tourism projects should ensure that local inputs are purchased for their projects.

A proper examination of local resources available will be beneficial for both the industry and the local residents. Usually, there is considerable local willingness to start producing new products if a market for these products exists. The tourism sector should also adopt measures to prevent foreign exchange leakage by a commitment to re-investment of a fair share of the locally accrued profit. We have already mentioned protected areas, training programmes on codes of conduct for tourists, or possible training of local employees, as projects in need of funds.

Initiatives towards more local community development projects should also be appropriate. The tourism industry should promote the establishment of small and medium-sized tourism enterprises which, compared to large-scale hotels etc., have far more moderate impacts on the environment. It is the industry's responsibility to act as a model for communities to show that it is possible to do business whilst protecting natural resources.

The industry should also promote and support local communities to start tourism-related businesses and grant access to low interest loans. It is the responsibility of the tourism sector to ensure total transparency in all transactions, and to prevent tourism projects from being used as projects for laundering illicit money, as well as to refuse using bribes as a means to obfuscate or avoid government rules and regulations. There should be a global boycott against those investors involved in such or other types of illegal activities.

Empowerment of residents at tourist destinations, through local participation, may be facilitated by providing written and legally binding contracts between local people and tourism investors. The contracts will help to avoid broken promises, which too many examples and previous experience prove to be a huge problem. In addition to the mentioned examples (providing proper information for tourists and establishing training programmes for residents), the tourism industry, through for instance the WTTC or the WTO with NGOs in the selection panels, could issue awards especially for sustainable tourism projects as an encouragement for investors.

Within the industry, it is important that both small and large-scale tourism operators are included in the collaboration and that they participate in solving problems related to tourism development. A sustainable development of the tourism industry can only be ensured through participation of all local residents in the destination countries. There is a need for a willingness and ability for the partners to work with this kind of bottom-up approach.

Governments in both destination and countries of origin of tourists and investors are responsible for providing appropriate legislation for sustainable tourism development, and to follow up the tourism projects with sufficient monitoring and appropriate sanctioning. Exchange of successful experiences of sustainable tourism projects is an important factor in this connection. Lastly, an interdisciplinary approach to the problem is necessary: using local, regional and/or international consultative forums.

International tourism plays an ambivalent role in contributing to cultural exchange and sustainable development. On the one hand, it involves a highly buffered, short-term consumer experience of other locales. Tourists can pay and leave, remaining isolated from negative impacts at the local level. On the other hand, tourism may increase recognition of the importance of respecting cultural diversity and developing an identity as a world citizen. It offers opportunities to educate consumers regarding responsible tourism and sustainable development.

Consumers can play a major role in the transformation of societies towards sustainability. While mass tourism in the past was rather producer-driven, the industry today is becoming increasingly consumer-driven.

In highly competitive tourism markets, well informed, responsible consumers can put increasing pressure on the industry to behave more responsibly. A number of official proclamations have affirmed every individual's right to rest and leisure including tourism. However, tourism remains an unobtainable luxury for the majority of the world's population. Tourists primarily originate from affluent industrialised societies where tourism has become a mass phenomenon.

Tourists' values, attitudes and behaviour are determined by their social environment, cultural identity and way of life which may be in conflict with local customs. Tourism is heterogeneous in nature, made up of many different types of traveller, seeking a wide range of tourism products. Demand is influenced by irrational factors, e.g. fashion and trends. Demand depends on the availability of time and money, on images, perceptions and attitudes. Tourists have various needs, desires and motivations, both of a 'push' and 'pull' nature.

While household incomes in major touristsending countries are declining, industry sales projections continue to grow, indicating increasing competition. The consumer mind is set on discount prices and "buy now/pay later" options. This poses serious threats, as prices already lag far behind any realistic accounting of tourism costs and impacts. Many of the demand patterns in tourism reflect the unsustainable lifestyles of industrialised consumer societies. Tourism acts as an agent in exporting these life-styles and consumerist attitudes to less industrialised societies via demonstration effects and modelling.

Tourism increases demand for imported consumer goods in the destinations, with detrimental effects on the environment, due to the ecological costs of transport and the high amount of waste generated. Increasing imports also reduce local/national economic gains, due to foreign exchange leakage. The over-consumption of resources by tourists and tourism infrastructure (e.g. the excessive use of water, firewood or food) is incompatible with sustainable development. The carrying capacity of natural environments is often exceeded with the addition of tourism demands.

Tourist demand for resources (land, water, energy, food) may also compete with the needs of local people and may increase social inequality, gender inequality and injustice. Tourist transport, especially air travel, is highly energy intensive and causes pollutant emissions. Many tourism activities such as skiing, boating, mountain hiking, motorised water-sports (e.g. jet skies), and trekking represent stress for fragile ecosystems. Tourists often lack information and awareness about their impact in a different culture and environment, about their impacts on socio-economic and socio-cultural development, and about the environmental costs of tourism.

While tourists may be open to learning, they are often unaware of inappropriate behaviour and have little guidance on how to improve them. Others may refuse to adapt to local life-styles (even when informed) insisting on their freedom to behave as they want. While the tourism industry may be willing to improve their products and services, there is a conflict between the industry's pursuit of economic gains and social and environmental responsibility. The industry lacks information on the requirements of sustainable tourism and on how to integrate economic forces with environmental and social requirements.

Tourists shopping for escapism generally abide by one fundamental consumer ethic: receipt upon payment. Consumer advocates may intervene where inferior customer service is delivered. However, the sustainability of corporate practices is self-regulated. This conflict of interest within the industry, and consumers' low awareness of tourism impacts, have led to a widespread abuse of 'green' labeling.

The mass media, especially television through films and reports about events, sights, etc. in other parts of the world, are increasingly influential on travel decisions and consumer behaviour in the destinations. However, these programmes often serve primarily as advertisements, painting images of destinations, rather than providing relevant information for potential travellers. There is a lack of reliable and appropriate (e.g. age and gender segregated) research data on the determinants of tourist demand, motivation and behaviour.

Few countries, whether tourist-sending or tourist-receiving, collect such data that are helpful under sustainable development criteria. Most studies of tourist behaviour focus on mainstream markets or market segments, rather than assessing or modelling sustainable alternatives. Governments in many tourist destinations and local communities have little or no information on what to expect from tourism and the incoming tourists, and how to influence and control tourism and guide tourist behaviour; They are controlled by international/ global institutions, the industry and the consumers.

Governments of the affluent countries are only beginning to look at the issues of outgoing tourism. They are not yet sufficiently aware of their responsibility and methods to influence tourist behaviour by political and legal guidelines/criteria and appropriate planning and policies. Trade unions have fought successfully for shorter working hours and more vacation. However, they need to take more responsibility for helping to create a leisure industry that is more sustainable.

Consumer behaviour can and must be influenced by:

— Fighting unsustainable forms and aspects of tourism, at the various levels, by sanctioning unacceptable behaviour and discouraging inappropriate consumer behaviour.

— Promoting responsible and sustainable patterns of behaviour, at the various levels, by promoting best practises and encouraging responsible consumer behaviour. There are different types of instruments and remedial measures available:

a) Legal measures (rules, regulations, sanctions);

b) Market based instruments, such as taxes to influence market prices;

c) Promotion of and (financial) support for best practice;

d) Industry self-monitoring/codes of conduct;

e) Information, education and research.

Agents and Partnership

Consumer behaviour in tourism is both a product and cause of policies by government and industry. Therefore, a comprehensive approach is required to solve the problems associated with market-driven tourism. Tourism should be viewed as a major development issue that all stakeholders need to be actively engaged with. To develop effective partnerships, the imbalance of power between the different stakeholders needs to be addressed.

UN action

— Establish an NGO tourism advisory group for UN to provide technical support, analysis, and strategic advice;

— Create a 'best practices' information clearing-house, in order to collect consumer information useful to understanding and positively influencing consumer behaviour and to make documentation accessible on an equitable basis;

— Initiate a broad information and awareness campaign to highlight damaging forms of tourism and impacts, providing tools for informed decision-making. Initially, target participants in the CSD and CBD processes to clarify roles and responsibilities;

— Research and develop effective certification schemes, form a technical group under the CSD to assess how certification can be improved, e.g. through the review of voluntary codes set up by CSD1998;

— Designate an 'ombuds' office jointly between the CSD, CBD, and UN-CHR to encourage diligent self-regulation and compliance with international standards for sustainable tourism;

— Develop guidance on tourism as an issue within Local Agenda 21 processes.

Governmental actions

— Introduce and enforce legislation to abolish child prostitution, implement effective control mechanisms, conclude judicial assistance agreements;

— Regulate tourist access to ecologically fragile or stressed natural areas;

— Tourist-sending countries: develop policies on outgoing tourism from a development perspective;

— Provide frameworks for ecologically appropriate pricing by strictly applying the polluterpays-principle to internalise external costs. This includes ecological tax reforms including the taxation of aviation gasoline and oil, removal of subsidies/other economic incentives with negative environmental impacts.

— Improve conditions for sustainable consumer behaviour by providing/promoting sustainable tourism facilities;

— Promote environmentally friendly modes of transport and transport concepts, reduce tourism-related traffic, shift demand to less environmentally damaging modes of transport;

— Promote renewable sources of energy (such as solar power), reduce the use of non-renewable energy and of limited local resources, through more sustainable practices/consumption patterns.

— Develop information and education programmes in co-operation with local stakeholders ensuring all stakeholders' involvement (e.g. women's); provide information to tourists on appropriate behaviour, e.g.

by establishing information centres in destinations, or by including briefing material for package tours;

— Take into account the specific information needs of various market segments, provide information to the local population on the opportunities and risks from tourism and on how to influence tourist behaviour;

— Adopt, observe, implement and promote codes of conduct, e.g. the planned WTO-OMT 'Global Code of Ethics for Tourism';

— Integrate sustainable development education including tourism in the curricula of schools at all levels, universities and training institutions, involving all stakeholder groups, create and promote open networks for information and research on sustainable tourism, disseminate and implement results;

Tourism industry action

— Promote sustainable tourism products, using market related instruments and incentives, such as contests, awards, certification, model projects, culturally sensitive quality labels covering both environmental and social sustainability;

— Reduce inappropriate consumption, use local resources in preference to imports in a sustainable manner; reduce and recycle waste, ensure safe waste disposal, develop and implement sustainable transport policies and systems, e.g. efficient public transport, walking, cycling in destinations;

— Provide tourists with authentic information, enabling them to understand all environmental and related aspects (e.g. human rights situation) of tourism when selecting any destination or holiday package; educate visitors in advance of arrival and give guidance on 'dos' and 'don'ts'; make tourists aware of their potential impact on and their responsibilities towards host societies;

— Provide information on respecting the cultural and natural heritage of destination areas; employ tour guides who portray societies honestly and dispel stereotypes;

— Ensure that the marketing of 'green' tourism reflects sound environmental policy and practice; use non-exploitative marketing strategies that respect people, communities and environments of destinations, dismantle stereotyping, integrate sustainable tourism principles when creating new marketing strategies;

— Train staff to foster tourist responsibility towards the destinations, encourage multi-cultural education and exchange;

— Actively discourage exploitative sex tourism, particularly sexual exploitation of children, and tourism which causes or contributes to social problems;

— Adopt, observe, implement and promote codes of conduct.

NGO action

— Disseminate information to a wide public about the complexity of tourism and about the objectives and criteria of sustainable tourism;

— Educate tourists to change consumption patterns and promote appropriate, environmentally and socially acceptable behaviour in the destinations;

— Launch broad awareness campaigns on the worst impacts of tourism, to be funded by international governmental and non-governmental agencies;

— Promote relevant research on tourism impacts, criteria for sustainable tourism and possibilities for implementation;

— Monitor tourism development, policy, industry initiatives, and local people's reaction to tourism development and policy, and implementation of stakeholder action.

Early tourism development has given little consideration to natural resource limitations, impacts on wildlife and indigenous cultures. The human environment and development has been largely ignored. Within the process of globalisation local communities' participation and nature conservation are threatened and often overlooked. If tourism is to be sustainable, it must improve the lives of local people, protect their environment and health, and offer them a better future.

In many instances, tourism can be seen as a vehicle to empower local communities and protect the environment through the development of new employment opportunities, the enhancement of local economies, preservation of indigenous knowledge and practices, public awareness and education. Sustainable tourism can create positive opportunities for community development in remote areas. The business sector can choose sustainable tourism over other more polluting ventures.

Long and short-term development plans should be developed so that tourism and its benefits are spread within the area. To develop tourism in a sustainable manner, it is necessary to define optimal tourism destinations in local areas and regions, ensuring enjoyment for the tourist and minimum impact or disruption for the environment and local communities. Complex and broad-based local communities' involvement in tourism development requires targeted investment strategies implemented by local decision-makers.

Those strategies do not exist in many areas and the development of tourism is not planned. Often, tourism investments are imposed from the outside, and the potential for sustainable forms of tourism is weakened. Alternatives to mass tourism (e.g. cultural and "ecotourism") can be influential in changing the nature of tourism. Tourism can benefit both tourists and local communities and allow for two-way interaction and education.

In order for tourism to become a sustainable industry, countries, states, regions, and individuals must work with new technology, natural resource management and marketing concepts. Ideally, participatory planning and implementation will be a part of Local Agenda 21 processes. To ensure community involvement and to safeguard local cultures, sustainable tourism development should therefore involve all stakeholders in tourism development at all appropriate levels, facilitate the development of tourism services that are planned, managed and reviewed by the host community in Local Agenda 21 processes. This will also ensure that tourism revenue stays in the host communities to enhance livelihoods and generate a profitable source of income, empower and motivate local groups to direct cross-cultural exchange in the way they wish and adopt practices which conserve, protect and preserve the environment.

Local and Regional Tourism Boards

These Boards should:

— promote sustainable tourism concepts in co-operation with local governments and all —stakeholders, in line with Local Agenda 21 priorities;

— work systematically to attract investment in sustainable tourism;

— help other institutions in developing marketing strategies and training programmes and developing educational materials;

— work together with different public institutions to involve all stakeholder groups in tourism activities, and bring greater benefits to the entire community; and

— co-operate with grass-roots organisations to develop employment strategies through sustainable tourism.

Institutional Action

The UN-CSD should:

— invite countries to integrate tourism into their sustainable development strategies for the 2002 review;

— ask the review progress in local communities involvement in tourism development in their country profiles to the preparatory meetings for Earth Summit III in 2002 as part of the review process;

— instruct DESA in co-operation with relevant UN agencies and convention secretariats, major groups and all stakeholders to develop indicators of sustainable tourism;

— invite convention secretariats and the Committee on the Environment of the WTO-OMC to report annually to the CSD;

— establish an international "ombuds" office to deal with human rights abuses and environmental destruction in tourism;.

— ask UNEP, through their Technology Industry and Economics Division, to work with industry associations at all levels, trade unions, local authorities and NGOs to develop a framework for 'good practice' and to develop a database on good practice, criteria, examples and analysis which should be accessible to governments and stakeholders alike;

— ask UNEP together with UNCHS, the Sustainable Cities Programme and relevant stakeholders to develop guidance notes on tourism within Local Agenda 21.

— ask the UN Regional Commissions to prepare a report for the preparatory meetings for Earth Summit III in 2002 on sustainable and community-based tourism activities within their region and to work with UNEP/WTO to develop regional agreements to address sustainable tourism.

— invite UNDP to share its work on guidelines for "good practice" and to involve indigenous peoples and local communities this work;

— ask the UNDP country offices to bring together UN agencies, bilateral donors and other stakeholders to work together on sustainable tourism, as well as involve the gender development programme in this process;

— ask UNDP to include sustainable tourism into its poverty alleviation strategies and programmes.

— ask the United Nations Conference on Trade and Development to integrate tourism into their development strategies and include a progress review on the role of indigenous and local communities' involvement in tourism for the Earth Summit III (year 2002) review, and to support community-owned and controlled initiatives in tourism and bio-diversity through its BIOTRADE initiative.

— invite environmental conventions and treaties secretariats to include community-based tourism in their action plans and programmes, and to promote it as an incentive for the conservation and sustainable use of bio-diversity.

Multilateral financing and assistance agencies should:

— provide funds for applied research through pilot projects to determine optimal mechanisms for tourism development in a range of differing circumstances;

— create small-scale credit lines to assist small enterprises to invest in tourism without excessive risk on personal property;

— support community controlled tourism initiatives that are directed to poverty alleviation, bio-diversity conservation and promotion of human rights;

— assess their projects' effectiveness on local, sub-national and national levels involving all stakeholders, and publish the results by the Earth Summit III in 2002;

— take part in a discussion forum on minimising leakage, with findings to be brought back to the finance discussion at CSD-8 in 20Possible outcomes include the development of a purchasing/

procurement strategy for the tourism industry, local/ national investment strategies, improved mechanisms for informed choice by consumers, and a linking of aid with capacity building in tourism-dependent areas.

Governments should, at national level

— establish/clarify institutional and departmental responsibility for developing outgoing tourism and harmonise institutional interventions;

— initiate the use of tourism for local economic development by involving all sectors alongside the tourist ministry; to build the capacity to work at the destination level, including product development and effective management of existing destinations;

— facilitate research grants on sustainable tourism, methodologies, impacts and analysis of good practice; finance pilot schemes to develop 'good practice' and establish systems for ongoing evaluation and monitoring;

— establish sustainable tourism policies and regulations, ensuring responsibly zoned development; natural and cultural heritage and resource conservation and protection;

— review land ownership in potential tourism areas and where possible transfer ownership to local communities and provide the necessary training for them;

— include the perspective of local and indigenous communities into local and national sustainable development strategies;

— increase funding for local NGOs to enable them to engage in a dialogue on tourism;

— support public education programmes which encourage responsible consumption, natural resource use, environmental protection and local culture conservation;

— give priority to the following investment suggestions: create funds to help tour operators improve their technical capacity for sustainable tourism development; create funds to develop recreational facilities for the public;

— encourage local banks and other lending institutions to set up regional investment funding programmes, including micro-credit programmes;

— create Regional Tourism Boards, fully staffed, to help in planning, promoting, regulating, and expanding sustainable tourism;

— initiate special marketing programmes by local governments and Tourism Boards, in which local tourism programmes will be advertised in the media;

— initiate programmes to improve the management of eco-tourism in protected areas;

— set up training programmes for guides, tour operators, marketers, etc.

Governments should, at local level

— harmonise laws on tourism including regulations, fee standards, licensing, etc. so that they will be more favourable to sustainable tourism in the region;

— ensure that tourism development is in line with Local Agenda 21 priorities and land-use plans and that the public can participate in local and regional decision making;

— regulate tourism to ensure that profits benefit local people and conservation efforts;

— Develop and support programmes to revitalise the diverse aspects of local cultures.

The tourism industry should

— reduce financial leakage and support local economies by buying food and resources locally, develop long-term partnerships with local operators, businesses and suppliers;

— train and hire local staff and contract with local businesses, promote management opportunities for women;

— prefer accommodations owned, built and staffed by local people, promote locally made handicrafts and traditional products;

— encourage clients to study and understand their destinations, respect local cultures and co-ordinate visits with local communities, authorities and women's organisations, being aware of and being sensitive to local customary laws, regulations and traditions, whilst respecting historical heritage and scientific sites;

— educate staff to avoid negative environmental and cultural impacts and create incentive schemes to promote sustainable behaviour.

NGOs should:

— initiate stakeholder dialogue on community involvement in tourism development, recognising social and gender divisions in communities;

— promote consultation processes in tourism planning, involving local communities;

— launch educational and awareness programmes on tourism for local communities, support and promote history research and museums;

— promote the respect for indigenous peoples and local communities' self-determination, autonomy and social and cultural integrity;

—strengthen their efforts to empower disenfranchised groups (in particular women) to become involved in local tourism planning and management;

— develop participatory programmes to support the integrity of local cultures and economies;

— support the sustainable resource use and initiate environmental actions on different levels to conserve the environment while the tourism is developing;

— analyse the experience with sustainable tourism in different parts of the world, in order to disseminate methodology/positive examples of community involvement in tourism;

— support the use of traditional knowledge, practices and innovation systems relevant for the conservation and sustainable use of biological resources and promote actions on different levels to eradicate poverty, protect human rights and conserve the environment while working in tourism.

There is an urgency to constructively shape tourism in order to support local development and conservation goals. UN bodies and institutions, governments, industry and civil society should co-operate to launch a dialogue process on sustainable tourism. This must be planned within the framework provided by the various UN treaties and declarations. All the stakeholders involved in and affected by tourism should be involved in the development of action plans for sustainable tourism. Identifying mechanisms to achieve sustainable development goals in tourism must be a priority for co-operation.

'Good practices' in conserving culture and nature while developing sustainable tourism should be collected worldwide, involving all stakeholders. This process should lead to a multi-stakeholder round-table on strategic planning of local community involvement in tourism to be organised by UNEP as a side event at the Preparatory meetings for Earth Summit III in 2002. There is an urgent need to assess the impacts of globalisation and the role of multilateral and bilateral development organisations in unsustainable tourism practices. An independent international assessment commission should be created under the CSD.

NGOs, indigenous peoples, women's organisations and local communities should be involved in this assessment process together with all other stakeholders. The UN Working Group on Indigenous Peoples should be invited to monitor impacts of tourism on indigenous peoples and local communities. The assessment is to be completed and published by the year 2002.

Coastal Tourism

The United Nations Commission on Sustainable Development in 1999 will address both Oceans and Seas and the review of SIDS. Therefore, it is recognising that: "The survival of small island developing States is firmly rooted in their human resources and cultural heritage, which are their most significant assets; those assets are under severe stress and all efforts must be taken to ensure the central position of people in the process of sustainable development." With these words, the Report of the Global Conference on the Sustainable Development of Small Island Developing States identifies the single most important issue to be borne in mind as we address the challenge of survival and development for our islands.

Article 25 of the Programme of Action from the United Nations Conference on the Sustainable Development of Small Island Developing States (SIDS) focuses our attention on another significant consideration: "Sustainable development in small island developing States depends largely on coastal and marine resources, because their small land area means that those States are effectively Costal entities" Tourism is one of many anthropogenic activities with a special focus on coastal areas.

The two most popular locations for holidaymakers are the mountains and the coast. The coastal area or zone (as it is often called) is hard to define as the area where fresh and salt waters mix, containing many complex, diverse and productive ecosystems on and offshore interacting with each other. New concepts including the whole watershed area seem to be the best approach, especially when aquatic pollution problems are considered. Most problems are related to conflicts between different uses and access restrictions. Tourism leads to increased traffic flow and overcrowding in already densely populated areas. Up to 130 tourists has been calculated per inhabitant in the most popular coastal regions. Therefore, tourism adds substantially to the following pressures:

— Pollution by waste water, garbage, heating, noise and traffic emissions;

— Encroachment of buildings, facilities and roads close to the coastline;

— Beach erosion due to building, dune removal and dredging;

— Excessive use of natural areas;

— Destruction of natural areas to accommodate tourism or other needs;

— Inter-sectorial competition and conflict over (marine and terrestrial) space;

— Exclusion of local communities from any role of significance in decision-making;

— The loss of natural and architectural heritage in the face of rapid expansion;

— Strain on public utilities and facilities;

— displacement of local population;

— Creation of restricted exclusive zones that are off-limits to the local people;

Additional typical tourism impacts are socio-economic conflicts as property and general costs of living increases, and social structure can be changed significantly, when summer guests overrun small communities. Foreign customs and expectations can create conflicts and a deterioration of cultural and regional values.

A major focus should be on the integration of tourism planning and operation of tourist facilities into local planning instruments. Local agenda 21 can play a key role here in ensuring the involvement of all stakeholders. Ideally, this would be done in the context of integrated coastal area management (ICAM). This instrument bridges sectorial approaches in order to avoid or mitigate user conflicts, and it ideally takes into account ecosystem features and physical, not man-made borders.

New tourism developments should be planned together with municipal, industrial, agri- / aqua-cultural and nature protection activities, to allow for multiple complementary uses and to segregate conflicting activities. Area development plans should inform sector plans which should then be incorporated into a coordinated national development plan. All planning should be accompanied by widespread public information dissemination and provide opportunity for discussion leading to integrated coastal zone management.

The tourism development strategy should protect local culture, respect local traditions and promote local ownership and management of programs and projects, so as to foster community stewardship of the natural resource base. Environmental Impact Assessment (EIA) on a strategic level as well as for projects is an invaluable tool for this stage. Criteria for planning and EIA should be:

— Strict environmental standards for solid, liquid and gaseous waste emissions;

— Taking the integrity of coastal values and resources into account;

— Enhancement of public transport infrastructure (train, boat, bike, bus);

— Locally adapted styles and maximum height/size limit for facilities;

— Setting of local/regional carrying capacities on a case-by-case basis;

— Limits to sale of property to foreigners;

— Maintenance of public access to the coastal strip;

— Safeguarding cultural values and customary uses.

During the operation of tourism facilities, several instruments can be applied to enable sustainable development. The details have to be developed according to the use, and together with the local community, the facility operator and local NGOs. Local Agenda 21 could play an important role here (They will be different for a diving site than for a big hotel complex). Modern instruments, which should be, and partly are, already applied in the tourism industry are:

— Introducing environmental management, (according to ISO 14.000 or the European EMAS Initiative);

— Increasing cultural and nature awareness of guests through interactions with local initiatives, guided nature walks, museums, etc.;

— Integrating the local economy by giving priority to local produce (e.g. fish, fruit, vegetables, furniture, and building materials).

However, all these efforts will be in vain, unless carrying capacity limits can be agreed upon in a dialogue and on a case-by-case basis. These limits have to follow sustainability criteria and have to come out of discussions on the development objectives and the natural and cultural values to be protected. They can be tiered in respect to nature used, number of beds and other facilities for guests, and amount of property to be sold to foreigners.

To diminish conflicts a better use of facilities over the year, instead of only in a short season of two to three months should be aimed at. These limits probably have to be stricter for "nature use". Here the introduction and implementation of ranger and guide systems together with limits, regarding the number of visitors, can lead to increased awareness and control at the same time. A simple example is the different approaches to beach litter: Instead of excessive beach cleaning of all organic matter, a plastic litter clean-up by volunteers plus hands-on teaching on the biota originally inhabiting the beach and its natural detritus (like algae and wood) could reinstate an appreciation of nature.

Institutional Actions

Actions on several levels are necessary. First and

foremost, the historically grown sectorial approach to managing coastal issues, relating to tourism and other uses, has to be changed substantially. Under the lead of one coastal agency, all stakeholders, especially local people and NGOs, and also sectorial agencies, small and medium enterprises and industry representatives should meet regularly to promote sustainable development of their coastal area. The planning process and the operation of tourism developments should reflect the country's commitment to the guidelines set out in international accords such as Agenda 21 and the SIDS Program of Action.

Depending on the region, this could mean enhancing human resource development including public awareness building and training; institutional strengthening and networking. Lessons learned in one community should be accessible to others. This will start the ICAM process, which is a goal-directed planning and decision-making process. ICAM leads to inter-agency and inter-sectorial collaboration, resulting in operational decision-making with strong public participation and feedback mechanisms. ICAM could mean in practice:

— To start an environmental management initiative through an award scheme;

— To raise an environmental tax from visitors for small projects, e.g. for funding ranger;

— Training or environmental training for tourism staff;

— To start joint actions with local fishermen, farmers, hotels, or other local initiatives;

— To develop a tourism master plan for the region.

In the long term, a development plan should be devised and discussed thoroughly in order to achieve a common understanding on the objectives and necessary restrictions. As all coastal areas contain particularly sensitive sites, environmental protection has to feature strongly in this planning process, with representatives from government nature protection agencies and NGOs having an equal standing with all other participants.

Depending on the nature of the coastline, regional and intergovernmental collaboration may be necessary in addition to local initiatives. For some issues, such as the reduction of pollution and especially "eutrophication", co-operation on a larger regional scale is necessary.

As integrated processes take time, tourism umbrella organisations should start with voluntary selfrestraint, until locally adapted objectives have been reached. In the north, which bears the brunt of world-wide tourism, a development of quality tourism should be the focus for the future instead of an increase in quantity. The term quality should include ecological and social carrying capacities at the same time as being economically sustainable.

CHAPTER 4

PROMOTION OF DESTINATION

Knowing how tourists inform themselves on a site they wish to visit will help identify where to focus promotional efforts: For example, since most "eco-tourists" wishing to see polar bears in Manitoba, Canada, seek information from travel agents, the site's managers are wise to send their promotional materials to travel agencies. However, since few travel agencies are able or willing to stock the full range of available brochures and are ill-prepared to deal with specialised inquiries, a more efficient approach may be to send agents a brochure and then contact them personally to brief them on the site's attractions and the logistics of reaching it.

Developing a theme using a site's central message for the park's promotion helps develop marketing and promotional materials: Combining a site's most attractive elements to develop slogans or "soundbites", will facilitate the design and creation of brochures and interpretation displays. For instance, a park could be "the best kept secret in the Caribbean", or the place where "billions of years of nature meet thousands of years of history".

An analysis of strengths, weaknesses, opportunities and threats (SWOT) can be used to identify gaps between a site's promotion strategy and tourism trends: A SWOT analysis is a marketing tool used to evaluate a site's promotional abilities by examining the strengths and weaknesses of its promotional organisation, financial and staff resources, and existing promotional strategy.

Strengths and weaknesses are considered factors over which the site has some control; opportunities and threats are external. Strengths and weaknesses include:

— the ways in which the site is being marketed, the size of the marketing budget, performance measures and the degree and nature of the staff's involvement in marketing efforts

— the site's tourism products, including the quality of service, image and reputation

— a profile of current visitors

— suppliers and the quality of goods and services they provide

— the people who handle any marketing for the site and the image they promote, for example, the way it is presented by tour operators compared with the site's own promotional materials Opportunities and threats include:

— political factors, including government legislation

— economic factors

— social factors

— competition, identifying competitors and analysing their strengths and weaknesses

Managers without sufficient time or staff to carry out promotional tasks may consider seeking outside assistance: Tasks such as writing to guidebook publishers, magazines and newspapers to publicise attractions and present management issues are time-consuming and vie for a manager's attention. An independent promotional organisation representing the different interest groups may provide a solution. Such a group can analyse a site's tourism market and management realities. It has the further virtue of being independent, so that it can bridge gaps between competing interest groups.

A group such as an NGO with ties to the site and that knows the tourism business, or a government group with a mandate to coordinate all the stakeholders could play this role. An independent organisation set up to facilitate tourism and park promotion at Lake Baikal, Russia, produced a guidebook giving the names of local tour operators and guides, and distributed it in North America, Europe and Japan.

If an outside organisation is solicited, it must be given clear direction so that its output reflects the site's goals and objectives. For example, if a goal is to support local entrepreneurs, such as ground operators, the organisation must ensure that it promotes both smaller local operators as well as larger or regional and national companies.

Developing a site's "tourism identity" is an essential element of a promotional strategy. This identity, which is based on the site's goals, objectives and market potential, becomes associated with the site in the minds of potential visitors. It could centre on a famous fresco or an endangered animal, for example, and be used to develop a logo for future promotional activities.

PROMOTING A SITE

International tourist guidebooks can be a free source of promotion: Guidebooks are a popular source of information for trip planning and are available for almost every country and region of the world. Because guidebook information is constantly changing, new editions are regularly updated, and editors are usually willing to publish information free of charge. This presents an opportunity to have information on a site and local attractions and services distributed to a wide audience.

Supplying information to travel magazines, newspapers, radio and the internet is another costeffective way to promote a site: Travel magazines and newspapers publish information on tourism attractions free of charge and local radio and television stations broadcast such information as a public service. These can all be useful sources of free publicity for the site. In-flight airline magazines reach a large public, and because they are published quarterly or bimonthly, articles remain in circulation for considerable periods. Most publications can be accessed by the internet and the information transferred in this manner.

Brochures can be used to distribute site information to a wide range of audiences: They can be mailed to national tourism offices, included in promotional information sent to tour operators, newspapers, magazines, radio and television stations and distributed to hotels. However, unlike other types of promotional material, brochures are costly to produce, and should be designed to remain valid over a long period of time. Most people who receive brochures read them. However, research has found that brochures are likely to exert more influence on people who have not visited a site before and less likely to attract repeat visitors.

Contacting tour operators directly is a useful means of interesting them in a site: Tour operators are always on the lookout for new attractions to sell to their clients. Operators, particularly companies that specialise in activities offered at the site, will appreciate receiving a brochure and any information about the local community. Direct contact with tour operators bypasses travel agencies and improves the chances of a positive response.

Producing an information package to area attractions and services can help direct benefits to local residents: If one of the goals of a site's tourism programme is to benefit local communities, a multi-lingual community guide sheet may be a valuable promotional tool. It can direct visitors to neighbouring destinations and attractions, providing a detailed picture of what the area offers, including dining, shopping and accommodations. The information is especially useful for attracting the independent traveller. Such a package should be distributed to key points such as hotels in major cities and at national tourism offices or embassies abroad.

If a site has internet, it can be distributed electronically. A guide can also be used as a management tool for bringing about desired visitor behaviour, by for example discussing cultural rules and taboos and good conservation practices. Such a guide can be produced by the community with the help of site management. A local NGO may provide free computer time and translating services. Selling the guide even if it is very simple may help pay for future copying expenses.

A 10-page guide which can be easily and cheaply copied may be all that is needed initially. The copy should be stored on a computer, so that the guide booklet can be easily updated whenever necessary. If and when the attraction becomes more popular, a more sophisticated guide could be written and sold to cover the costs of publication.

National tourism offices or embassies can be a free and effective means of distributing promotional materials: Tour operators are always on the lookout for new attractions to sell to their clients. Operators, particularly companies that specialise in activities offered at the site, will appreciate receiving a brochure and any information about the local community. Direct contact with tour operators bypasses travel agencies and improves the chances of a positive response.

Holding a press day can be an effective way to introduce a site to the media: The day can be scheduled to coincide with a cultural celebration at the site, or it could be a yearly event held to mark the beginning of the tourist season. Tour operators, hotel owners and government officials who belong to the site's advisory group can be recruited to play a role.

These stakeholders usually have press contacts and may be interested in obtaining media coverage of their activities or businesses. National tourist offices sometimes organise familiarisation tours for travel writers whose expenses paid by the government or large tourist enterprises. To get a site included on a familiarisation tour is not easy, but the manager may approach the tourism ministry or perhaps a hotel chain with promotional materials.

If no outside funding is available stakeholders may be able to offer or raise financial support. If foreign press are invited, local business people are more likely to contribute time and resources to the event. Familiarisation visits for the international media are most successful if the journalists invited have special interests that match the activities of a site, such as the theatre or marine protection. One method of identifying appropriate journalists is to find their by-lines in the international press.

DESTINATION MARKETING

Marketing is one of the main ways for destinations to inform and entice potential tourists and to gain competitive advantage. However, many service industries such as tourism have traditionally used marketing less than manufacturing firms, as they felt it was too expensive, time-consuming, unnecessary, and unprofessional, relying primarily on an established reputation to attract business. And there are still those who consider marketing unprofessional, particularly within the area of advertising. Such detractors hold on to the belief that marketers will do anything to sell their products or services, with their number one goal being the making of a "quick buck."

They are seen as having a complete lack of respect for customers' opinions, desires and intellects, and the environment or society as a whole. But this is an unfair view of many of today's marketers, because in a true marketing philosophy, customer satisfaction is key. Some have noted that marketing also can be used to protect the environment, improve quality of life, and help society as a whole. Marketers can use demand management to increase, decrease, or shift demand for a product or service either temporarily or permanently. In the case of tourism, demarketing can be particularly useful, as it can be used to even-out demand (i.e., increase off-season visits, and limit high-season visits, thus reducing congestion, crowding and environmental impacts), to restrict access to sensitive areas, and to inform and educate tourists about problems facing various areas.

Tourism destinations that adopt a modern marketing philosophy "that focuses on the satisfaction of tourist needs and wants while respecting the long-term interests in the community" will benefit not only themselves, but consumers, the environment, and society. This is corroborated by Poon who believes that "[n]ew tourism can play a leading role in providing and promoting more sustainable patterns of development and in saving Planet Earth." Thus, tourism marketing can and should assume an important role in education and conservation, because in the tourism industry, there is much more to gain (or lose) than just profits.

In these days of increased amounts of leisure time, higher standards of living, greater quality of life, higher expectations, and increasing choices (at least in so-called "developed countries"), tourism destination marketers must work harder to provide tourist satisfaction and to ensure they obtain and retain their share of the market. But tourism marketers should be sensitive to the new situation in which they are marketing. They must realize that tourism can and does have a sizeable impact on the environment, and tourism should not be promoted without full knowledge and understanding of that fact.

Certainly not all regions are ready or willing to accept and develop tourism. Nor should they, as tourism does not always have a positive effect. But in many areas, tourism marketing can make a significant contribution to the quality of life of residents and tourists alike. Destinations that have chosen to embrace or at least accept tourism as a valuable industry must find a way to compete and succeed, and to protect the environment from the negative impacts of tourism. Adoption of a marketing philosophy is the key to success, and tourism marketers that adopt the societal marketing concept will be better off in the future, as consumers are becoming more educated and concerned about choosing products and services that benefit rather than harm the environment.

Marketing is defined most simply as "providing the right products [or services] at the right price in the right place and promoting them in a way that will appeal to the target market". More specifically:

> "marketing is a managerial process involving the setting of organizational goals and objectives, analysis, planning, and implementation. It is a set of activities that results in the formulation of plans and programs. Through these activities an organization seeks to bring about a voluntary exchange of values by providing benefits to its clients and potential clients and, through this, benefits to the organization and its constituent parts or members".

Marketing can be visualized at three levels. Firstly, any "exchange" of products or services in order to satisfy needs and wants is considered marketing. Secondly, marketing is a "system," which includes the providers of goods and services (i.e., the industry), those purchasing the goods and services (i.e., the market), and those responsible for delivering goods and services from the producers to the consumers. The marketing system also encompasses the flows of money, communications, and information between the industry and the market, and the surrounding environment in which these flows occur. Thirdly, a marketing "management philosophy" is one of five management philosophies, including the "production concept," the "product concept," the "selling concept," the "marketing concept," and the "societal marketing concept", that may be adopted by organizations involved in exchanges with consumers.

Organizations that focus on providing their products and services in the most efficient manner possible are said to have a "production" orientation, whereas organizations that concentrate their efforts on producing the best product possible have adopted a "product" orientation. The "selling" philosophy involves "large-scale selling and promotion effort[s]" in order to stimulate purchases. A "marketing philosophy" involves "determining the needs and wants of target markets and delivering the desired satisfactions more effectively and efficiently than competitors do". Some companies go further by adopting a "societal marketing concept" in order to "deliver the desired satisfactions more effectively and efficiently than competitors in a way that maintains or improves the consumer's and society's well-being".

According to this philosophy, marketers should make every effort possible to find out what it is that consumers really want and need, and then endeavour to provide these products and services in an ethical and socially-responsible way. One example of the societal marketing concept for tourism can be seen in the case of bike tours of Africa. The tourist experiences the outdoors, improves his/her well-being by obtaining exercise, learns about the history, culture, ecology, and economics first-hand, all the while avoiding the pollution and environmental damage that would be produced by renting a vehicle. The marketing system comprises many complex, interrelated elements and processes. Despite the fact that the individual, specialized elements in a marketing process vary, and the order in which the steps should be followed is flexible, there is a general consensus on the process to be followed regardless of the product or service being marketed.

Strategic marketing planning is the first step in the marketing process, and involves developing the business portfolio, creating the mission statement, determining goals and objectives, and designing functional strategies for each department of the business (e.g., human resources, accounting, purchasing). A business portfolio is "the collection of businesses and products that comprise the company". The mission statement is a statement of a company's overall reasons for doing business, and provides guidance for all the various departments, products, and services which make up the company. Goals and objectives are set in order to help the company and its various departments fulfill the mission statement, and to provide direction for every aspect of the business. Functional strategies are plans which help each business unit to achieve its goals and objectives.

Another major step in the marketing process is the selection of the target market, defined as the group of consumers sharing similar characteristics or needs that the company has chosen to satisfy. This in turn is made up of four steps: "demand measurement and forecasting;" "market segmentation;" "market targeting;" and "market positioning". Demand measurement involves determining whether or not there exists a market for the product or service at the present time, and forecasting is used to estimate the demand for the product or service in the future. As it is nearly impossible to satisfy every consumer with a particular product or service, market segmentation is performed to identify "distinct groups of buyers with different needs, characteristics, or behaviours who might require separate products or marketing mixes".

The selection of the particular markets to be satisfied by the company's product or service is called market targeting, and is followed by marketing positioning, which involves determining the distinctive position (e.g., most luxurious, most economical) the product or service will occupy in the market relative to competing products or services. The development of "competitive marketing strategies" requires the examination and evaluation of competitors so as to discern "areas of potential advantage and disadvantage". This is followed by the development of the "marketing mix," which is "the set of controllable tactical marketing tools — product, price, place, and promotion — that the firm blends to produce the response it wants in the target market".

The marketing mix is of great importance as "[i]t determines how the marketing budget is allocated, forms the foundation of the marketing plan's strategy, and provides the marketing manager with the techniques to optimise his [sic] budgetary expenditure". "Product" refers to the product or service that the company has chosen to offer to its target markets, and the "price" is the amount that consumers will have to pay to obtain the product or service. "Place" refers to the physical location in which consumers may access the product or service, and encompasses the distribution of the product or service. Lastly, "promotion" involves the activities that the company undertakes in order to make consumers aware of its products and services.

Businesses also must undertake the management of their marketing efforts, which includes analysis, planning, implementation and control. Marketing analysis involves "complete analysis of the company's situation . . . to determine which opportunities it can best pursue". Through the process of marketing planning, a company develops a marketing plan, which "will help the company attain its overall strategic objectives" and includes an "executive summary, current marketing situation, threats and opportunities, objectives and issues, marketing strategies, action programs, budgets, and controls". The third step in marketing management is implementation, which involves "turn[ing] marketing strategies and plans into marketing actions to accomplish strategic marketing objectives". Lastly, marketing control is used to evaluate the performance of the plans and strategies against preset goals.

In this way, marketers may analyse the performance of their plans, and then take "corrective actions" in order to improve future performance. The preceding description of the marketing process highlights the fact that marketing is a complex, time-consuming, and expensive undertaking, made even more so because it occurs in an environment that is constantly changing, and involves competitors that are trying to gain competitive advantage. Businesses (and tourist destinations) must realize the importance of their marketing efforts, and continually monitor and modify their marketing strategies and plans in order to survive in this competitive environment.

Marketing Strategies

Marketing involves the creation of an image of a product

or service. In the case of tourism marketing, the product is "the destination itself", or "an experience of place (location and people) at a particular time". Thus, the purpose of tourism marketing is to create a desirable image of the tourism destination in the minds of potential tourists, with the goal of enticing tourists to select the destination for their next holiday. As Ashworth affirms:

> "the demand for holidays emanates from a consumer reaction to perceptions of anticipated tourism experiences which are inextricably place-bound . . . the tourism product is a set of such experiences packaged as a destination place and marketed largely through images of that place."

Murphy agrees, stating that "tourism is built upon imagery." However, a desirable image is not enough. Kotler et al. stress that destination images must also be simple, appealing, distinctive, believable, and above all valid, as deceptive or unrealistic images can lead to tourist disappointment and dissatisfaction, loss of repeat business, bad "word-of-mouth" advertising, and a poor reputation. Thus, the formation of a desirable and realistic image of the tourism destination is of the utmost importance in tourism marketing. Despite the unusual nature of the product, the principles of tourism marketing are the same as for the marketing of other products and services, however, "differences occur in the application of the theory".

Tourism is a service, and must be marketed accordingly. Services are "products purchased through an exchange transaction that does not confer ownership but permits access to and use of a service at a specified time in a specified place". Hence the four special characteristics of tourism: "intangibility," "perishability," "inseparability," and "heterogeneity". Middleton discusses three other important characteristics of tourism services, namely "seasonality and demand fluctuations," the "interdependence of the tourism product" and the "high fixed costs of service operations." Demand for tourism products and services varies on a daily, weekly, monthly, and yearly basis (termed "seasonality"), mainly as a result of varying climatic conditions and the patterns of the school and business year. "Interdependence" occurs because when tourists visit a destination their experience is made up of several services, such as accommodation, transportation, and attractions.

Tourism services have "high fixed costs," meaning that in order to perform a tourism service, the fixed costs are practically identical regardless of how many people use the service. For example, to operate a hotel, overhead costs are virtually the same, regardless of whether there is 30% or 70% occupancy on a particular day. Wheeler describes the tourism industry as "volatile," because it is "affected by world events and the health of national economies." The horrible incidents of September 11, 2001 are an extreme example of the tourism industry's volatility. The terror attacks significantly impacted tourism in New York, which suffered a loss of almost $1 billion, and in the entire travel sector.

When marketing tourism, the marketing mix (which includes the variables of product, price, place, and promotion - the "4 Ps") must be applied appropriately and may be expanded to include "people" and "physical evidence". Within tourism marketing, the marketing mix elements are important because they communicate to consumers what type of tourists particular destinations are trying to attract. The marketing mix is closely related to the "scale" of tourism to be marketed, as each of the marketing mix elements will vary depending on the scale of the tourism product being marketed. Obviously, the overall marketing mix, including such things as price and promotion will differ greatly, depending on the scale of the tourism product. For example, a souvenir store (large-scale) versus Canada as a tourism destination (small-scale).

The "product" of tourism is different in nature than other products. The product of tourism is "a satisfying experience at a desired destination" and "a bundle of benefits", and is intangible, inseparable, perishable, and heterogeneous. Furthermore, "the tourist travels to the destination area where the product is experienced". More generally, the product of tourism is space and place, and tourism destination marketers can be considered "place marketers", or "experience" marketers.

The "price" of tourism is highly variable due to the interdependent and seasonal nature of tourism services. Heath & Wall state that, "[u]nderstanding the composition of and interrelationships among regional tourism products is . . . an important prerequisite to the development of an effective pricing strategy." Variable pricing strategies play an important role in demand management, as lower prices can be used to attract tourists to various destinations during their "off-seasons." In the same way, higher prices can be used to limit visitors in peak seasons. The element of "place" in the marketing mix refers to the distribution of the product, and includes "the location of all the points of sale which provide prospective customers with access to tourist products".

The fourth 'P' in the marketing mix refers to "promotion," which is the most visible element in the marketing mix, because "advertising and other promotional activities are the primary means of communication with tourists in target markets". Promotion consists of personal selling, sales promotion, public relations, and advertising. "People" refers to staff who deal with customers, and the customers (or tourists) themselves. "Physical evidence," the sixth marketing mix element, includes "physical characteristics" that influence "a company's atmosphere, image and identity and can affect consumers' judgments and perceptions about the service product they receive and about the service organisation itself". Integrated marketing communication should be used to coordinate all direct and indirect contact that consumers will have with a company's message. In integrated marketing communication, the "4 Ps" become the "4 Cs" - consumers (rather than products), cost (rather than price), convenience (rather than place), and communication (rather than promotion).

MATERIALS FOR PROMOTION

The most visible tourism marketing materials are those involved in the process of promotion, as its purpose is to create and increase awareness of a business' products or services and involves communicating with prospective clients. Promotion encompasses the areas of personal selling, direct marketing, sales promotion, public relations, and advertising and of these, advertising is usually the most obvious as it is conducted on a larger scale than the other four. Personal selling consists of one-on-one interactions between a company's salespersons and their prospective clients, and is one form of direct marketing, which involves communicating with potential customers, usually by direct mail and telephone, and measuring the response.

Public relations involves "building a good reputation and image", and "handling or heading off unfavourable rumours, stories, and events". Sales promotion includes "short-term incentives to encourage purchase or sales of a product or service", such as rebates, coupons, or contests. Advertising can occur through a number of different media, including print materials (such as brochures, magazines and newspapers), direct mail (flyers, announcements), television commercials, videos, radio advertisements, window displays, and through the newest communication channel: the Internet. These advertisements usually consist of pictures, graphics, drawings, videos, maps, animation, and text, in varying amounts depending on the advertising channel employed.

Consumers access marketing materials by either seeking them out, coming across them while pursuing other activities, or receiving them directly from the company undertaking the advertising effort. Once discovered, they can choose either to ignore the information, to express interest, to request further information, or to put the information to use. In addition, marketing may be either direct or indirect. Direct marketing is that which attempts to make a sale immediately, whereas indirect marketing is aimed at making a sale eventually.

Images of space and place play a prominent role in promotional materials, as their goal is the creation of a desirable image of the destination region, with the hope of causing consumers to seek further information and eventually select the destination as the site for future tourism experiences. Images are created through textual description, pictures, drawings, graphics, maps, music, audio, video, and animation.

CHAPTER 5

TOURISM AND AIR TRAVELLING

The expansion of tourism by air has been described as being "beyond the wildest expectations of travellers at the beginning of the twentieth century". Thus, international tourist arrivals increased from 25 million in 1950 to 664 million in 1999, corresponding to an average annual growth rate of 7%. Wheatcroft, writing for the World Tourism Organization (WTO), states that the WTO has long recognised that aviation and tourism are interdependent segments of a single travel and tourism industry. Further, "aviation and tourism must continue to work together for the optimum development of world travel".

Consequently, the boundaries between tourism, travel, leisure and accommodation are now quite unclear. For example, airline passengers are encouraged to join frequent flyer programs with rewards related to distance travelled, and "fly-buy" schemes linked to credit cards underline the link between the consumption of both travel and non-travel items. The driving force behind such travel and tourism developments is primarily the global economic system, with the process of globalisation also being facilitated by forces of social and cultural change that are linked to the development and impact of information technology and the mass media.

Indeed, increased economic globalisation assumes increasingly mobile societies. Local, previously relatively isolated and inaccessible places are now subject to global processes, and these have diverse economic, cultural and ecological consequences. Thus, the context for changes in tourism and travel is one of globalisation and international business motivation, supported in turn by compliant political systems. The World Travel and Tourism Council (WTTC) estimated that the travel and tourism industry:

— contributed 11.7% to the world's GDP in 1999

— directly or indirectly accounted for almost 200 million jobs worldwide, or 8% of the world's total employment in 1999

— will employ 254 million people by 2010.

In a position statement on air transport and freer world trade, the WTTC calls for a liberalisation of trade, transport and telecommunications. In relation to air transport in particular, the Council states: "a freeflowing [sic], competitive air transport system is fundamental to this development. It will fuel markets through price competition and service innovation". A more recent statement says: "we must look beyond the immediate outlook, towards a future vision of substantial air travel growth and to make the investments essential for its achievement".

Some elements of the associated WTTC action plan to achieve this vision include the presentation of persuasive arguments to show how air travel can be part of a sustainable economy without penal taxation; putting the case for the urgent need for new aviation infrastructure, including long-term airport plans for the next 20 to 30 years for all regions; and a worldwide public relations campaign to gain the support of "opinion formers" for such an action plan, including support from the policy agendas of governments. In the early 1990s, air arrivals accounted for 70% of tourist arrivals in at least 20 major countries that are popular with tourists, with 10 such countries (including Australia, New Zealand and Japan) reporting almost all international arrivals by air. This relationship is not as strong in Europe, where cars are more commonly used to make the relatively short trips across borders, and air travel accounts for only a quarter of international arrivals.

In keeping with the World Tourism Organization's bias towards the "economic objectives of tourism policies as paramount", the same author concludes that many governments are recognising the need to modify protectionist aviation policies in order to facilitate the growth of tourism, both domestically and internationally. Understandably, the terrorist events of 11 September, 2001 in the USA had a strong negative impact on travel and tourism, although the World Travel and Tourism Council's longer-term forecasts after 11 September were still very strong. Nevertheless, perceived threats to tourism led to the formation of an industry coalition, with the WTTC, of travel and tourism associations from around the world (representing airlines and airports, manufacturers, hotels and restaurants, tour operators and retail agents, travel related services, and credit card and rental companies). Thus, the tragic events of 11 September have both made more transparent and galvanised the web of business and economic interests surrounding aviation travel in the context of a global economic system.

More recently, just as the tourism and travel industry was beginning to overcome the downturn linked to the events of 11 September, 2001, it was challenged by the ramifications of further significant reductions in travel related to the 2003 war in Iraq and the spread of the disease Severe Acute Respiratory Syndrome (SARS). International travel fell 15 to 20% during the war, and US airlines sought US$3 billion from the US government in order to survive financially. Other airlines, for example Qantas and British Airways, announced job cuts in response to the downturn. The SARS related reduction in tourism to tourism-intensive economies such as China, Hong Kong and Singapore also significantly affected a variety of tourism, travel, entertainment and retail businesses. Global financial analysts at Morgan and

Stanley expressed this in April 2003 as a 0.4% reduction to their Asian growth forecast for 2003.

TRAVEL FORECASTING

The use of tourist arrivals and tourist receipts as indices of global travel forecasts is one way of estimating demand in the future and of understanding past trends, and the World Tourism Organization collects these for this purpose. These data show that the number of international tourist arrivals (i.e. arrivals from abroad) has increased by an average annual growth rate of 6.9% since 1950, from 25 million international arrivals in 1950 to 664 million in 1999 (Figure 1). Parallelling this increase is the increase in tourism receipts from $US 2.1 billion in 1950 to $US 455 billion in 1999.

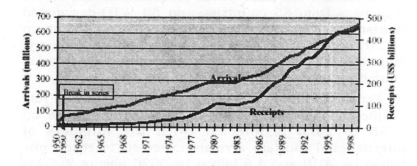

Figure 1. International tourist arrivals and tourism receipts, 1950-1999.

The usual upward trending graph of international arrivals and receipts from tourism followed an anomalous path after the terrorist events of 11 September, 2001, the Bali attack on 12 October, 2002, and the war in Iraq and the spread of SARS in 2003. The World Tourism Organization commented that "it is difficult to find a concrete confidence crisis that can compare with what the world experienced in 2001".

However, WTO still tends to promote an optimistic assessment of future trends, reporting that the 693 million international tourist arrivals in 2002 corresponds to a decrease of 0.6% or 4 million down from the 697 million arrivals in 2000. The general tenor of argument used by business driven interests is that after terrorist shocks and other such events, recovery occurs relatively quickly, and air travel rises eventually to new heights of activity, as pent-up demand due to postponed travel is observed. Even with such setbacks it is argued that tourism proves to be a resilient and stable economic sector with confidence that the growth of tourism will return to normal.

The World Tourism Organization's Tourism 2020 Vision program of research is an extension of its earlier work on tourism forecasting, which produced a series of forecasting reports for each of six WTO regions and a global volume. The 2020 Vision program analysed survey responses from 85 countries and 50 WTO-designated tourism "visionaries", who were selected from tourism and travel companies, suppliers to the tourism industry, and researchers, writers, publishers and academics in tourism, economics and politics.

For the medium term, an average annual growth rate of international tourism arrivals of 4.1% for the period 1995 to 2020 is forecast, with the numbers of international tourism arrivals expected to reach one billion by 2010 and 1.6 billion by 2020 (Figure 2). This forecast was reaffirmed despite the events of 11 September, 2001.

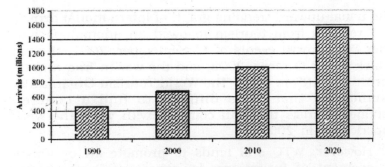

Figure 2. Actual and projected international tourist arrivals worldwide.

The Vision program also predicts that from 1995 to 2020 there will be a rise in the long-haul share of arrivals, with tourists travelling further afield. Hence the intraregional/long-haul travel ratio is expected to increase from 82:18 in 1995 to 76:24 in 2020. Of the 1.6 billion worldwide arrivals in 2020, 1.18 billion are expected for intraregional travel and 377 million are expected to be long-haul travellers. This corresponds to an average worldwide annual growth rate of 3.8% for intraregional travel and 5.4% for long-haul travel.

As foreshadowed above, an aspect of tourism forecasting that is problematic concerns the long-term volatility of tourism demand related to a variety of shocks from external events. Examples include the worldwide petroleum shortages in 1973-74 and 1979-80; the Chernobyl nuclear accident in 1986 coupled with the US-Libyan conflict; the Gulf War in 1991; the terrorist events of 11 September, 2001 in the USA; and the 2003 war in Iraq and the global spread of the disease SARS. These events significantly reduced international travel and tourism following their occurrence, as well as impacting on domestic tourism. Such sporadic events are usually impossible to forecast, and their potential effects are obscure.

Nevertheless Frechtling's work encompasses a range of qualitative and quantitative methods that extend beyond extrapolative or time series methods, and adopts a view of the future as being neither totally predictable nor unpredictable. In his view, forecasts are seen to be useful and feasible by considering the future to be somewhat predictable and somewhat alterable. Further, complexity is acknowledged in that tourism demand is seen at times to be volatile, with a wide range of factors influencing tourism behaviour. Of particular relevance to Australia is the WTO region labelled East Asia and the Pacific. This covers the subregions of North Eastern Asia, South Eastern Asia and Oceania.

Tourist arrivals in the East Asia and Pacific region grew at an average of 7.4% per year in the decade 1990-

2000, in spite of financial crises and violence in many countries. This puts growth in the East Asia and Pacific Region well above the world average growth rate of 4.3% per year. Looking ahead, WTO forecasts 195 million arrivals in this region by 2010 and 397 million arrivals by 2020, corresponding to an average increase of about 6.5% per year from 2000 to 2020, the highest regional growth rate. Of the 1.56 billion tourist arrivals forecast worldwide for 2020, the East Asia and Pacific region is expected to contribute about 25%. These projections are driven by expected large increases in China, Hong Kong and Macau and by strong growth in South East Asia.

In the case of Australia, international tourist arrivals are closely linked with the global international tourist market (although Australia occupies a comparatively minor quantitative position in the world travel market). Further, an expected increase in the Asia and Pacific region over the next decade is likely to benefit Australia through intraregional travel. In the ten years from 1989 to 1999, international tourist arrivals to Australia more than doubled from 2.1 million to 4.5 million visitors. However, although numbers increased by 10.6% to 4.9 million arrivals in 2000, subsequent years had decreases (2001 was -1.5% from 2000; 2002 was -0.3% from 2001) as a result of travellers' reluctance to travel in times of uncertainty.

As a result of the series of negative shocks to the travel sector since 2001, the Tourism Forecasting Council (TFC) expected international travel to Australia to fall by 5.3% to around 4.6 million visitors in 2003, the lowest since 1999 and the third year in a row that inbound travel has contracted. Nevertheless, the TFC suggested that inbound travel to Australia would increase by 9.8% to just over 5 million visitors in 2004, assuming that confidence for international travel returns. Further, assuming a continuation of the previous "normal" trend, international tourist arrivals are expected to grow at about 5% per annum to reach 6.8 million visitors in 2010. This represents a significant downward shift from the forecast 9.4 million visitors for 2010, as made in the similar TFC report immediately after 11 September.

Outbound travel was similarly forecast to fall significantly by 4.2% in 2003, but is expected to strongly recover in 2004, increasing by 8.7% assuming the usual confidence levels to travel return. Outbound travel is projected to reach 4.6 million resident departures by 2012, with average growth of 2.9% between 2002 and 2012. To put this trend in perspective in relation to its resource and greenhouse implications, a related CSIRO study of Australian tourism trends estimates that international air departures in 2020 would require about 230 petajoules per year for fuel. This represents about one quarter of the current requirements for the total transport task (passenger plus freight) for the Australian economy.

Projecting further ahead, the study suggests that by the year 2050, the energy required for international departures could exceed 400 PJ per year. Another study conducted by the CSIRO investigated Australian inbound tourism to 2020, but used a different set of modelling assumptions than the Tourism Forecasting Council. The more conservative forecast of 11.2 million arrivals by 2020 (compared with 4.2 million in 1996) serves to highlight the variability in visitor numbers that could be created by a worldwide economic recession, or sudden increases in oil prices.

Given the range of factors involved in forecasting tourism demand, it is not surprising to find quite different forecasts depending on the models and variables used. For example, the earlier mentioned forecast for Australian inbound tourism by the Tourism Forecasting Council projected 9.4 million tourist arrivals by 2010. This can be compared with the figure of 11.2 million arrivals by 2020 in the CSIRO study. The CSIRO study recognised the dangers of simple models in such a complex area, suggesting that the problem of unrepresented variables is often severe. Nevertheless it used a relatively simple model that explains about 90% of the variations in visitor numbers using GNP per capita, population, and settler ratios, to make projections for 2020. However, the authors comment: "at best, statistical models can find strong patterns in the data consistent with expert views on the nature of the industry and which may have some predictive value".

RAMIFICATIONS

Aviation travel is clearly inextricably bound up with larger economic and political processes, including that of economic globalisation-and in particular the globalisation of tourism. However, transport, and in particular aviation travel, as a subsystem of tourism, has been largely unexamined systemically, especially in relation to ecological sustainability. Rather, aviation is often viewed. simply as a strong instrument for the promotion of economic globalisation. An analysis of the tourism literature suggests that it is primarily constructed within a framework emphasising business and economics.

Tourist travel (including air travel) is a major source of environmental problems, thus linking the notions of sustainable tourism and sustainable mobility. 40 to 60% of the environmental loads linked to tourism are from the transport of tourists between their homes and the tourist region, as well as from local transport within the destination area. In the case of aviation, Hoyer argues for strong measures, including environmental taxes, to reduce the volume of international tourist travel by aircraft. This is because of the increase in the global impacts of such activity and the large tourism contribution to such international and long-distance flights.

More radically, Hoyer argues for new forms of tourism other than those based on auto- and aeromobility, as well as questioning the priority given to time efficiency as a value. Such measures naturally are inimical to the objectives of the aviation industry. For example, the Scandinavian Airlines System (SAS) opposes the use of environmental taxation in spite of its notable efforts to reduce environmental impacts. Nevertheless, the management of SAS admits that future growth in air transport, largely linked to tourism, will only increase environmental impacts.

Later work focuses on the issue of increasing travel to international meetings and conferences as "one of the environmentally most worrying changes in the mobility of post-industrial society". The authors contrast the globalisation and regional competition issues that encourage cities and institutions to put themselves on the conference map, with the environmental and social consequences involved. The radiative forcing index for aviation points to a multiplier effect of at least 2.7 for CO_2 emissions from aircraft, meaning that for each individual conference participant a global warming impact results that is typically equivalent to at least one, if not two or more years of total mobility for all other purposes in terms of comparative impact, depending on the distance travelled.

Another study on international passenger travel to New Zealand found that national energy use would increase by 6% if international air travel were to be included in national inventories. This energy use corresponds to an additional 1.9 million tonnes of carbon dioxide emissions. Although concentrating on energy use and CO_2 emissions per se because of the uncertainties associated with the full impact of aircraft emissions, she does acknowledge that her approach is a conservative one and that the impacts on the atmosphere are possibly considerably underestimated. Recent policy discussion in the UK involving the Departments of Transport and Treasury and the Royal Commission on Environmental Pollution confirms the likely underestimation inherent in Becken's methodology.

As part of a study by CSIRO on the opportunities and challenges for Australian tourism in the longer term, the primary energy and greenhouse gas emissions for the tourism sector were estimated at the national level. In 1995, tourism contributed around 80 million tonnes of

CO_2 equivalent of greenhouse emissions. For comparative purposes, total industrial activity and personal consumption in Australia contributed 575 million tonnes of CO_2 equivalent greenhouse gases. Across a range of consumption categories linked to tourists, the largest category for primary energy consumption for both international and domestic tourists is air transport.

Two categories of tourist consumption, "air transport" and "recreation and other services" each account for around 23% of the total domestic and international tourist greenhouse emissions (or 46% of the total for both categories). The authors underline the significance of these findings given that the externalities of world greenhouse issues are increasingly likely to be internalised in the structure of every industry, and especially one in which transport and air travel are integrally involved. "Sustainable tourism" is therefore becoming a contested concept like sustainability, being interpreted differently by different groups with opposing values.

The latter challenge the paradigm on which economic, social and political development is based, questioning the values of society as much as those of tourism. Organisations such as the World Tourism Organization (WTO) are associated with the pole concerned with mass tourism and strong economic growth, and especially with the globalisation of economic activities such as the growth of international tourism and long-haul tourist travel. It is true of course that some of the language used by WTO is typical of the "reassurance" and "balance" orientation characteristic of sustainable development and sustainable tourism discourses.

For example, in a document on international tourism, WTO speaks of "the continued need to combine sound economic development with the protection of natural resources". Similarly, the need for limits on tourism development is acknowledged by reorienting the industry's priorities and practices towards an acceptable balance between viable growth and environmental sustainability over the long term. Tourism clearly counts as one of the most remarkable economic and social phenomena of the last century. It will undoubtedly keep this position for the century to come. Every year a bigger portion of the world population takes part in tourism activity and for the majority of countries tourism has developed as one of the most dynamic and fastest growing sectors of the economy.

Even after the events of 11 September, 2001, the World Tourism Organization looked forward to "a return of consumer confidence in the travel industry" as the desire to travel for leisure or business reasons is a "social paradigm ... now deeply embedded in our modern lifestyles". Nevertheless since the 1990s, the image of tourism has been changing, to some extent, from a "smokeless industry" to one implicated in an array of global and local ecological concerns. This is reflected in terms such as "eco-tourism", "green tourism", and "sustainable tourism" and in a number of recent books e.g. Holden and journals e.g. Journal of Sustainable Tourism.

Although some are anxious to present these alternative forms of tourism as more sustainable by labelling them "appropriate", "responsible", and "soft", Wheeller has argued that such labelling distracts us from addressing "the real problem of mass tourism-the massive volume and, globally, the growing absolute number of tourists", with all of its associated cultural and ecological impacts.

Moreover, an OECD case study on tourism travel argues that the scale and extent of tourism-related travel are integrally linked with the rising number of air departures to far-off destinations. Combining the significant volume of people and demand pressure with an increasing propensity to travel further, as with long-haul holidays, is thus a prescription for significant ecological impact.

On the other hand, the Royal Commission on Environmental Pollution has also drawn attention to the particular problems associated with short-haul flights (800 km or less), which have a much higher proportional fuel use per passenger than medium- and long-haul flight distances.

The high rate of fuel burn during take-off and landing represents a disproportionate fuel usage for short flights, with for example, 20% of the fuel used for a 500 km flight between Stansted and Edinburgh, being required to get airborne and land. Such profligate fuel use is used to support policy arguments encouraging modal shifts, for example to rail, given the considerable environmental benefits achievable. The Commission suggests this approach both for domestic travel within the UK and for the shorter journeys to Europe. Sustainable tourism scenarios and principles as generally framed to date therefore do not appear to be getting to grips with the ecological ramifications of growth scenarios for the future.

Conventional Oil

Another major energy issue that has significant implications for aviation, in addition to the question of climate change, is the continuing availability of conventional oil. There is a growing literature pointing to a near to medium term supply problem. The main source of this view is a group of retired oil geologists freed from corporate commercial and political constraints e.g. Campbell and Laherrere, Deffeyes. Such a perspective is also increasingly appearing in a range of popular social and scientific analyses e.g. Heinberg, Rifkin. It is further supported by specialist groups such as the Oil Depletion Analysis Centre associated with the University of Reading in the UK, and in Australia at Murdoch University.

The above analyses essentially point to a near to medium term rapid decline in conventional oil production, a relatively modest contribution from non-conventional oils to partially offset conventional oil's decline, and a decline in conventional gas production from about 2020. Another experienced geoscientist Les

Magoon has coined the term, the "Big Rollover", for the point in time when the world demand for conventional oil outstrips the capacity to produce it. This peak in production followed by a steady decline is generally estimated to be around the 2010 or thereabouts, although various estimates between 2003 and 2020 have been suggested.

Given the central role of oil in modern economies, and given that oil currently provides 90% of transport fuel, Magoon and others conclude that the arrival of such a time will be a major turning point in history. The critical issue is not an immediate running out of oil but rather the discontinuity created when humankind's ascent up the "oil production" mountain flips over to the descent down the mountain. A complex range of issues surrounds this issue, including the reliability of forecasting. For example, when M. King Hubbert in 1956 predicted correctly that oil production in the USA would peak in the early 1970s, almost everyone inside and outside the oil industry rejected his analysis.

Similarly, now that analysts have applied Hubbert's method to world oil production with an increasing consensus on an emerging oil crisis, such questions seem to be ignored by the popular press and mainstream politicians. This is partly due to the word "decline" being politically incorrect in the present culture of continuing growth. Against this contention, however, is the often-put argument that the cause of the 2003 war in Iraq was linked in part to an interest in longer-term influence over oil supplies and to the US transportation sector's heavy dependence on oil. With the arrival of the "Big Rollover", the geopolitical consequences of rising oil prices and the fact that demand will not be met, are likely to be far-reaching.

They include the likelihood of inflation, recession, and international tension, given that the remaining reserves are primarily in the Middle East. In addition, definitional problems including the reliability of official statistics, have been critiqued. Thus the notion of "proved reserves", for example, gives rise to "reserve growth", with OPEC misreporting its oil reserves because its quotas depend upon reported reserves. The Association for the Study of Peak Oil, a network of scientists in universities and government departments, particularly in Europe, is focusing on such complexity, and two international workshops have now been held, one in 2002 with a second one held in May 2003.

CHAPTER 6

LODGING, STAFFING AND HOUSEKEEPING

A hotel is an establishment that provides lodging, usually on a short-term basis. Hotels often provide a number of additional guest services such as a restaurant, a swimming pool or childcare. Some hotels have conference services and encourage groups to hold conventions and meetings at their location. Hotels differ from motels in that most motels have drive-up, exterior entrances to the rooms, while hotels tend to have interior entrances to the rooms. The word hotel derives from the French hôtel, which originally referred to a French version of a townhouse, not a place offering accommodation (in contemporary usage, hôtel has the meaning of "hotel", and hôtel particulier is used for the old meaning).

Basic accommodation of a room with a bed, a cupboard, a small table and a washstand only has largely been replaced by rooms with en-suite bathrooms and climate control. Other features found may be a telephone, an alarm clock, a TV, and broadband Internet connectivity. Food and drink may be supplied by a mini-bar (which often includes a small refrigerator) containing snacks and drinks (to be paid for on departure), and tea and coffee making facilities (cups, spoons, an electric kettle and sachets containing instant coffee, tea bags, sugar, and creamer or milk).

The cost and quality of hotels are usually indicative of the range and type of services available. Due to the enormous increase in tourism worldwide during the last decades of the 20th century, standards, especially those of smaller establishments, have improved considerably. For the sake of greater comparability, rating systems have been introduced, with the one to five stars classification being most common. One of the most critical challenges facing lodging managers today is the development of a responsive organizational structure that is committed to quality.

The organizing process of a lodgind establishment involves dividing . tasks into jobs, specifying the appropriate department for each job, determining the optimum number of jobs in each department, and delegating authority within and among departments. The framework of jobs and departments that make up any organization must be directed toward achieving the organization's objectives.

JOB SPECIALIZATION

As there are types of lodging organizations, there are as many degrees of job specialization within the lodging industry. One extreme is the case of a hotel where the owner/operator is responsible for checking in the guests, servicing their needs, taking care of the housekeeping for the guest rooms, maintaining the building and grounds, and checking out the guests. There is, to be sure, much to recommend this method of work. It is rewarding to have total control over a project from beginning to end, and many people find it motivating to see the results of their efforts. However, as the demand for additional products or services increases, it becomes more and more difficult for an individual to do his or her job well. One benefit of the increased workload is increased revenue, which would enable the individual hotel operator to add housekeeping staff, one or more front desk agents to check in and check out the additional guests, and engineering and maintenance personnel to care for the building and grounds.

Specialization increases worker productivity and efficiency. On the other hand, delegating jobs increases the need for managerial control and coordination. Someone has to make sure that housekeeping staff come in after the painters have repainted a roo, not before! A crucial element of hotel and lodging management is coordinating the many specialized functions within hotels so that the organization runs smoothly.

Specialization has its own set of problems; it can result in workers performing the same tasks over and over again. A point can be reached where the degree of specialization so narrows a job's scope that the worker finds little joy or satisfaction in it. Signs of overspecialization include workers' loss of interest, lowered morale, increasing error rate, and reduction in service and product quality. One solution to this problem is to modify jobs so that teams can perform them. Instead of a single guest room attendant being assigned to a group of rooms, a work team in a hotel housekeeping department might clean all of the rooms on a particular floor.

Some establishments use teams regularly throughout the organization; others use teams more selectively. Teams can be directed by a manager or can be selfmanaged. The idea behind self-managed work teams is for workers to become their own managers, which increases their self-reliance as well as develops a talent pool. A concept called the quality circle is based on the belief that the people who actually do the work, rather than their managers, are the ones who are best able to identify, analyze, and correct problems they encounter. The quality circle is a group of employees, usually fewer than ten, who perform similar jobs and meet once per week to discuss their work, identify problems, and present possible solutions to those problems.

General Manager (GM)

The general manager (GM) is responsible for defining and interpreting the policies established by top management.

The general manager serves as a liaison to the hotel's owner or corporate parent, sets (or communicates) the overall strategic course of the hotel, sets hotel-wide goals, coordinates activities between departments, and arbitrates interdepartmental disputes. It is common practice in a large, full-service hotel for a director of public relations to report directly to the GM. The GM also has corporate-level responsibilities, participates on civic boards and committees, and engages in industry-related activities such as serving on the local tourism commission or hotel-motel association. In addition to possessing a high level of technical skill, the general manager must also be decisive, analytical, and skilled with both computers and people. He or she must be able to see the big picture and how all of the parts of the hotel fit into the overall organisation.

Resident Manager

An executive may be promoted to relieve the general manager of some operational duties. This is often accomplished by elevating the duties and responsibilities of one particular department head without relieving that person of regular departmental duties. The title of this position is usually resident manager. It is quite common (and logical) for the general manager to select the manager of the rooms department to be resident manager.

Responsibilities of the resident manager include serving as acting GM in the GM's absence, representing the GM on interdepartmental hotel committees, and taking responsibility for important special projects such as major hotel renovations, VIP guests, and operating reports that require in-depth analysis for the regional or corporate offices.

Rooms Department

Responsibilities of the rooms department include reservations, guest reception, room assignment, tracking the status of rooms, prompt forwarding of mail and phone messages, security, housekeeping of guest rooms and public spaces such as lobbies, and answering guests' questions. To perform these many duties effectively, the rooms department may be divided into a number of specialized subunits. To complicate matters, in many instances these subunits are also referred to as departments.

The laundry department is responsible for cleaning and pressing all the hotel's linens and employee uniforms as well as guest laundry. Because of its specialized function, little of the knowledge and skills required to manage a laundry operation is transferable to other areas of hotel operations. The front office is one of the most important departments in a hotel, as it often offers the only contact between guests and staff. A hotel's front office is where guests are greeted when they arrive, where they are registered and assigned to a room, and where they check out.

Usually, the telephone operator, other guest communications functions, and the bell staff or those employees responsible for delivering luggage and messages and attending to special guest requests also fall under the front office umbrella. The reservations department takes and tracks the hotel's future bookings. The housekeeping department is responsible for cleaning guest rooms and public spaces. Because of their specialized nature, the security and engineering departments are discussed in separate sections. A great deal of interdependence exists among the subunits of the rooms department. The front office must let reservations know whenever walk-in guests register. A similar level of cooperation is required between the front office and housekeeping. When a guest checks out, the front office must inform housekeeping so that the room may be cleaned. Once a room is cleaned, housekeeping must inform the front office so that the room may be sold. Certain tasks within the rooms department must occur in a specific order.

Housekeeping cannot properly provision a guest room if the laundry does not supply enough clean towels or bed sheets. Engineering cannot replace a defective light switch in a guest room if housekeeping does not report the problem. Effective management of this busy department calls for standardized plans, procedures, schedules, and deadlines, as well as frequent direct communication between the executives who manage the key operating units of the rooms department.

The hotel and lodging business is vulnerable to security and safety problems. Problems can be created by guests, employees, or intruders. Security breaches can result in embezzlement, theft, arson, robbery, and even terrorism. Depending on the size of a hotel or a lodging establishment, the security function may be handled by a fully staffed department on site, contracted to an outside security company, or assigned to designated staff members sonnel in the rooms department.

In a larger, full-service hotel, the director of security may report directly to the general manager. In smaller hotels, the security function might become a task of the rooms department. Engineering department's responsibilities include preventive maintenance; repair; replacement; improvement and modification to furniture, fixtures, and equipment (FFE); and ensuring uninterrupted provision of utilities (gas, electricity, water).Preventive maintenance involves routine checks and inspection of the key components of all equipment.

Maintenance of recreational facilities may be part of the engineering department's responsibilities. In particular, swimming pools require extensive maintenance to ensure proper filtration and to prevent the accumulation of algae and other conditions unsuitable for swimming. Prompt repair minimizes loss of productivity in other hotel operating departments and inconvenience to hotel guests. When a particular FFE has reached the end of its useful life and repair is no longer cost-effective, replacement is indicated. Improvement projects enhance the existing operation or reduce operating costs of the facility.

Modification projects alter the existing operation to accommodate one or more new functions. One hotel might have a large engineering staff that includes plumbers, carpenters, painters, electricians, and other technicians. Another might have maintenance personnel who have general knowledge and understanding of the hotel's operations but rely on outside contractors for specialized jobs. In larger, full-service hotels, engineering may be a separate department, with a director who reports directly to the resident manager.

Food and Beverage Department

The primary function of the food and beverage department is to provide food and drink to a hotel's guests. In earlier times, when an inn had a single dining room that could hold a limited number of guests, this was a fairly simple task. Today, however, providing food and drink is much more complicated. A large hotel might well have a coffee shop, a gourmet restaurant, a poolside snack bar, room service, two banquet halls, and ten function rooms where food and beverages are served. It might also have a lounge, a nightclub, and a lobby bar. On a busy day, it's quite likely that functions will be booked in many outlets at the same time.

In addition, some outlets may have multiple events scheduled for a single day. As you can see, there is great diversity in the types of activities performed by a food and beverage department, requiring a significant variety of skills on the part of its workers. Because of the diversity of services provided, the food and beverage department is typically split into subunits. The executive chef, a person of considerable importance and authority in any full-service hotel, runs the food production, or kitchen, department.

A variety of culinary specialists who are responsible for different aspects of food preparation report to the executive chef. The actual serving of food in a large hotel's restaurants is usually the responsibility of a separate department, headed by the assistant food and beverage director. The food service department is composed of the individual restaurant and outlet managers, maitre d's, waiters, waitresses, and bus help. Because of their special duties and concerns, many large hotels have a separate subunit that is responsible only for room service. Because of the high value and profit margins associated with the sale of alcoholic beverages, some hotels have a separate department that assumes responsibility for all outlets where alcoholic beverages are sold.

The person responsible for this department is the beverage manager. Most full-service hotels also do a considerable convention and catering business. The typical convention uses small function rooms for meetings and larger rooms for general sessions, trade shows, exhibits, and banquets. As a hotel or lodging business increases the use of its facilities for conventions and meetings, it may form a separate convention services department.

The convention services department and its personnel are introduced to the client, a meeting planner, or an association executive by the marketing and sales department. The convention services department then handles all of the client's meeting and catering requirements. Individually catered events include parties, wedding receptions, business meetings, and other functions held by groups. To provide for the unique needs of these types of customers, hotels often organise separate catering and convention departments. Depending on the size of the hotel, the job of cleaning the food and beverage outlets themselves as well as of washing pots and pans, dishes, glasses, and utensils is often delegated to a subunit known as the stewarding department. It is only through continuous cooperation and coordination that a hotel's food service function can be carried out effectively.

A guest who is dining in a hotel restaurant requires the joint efforts of the kitchen, food service, beverage, and stewarding departments. A convention banquet cannot be held without the efforts of the convention and catering department along with the food production, beverage, and stewarding departments. The sequence of events and cooperation required among the food and beverage staff is even more important than in the rooms department, thus increasing the importance of communication between managers and employees alike. Another challenge faced by management is the diversity of the employees in the food and beverage department; the dishwasher in the stewarding department is at a dramatically different level than the sous chef in the kitchen. The primary responsibility of the sales managers who make up the marketing and sales department is sales, or the selling of the hotel facilities and services to individuals and groups. Sales managers sell rooms, food, and beverages to potential clients through advertising, attendance at association and conference meetings, and direct contacts.

Marketing and Sales Department

The marketing and sales department is removed from most of the day-to-day operational problems faced by other departments. The division of work among the sales managers is based on the type of customers a hotel is attempting to attract. Individual sales managers often specialize in corporate accounts, conventions, or tour and travel markets. Sales managers' accounts are sometimes subdivided along geographical lines into regional or national accounts.

Human Resource Department

The three functions of the human resources department are employee recruitment, benefits administration, and training. The director of human resources is also expected to be an expert on federal and state labor laws and to advise managers in other departments on these topics. The human resources department's major challenge is in its interactions with other hotel departments. Although the human resources department recruits, interviews, and screens prospective employees, the final hiring decision rests within the department in which the potential employee will be working. The same is true of promotion and disciplinary decisions; the human resources department's input is, in most cases, limited to advice and interpretation of legal questions. The human resources department's effectiveness depends on its manager's ability to form effective working relationships with managers of other departments.

Accounting Department

The accounting department's traditional role is recording financial transactions, preparing and interpreting financial statements, and providing the managers of other departments with timely reports of operating results. The accounting department combines staff functions and line functions, or those functions directly responsible for servicing guests. Other responsibilities, carried out by the assistant controller for finance, include payroll preparation, accounts receivable, and accounts payable. Another dimension of the accounting department's responsibilities deals with various aspects of hotel operations, cost accounting, and cost control throughout the hotel. The two areas of central concern to the accounting department are rooms and food and beverage.

The accounting department's front office cashier is responsible for tracking all charges to guest accounts. At the close of each business day, which varies by hotel but typically occurs at midnight or after the bulk of guests' transactions have been completed, the night auditor is responsible for reconciling all guest bills with the charges from the various hotel departments. Although the front office cashier and the night auditor physically work at the front desk and, in the case of the cashier, have direct contact with guests, they are members of the accounting department and report to the assistant controller of operations.

The food and beverage department may be responsible for food preparation and service, but the accounting department is responsible for collecting revenues. The food and beverage controller and the food and beverage cashiers keep track of both the revenues and expenses of the food and beverage department. The food and beverage controller's job is to verify the accuracy and reasonableness of all food and beverage revenues. In addition to tracking and preparing daily reports on the costs of the food and beverages used in the hotel, in many cases the accounting department is also responsible for purchasing and storeroom operations. Finally, the director of systems is responsible for designing the accounting and control systems used throughout the hotel.

The accounting department is anything but a passive staff unit contending with routine recordkeeping. The accounting department is also responsible for collecting and reporting most of a hotel's operational and financial statistics, which provide important data for decision making and budget preparation purposes. The head of the accounting department may report not only to the hotel's general manager but also to the hotel chain's financial vice president or to the hotel's owner. The reason for this dual responsibility and reporting relationship is to afford the hotel corporation an independent verification of the financial and operating results of the hotel.

Authority

Authority is the organisationally sanctioned right to make a decision. Authority can be distributed throughout an organisation or held in the hands of a few select employees. The delegation of authority creates a chain of command, the formal channel that defines the lines of authority from the top to the bottom of an organisation.

The chain of command specifies a clear reporting relationship for each person in the organisation and should be followed in both downward and upward communication. Following the chain of command enables each new employee, no matter what his or her position, to know exactly for whom and to whom he or she is responsible.

When designing an organisational structure, managers must consider the distribution of authority. Decentralization is the process of distributing authority throughout an organisation. In a decentralized organisation, an organisation member has the right to make a decision without obtaining approval from a higher-level manager. Centralization is the retention of decision-making authority by a high-level manager. Traditionally, hotel and lodging management has been very centralized, probably due to its roots in small, owner-operated lodging.

In recent years, as the hotel and lodging industry has expanded, decentralization has become a more frequent style of operation. Decentralization has several advantages. Managers are encouraged to develop decision-making skills, which help them advance in their careers. The autonomy afforded by this style of operation also increases job satisfaction and motivation. When employees are encouraged to perform well, the profitability of the organisation increases.

Many hotel and lodging organisations have begun to empower employees and supervisors to make decisions that typically have been made by managers. One example that we have already discussed is the use of the quality circle. For example, if a front desk agent determines that a guest's bill is incorrect, in a decentralized organisation the agent has the power to make the correction immediately. If that same front desk agent determines that a guest's stay has been unsatisfactory, he or she has the power to reduce the guest's bill by an amount previously specified by management. Additional challenges, control of the process, and quality assessment become part of everyone's job, and each employee is given the authority to take positive actions that will lead to high quality and improved performance.

Controlling Organisation

It refers to the number of people who report to one manager or supervisor. A wide span of control results in a flat organisation that is, a large number of employees reporting to one supervisor. A narrow span of control results in a tall organisation, in which a small number of employees report to a supervisor, necessitating a larger number of supervisors. No formula exists for determining the ideal span of control.

The factors determine the most appropriate span of control are: task similarity, training and professionalism, task certainty, frequency of interaction, task integration, and physical dispersion. When a large number of employees perform similar tasks, the span of control can be increased. When the employees perform very different tasks, the supervisor must give each subordinate more individual attention in order to keep in touch with the different types of tasks; this requires a narrower span of control. For example, the rooms department manager might easily manage the front desk agents and housekeepers until the brand standards for check-in or checkout of a guest increase in complexity and the standards for the various types of rooms and their cleaning procedure increase in detail. At this time, the rooms department manager's span of control must be narrowed.

The better trained and more skilled a subordinate is, the less supervision is required. For example, a front desk agent might require a higher level of training and skill than a room service waiter. Thus, a front desk supervisor can supervise more employees (wider span of control) than the room service supervisor (narrower span of control). Task certainty refers to the predictability of a task. Routine tasks allow management to devise standard procedures for subordinates to follow, minimizing questions about the job and widening the span of control. On the other hand, close supervision is called for when tasks are ambiguous and uncertainty is great. For example, the task of checking a guest in or out of the hotel can be documented and standard procedures can be created, so the front desk manager can have a relatively wide span of control over the front desk agents. However, because of the diversity of customers the sales manager encounters, the tasks of a hotel sales manager are less certain. The director of sales is responsible for coaching the sales managers, observing sales calls, and ensuring deal closings; these tasks require a hands-on approach that limits the number of employees the director of sales can handle, narrowing the span of control.

If the supervisor-subordinate relationship requires frequent interaction, the span of control must be narrow. If interaction is infrequent, the span of control can be wide. For example, the hotel controller must review regularly the status of collections and payments with staff. In contrast, the frequency of interaction between the chief engineer and his or her subordinates is directed by written work orders in most circumstances and thus requires less direct communication, enabling a wider span of control.

If the supervisor must integrate and coordinate the tasks of subordinates, the span of control narrows. For example, in the production of a meal for one table of four guests with different appetizers, salads, and entrées, the chef must have a narrow span of control to ensure that each component of the meal is assembled correctly and delivered to service personnel on a timely basis. The span of control of the executive housekeeper can be much wider because the procedure for cleaning and preparing each guest room is similar, if not exactly the same, for every room.

Physical dispersion refers to the distribution of employees within the lodging establishment. For example, if the executive housekeeper has guest room attendants on 20 floors in two buildings and the front desk manager has all front desk agents located in one place, the span of control would narrow for the executive housekeeper and widen for the front desk manager. The ideal number of people that one person can supervise depends on a variety of factors. Consistent with trends in organisational structure such as teams, quality circles, and employee empowerment, many hotel and lodging organisations are widening their span of control. The objective behind these trends is to develop a flatter, more responsive organisational structure in which employees can make decisions without going through several levels of management.

One of the most important strength of a functional organisational design is efficiency. The performance of common tasks allows for work specialization, which increases overall productivity. Workers develop specialized skills and knowledge more rapidly. Training is easier because of the similarity of tasks and the resulting opportunities for inexperienced workers to learn from experienced workers. This helps new employees quickly learn the kinds of behavior that lead to success and promotion.

Coordination of activities within functional departments is easier than in more broadly based organisations. A functional organisation fosters efficiency, teamwork, and coordination of activities within individual units. However, the functional organisation's most important strength is also the source of its great-est shortcoming. The success of a hotel as a business is measured by its overall performance and not by the performance of any one department.

A hotel with spotless guest rooms will not be successful if guests' front desk experiences are not up to par. Even if guests' dining experiences are superb, the hotel will fall flat on its face if its rooms are dismal. It is sometimes difficult for each department to fully appreciate its role in the overall success of the organisation. It is vital that each department keep in mind the hotel-wide goals of customer service and profitability rather than focus narrowly on its own concerns. Some means must be found to coordinate the activities of functional departments and to set hotel-wide strategies and goals. A hotel's functional organisation demands strong leadership. New initiatives in hotels often require cooperation and coordination between functional departments. New ideas tend to be stillborn if department heads lack a hotel-wide perspective or have difficulty coordinating their activities.

The tendency to concentrate on doing things right often overshadows the organisation's ability to do the right thing.The GM, as the chief executive of the hotel, emerges as the single person capable of providing the overall organisational direction, decision making, coordination, and arbitration needed to make a hotel's functional departments work together effectively. A hotel simply cannot run itself from the departmental level. Thus, the GM must be a strong leader to be effective.

The executive operating committee (EOC) of a hotel, made up of the general manager and senior executives from each department, is designed to increase the level of coordination between departments. There is no standard membership for this committee, but it usually comprises those executives who report directly to the general manager. The EOC is also responsible for a hotel's major budgetary units, such as the food and beverage and housekeeping units. EOC functions depend on how the hotel GM chooses to use the group, the GM's style, and the structure of other management meetings in the hotel. Typically, the EOC meets weekly, focusing on matters ranging from day-today operational issues to comparing budgets with actual operating results.

Staff Meetings

Many hotels increase communications through an elaborate structure of additional committees and meetings, including some or all of the following: operations, staff, sales forecast and marketing, departmental, subdepartmental, credit, safety, energy conservation, and employee meetings. The operations committee comprises the general manager, department heads, front office manager, manager on duty, and representatives from housekeeping, security, engineering, and food and beverage. This committee might meet four or five times per week for 15 to 20 minutes to review upcoming activities and assess the results of previous activities. The staff committee might include the GM, department heads, and all subdepartment heads who report to the department heads. This committee, which might meet weekly for one or two hours, reviews the prior week's performance, the current week's activities, the next week's plans, and special projects. The staff committee also presents performance awards to employees.

The sales forecast and marketing committee might meet one to four times per month for several hours so the GM and department heads can review room demand for the coming 90 days and devise strategies to increase room nights (and thus bring in more revenue) and to increase average daily rates by up-selling potential guests to higher-rated rooms with perhaps more amenities or services. The departmental committee consists of the department head and his or her subdepartment heads, managers, and supervisors.

Meeting once or twice per month for an hour or so, the group reviews departmental issues. Similarly, subdepartment committees meet monthly for about an hour so the subdepartment head, managers, and supervisors can address issues unique to their subdepartment, such as the selection of a new type of floor cleaner by the housekeeping department or a more energy-efficient light bulb by the engineering department. The credit committee includes the general manager, the controller, sales, the front office, reservations, catering, and the credit manager. Meeting monthly for an hour, the committee reviews those guests and clients of the hotel who were granted credit but have not settled their account. The safety committee typically comprises representatives from human resources, food and beverage, housekeeping, and engineering. Meeting monthly for an hour or so, the committee reviews safety programs and safety records, addresses problems, and discusses the implementation of new safety regulations.

In some full-service hotels, an energy conservation committee includes the chief engineer, resident manager, food and beverage staff, human resource representatives, rooms staff, and housekeeping representatives. The committee typically meets monthly for an hour to discuss strategies and programs for controlling energy costs. Most full-service hotels convene a monthly meeting or at least an annual meeting of all hotel management and employees to review performance and to distribute awards. This event ranges from an hourlong meeting to a company-wide celebration lasting several hours.

As new business practices are evolving as fast as our technologies, resistance to change has become a primary cause of business failure. The future success of a hotel will be driven in large part by the ability to foresee and capitalize on change. As we go through global transitions, the successful hotel will examine the key factors that will not only define success but also the ability to survive in coming years. These key organisational trends must be acknowledged by the successful hotel organisation: visionary leadership, globalization, diversity, flexibility, flat structure, customer focus, zero defects, network orientation, and being in the information fast lane.

The organisation must be able to respond to increasingly globalized sales, the movement to maintaining sales offices in many countries and hotel properties across the globe, and an increasingly globalized labor market. Intercontinental Hotels Group recently introduced a new organisation structure to more efficiently use regional and global resources to drive higher levels of innovation, customer focus, and revenues. Diversity means the organisation must respond to a workforce that is heterogeneous sexually, racially, and chronologically; innovation and conflict/communication issues; and different styles of interaction, dress, presentation, and physical appearance. Flexibility in the modern hotel organisation means assuring that systems, processes, and people can respond differently to different situations; fewer detailed rules and procedures; greater autonomy and encouragement of initiative; customizing employment relationships to include telecommuting and job-sharing; and lifetime employability rather than lifetime employment. The trend toward flatness in hotel organisations means fewer levels of management, workers empowered to make decisions, and fewer differences in responsibility.

The organisation's employees need to believe in a sense of entrepreneurship that reacts proactively to market diversity. Traditional organisations that follow well-documented rules must give way to leaders who can balance a sense of discipline with one of flexibility. If the customer is king or queen in the 21st century, hotel organisaions will be best served by focusing less on their hotel assets as measures of success and more on their customers. This involves a fundamental shift from viewing the real estate asset as the wealth creator to seeing the customer as the key to building shareholder wealth.

A customer focus must reflect business decisions at all levels of developing and operating a hotel organisation. Pursuing such a course will inevitably impact shareholder wealth. Today's hotel organisation must recognize the need for visionary leadership. The old command-and-control model of leadership is giv-ing way to a focus on leadership in ideas, information, inspiration, vision, and teamwork.

A failing hotel organisation is overmanaged and underled. The networked hotel organisation can facilitate direct communication across unit and property boundaries, ignoring the chain of command; cross-unit team structures; outsourcing and downsizing; strategic alliances with competitors and others; customization; and decentralization.

Being in the information fast lane is critical. The traditional role of information technology as a back office support for accounting and bookkeeping has clearly moved to front and center stage. Information technology today influences all aspects of business from corporate strategies to organisational structure. Technology was once viewed as a way to reduce costs by replacing people. That attitude has been firmly supplanted by the idea of seeking information technology support for the creative work all organisations must pursue. Information technology must enable organisations to react more speedily to market needs and, of course, produce the fulfillment of customer demands both quickly and accurately. To do this it must operate on a decentralized basis. Information technology delivers, but it has to deliver the right information to the right people at the right time.

STAFFING OPERATIONS

Job analysis is an ongoing process, as many jobs change with improvements in technology and pressure to improve product quality. The job analysis is the basis for the job description and job specification. A job description includes the job title, pay, a brief statement of duties and procedures, working conditions, and hours. The job specification is an outline of the qualifications necessary for a particular job. In response to the limits of specialization, organisations can redesign jobs to improve coordination, productivity, and product quality while responding to an employee's needs for learning, challenge, variety, increased responsibility, and achievement. Such job redesign often involves job rotation, the systematic movement of employees from one job to another; job enlargement, an increase in the number of tasks an employee will do in the job; job enrichment, the attempt to give the employee more control over job-related activities; and flextime, a flexible work schedule that permits employee input in establishing work schedules. In team-driven job redesign, a concept similar to job rotation, employees can transfer back and forth among teams that provide different services or products.

Hotels recruit employees from a variety of sources. Newspapers and employee referrals are used to recruit nonskilled hourly employees. Supervisory and management employees generally are recruited through colleges and universities, promotions from within, professional associations, and management recruiters. Hotels that take more time in making their selections are more successful in retaining employees.

Discussions of employee training and development often concentrate on training techniques without giving a full explanation of what a hotel is trying to accomplish. As training and development impart job skills and educate employees, supervisors, and managers, they also improve current and future employee performance, which affects the bottom line.

Effective training includes problem solving, problem analysis, quality measurement and feedback, and team building. Performance evaluation, also called performance appraisal, is the systematic review of the strengths and weaknesses of an employee's performance. The major difficulty in a performance appraisal is quantifying those strengths and weaknesses. The performance of some jobs is easy to quantify, while for others it is more difficult. An important part of the appraisal process is a well-established job description, so that the employee and the supervisor have similar expectations.

Compensation includes the monetary and nonmonetary rewards that managers, supervisors, and employees receive for performing their jobs. In order to set compensation levels, the human resources department must periodically conduct job evaluations, which determine the value of the job to the hotel. Knowledge of the value of the job to the organisation and of wage rates for each job classification allows the hotel to establish a fair compensation policy.

There are several activities involved in staffing a housekeeping operation. Executive housekeepers must select and interview employees, participate in an orientation program, train newly hired employees, and develop employees for future growth.

Employees Selection

Each region has its own demographic situations that affect the availability of suitable employees for involvement in housekeeping or environmental service operations. For example, in one area, an exceptionally high response rate from people seeking food service work may occur and a low response rate from people seeking housekeeping positions may occur. In another area, the reverse may be true, and people interested in housekeeping work may far outnumber those interested in food service.

Advertising campaigns that will reach these employees are the best method of locating suitable people. Major classified ads associated with mass hirings will specify the need for food service personnel, front desk clerks, food servers, housekeeping personnel, and maintenance people. Such ads may yield surprising results. If the volume of response for housekeeping personnel is insufficient to provide a suitable hiring base, the following sources may be investigated:

— Local employment agencies
— Flyers posted on community bulletin boards
— Local church organizations
— Neighborhood canvass for friends of recently hired employees
— Direct radio appeals to local homemakers
— Organizations for underprivileged ethnic minorities, and mentally disabled people

If these sources do not produce the volume of applicants necessary to develop a staff, it may become necessary to search for employees in distant areas and to provide regular transportation for them to and from work. If aliens are hired, the department manager must take great care to ensure that they are legal residents of this country and that their green cards are valid.

More than one hotel department manager has had an entire staff swept away by the Department of Immigration after hiring people who were illegal aliens. Such unfortunate action has required the immediate assistance of all available employees to fill in. Whether you are involved in a mass hiring or in the recruiting of a single employee, a systematic and courteous procedure for processing applicants is essential. For example, in the opening of the Los Angeles Airport Marriott, 11,000 applicants were processed to fill approximately 850 positions in a period of about two weeks. The magnitude of such an operation required a near assembly-line technique, but a personable and positive experience for the applicants still had to be maintained.

The efficient handling of lines of employees, courteous attendance, personal concern for employee desires, and reference to suitable departments for those unfamiliar with what the hotel or hospital has to offer all become earmarks for how the company will treat its employees. The key to proper handling of applicants is the use of a control system whereby employees are conducted through the steps of application, prescreening, and if qualified, reference to a department for interview. Even though an employee may desire involvement in one classification of work, he or she may be hired for employment in a different department. Also, employees might not be aware of the possibilities available in a particular department at the time of application or may be unable to locate in desired departments at the time of mass hirings.

Employees who perform well should therefore be given the opportunity to transfer to other departments when the opportunities arise. According to laws regulated by federal and state Fair Employment Practices Agencies (FEPA), no person may be denied the opportunity to submit application for employment for a position of his or her choosing. Not only is the law strict on this point, but companies in any way benefiting from interstate commerce may not discriminate in the hiring of people based on race, color, national origin, or religious preference. Although specific hours and days of the week may be specified, it is a generally accepted fact that hotels and hospitals must maintain personnel operations that provide the opportunity for people to submit applications without prejudice.

Orientation

A carefully planned, concerned, and informational orientation program is significant to the first impressions that a new employee will have about the hospital or hotel in general and the housekeeping department in particular. Too often, a new employee is told where the work area and restroom are, given a cursory explanation of the job, then put to work. It is not uncommon to find managers putting employees to work who have not even been processed into the organization, an unfortunate situation that is usually discovered on payday when there is no paycheck for the new employee.

Such blatant disregard for the concerns of the employee can only lead to a poor perception of the company. A planned orientation program will eliminate this type of activity and will bring the employee into the company with personal concern and with a greater possibility for a successful relationship. A good orientation program is usually made up of four phases: employee acquisition, receipt of an employee's handbook, tour of the facility, and an orientation meeting.

Once a person is accepted for employment, the applicant is told to report for work at a given time and place, and that place should be the personnel department. Preemployment procedures can take as much as one-half day, and department managers eager to start new employees to work should allow time for a proper employee acquisition into the organization.

At this time it should be ensured that the application is complete and any additional information pertaining to employment history that may be necessary to obtain the necessary work permits and credentials is on hand. Usually the security department records the entry of a new employee into the staff and provides instructions regarding use of employee entrances, removing parcels from the premises, and employee parking areas.

Application for work permits, and drug testing, will be scheduled where applicable. All documents required by the hotel's health and welfare insurer should be completed, and instructions should be given about immediately reporting accidents, no matter how slight, to supervisors. The federal government requires that every employer submit a W-4 (withholding statement) for each employee on the payroll. Mandatory deductions from pay should be explained (federal and state income tax and Social Security FICA), as should other deductions that may be required or desired.

At this time, some form of personal action document is usually initiated for the new employee and is placed in the employee's permanent record. When a change has to be made, such as job title, marital status, or rate of pay, the PAF is retrieved from the employee's record, changes are made under the item to be changed, and the corrected PAF is used to change the data in the computer storage. Once new information is stored, a new PAF is created and placed in the employee's record to await the next need for processing. A long-time employee might have many PAFs stored in the personnel file.

Familiarization of Facilities

Upon completion of the acquisition phase, a facility tour should be conducted for one or all new employees. For new facilities, access to the property should be gained within about one week before opening, and many new employees can be taken on a tour simultaneously. It is possible for employees to work in the hotel housekeeping department for years and never to have visited the showroom, dining rooms, ballrooms, or even the executive office areas.

A tour of the complete facility melds employees into the total organization, and a complete informative tour should never be neglected. For ongoing operations, after acquisition, the new employee may be turned over to a department supervisor, who becomes the tour director. An appreciation of the total involvement of each employee is strengthened when a facilities tour is complete and thorough. If necessary, the property tour might be postponed until after the orientation meeting; however, the orientation activity of staffing is not complete until a property tour is conducted.

Orientation Meeting

The orientation meeting should not be conducted until the employee has had an opportunity to become at least partially familiar with the surroundings. Employee orientation meetings that are scheduled too soon fail to answer many questions that will develop within the first two weeks of employment. The meeting should be held in a comfortable setting, with refreshments provided. It is usually conducted by the director of human resources and is attended by as many of the facility managers as possible.

Most certainly, the general manager or hospital administration members of the executive committee, the security director, and the new employees' department heads should attend. Each of these managers should have an opportunity to welcome the new employees and give them a chance to associate names with faces. All managers and new employees should wear name tags. In orientation meetings, a brief history of the company and company goals should be presented.

Although the new employee will be gaining confidence and security in the position as training ends and work is actually performed, informal orientation may continue for quite some time. The formal orientation, however, ends with the orientation meeting. Finally, it should be remembered that good orientation procedures lead to worker satisfaction and help quiet the anxieties and fears that a new employee may have. When a good orientation is neglected, the seeds of dissatisfaction are planted.

Training

The efficiency and economy with which any department will operate will depend on the ability of each member of the organization to do his or her job. Such ability will depend in part on past experiences, but more commonly it can be credited to the type and quality of training offered. Employees, regardless of past experiences, always need some degree of training before starting a new job. Small institutions may try to avoid training by hiring people who are already trained in the general functions with which they will be involved.

However, most institutions recognize the need for training that is specifically oriented toward the new experience, and will have a documented training· program. Some employers of housekeeping personnel find it easier to train completely unskilled and untrained personnel. In such cases, bad or undesirable practices do not have to be trained out of an employee.

Previous experience and education should, however, be analyzed and considered in the training of each new employee in order that efficiencies in training can be recognized. If an understanding of department standards and policies can be demonstrated by a new employee, that portion of training may be shortened or modified. However, skill and ability must be demonstrated before training can be altered. Finally, training is the best method to communicate the company's way of doing things, without which the new employee may do work contrary to company policy.

First Training

First training of a new employee actually starts with a continuation of department orientation. When a new employee is turned over to the housekeeping or environmental services department, orientation usually continues by familiarizing the employee with department rules and regulations. Many housekeeping departments have their own department employee handbooks.

Systematic Approach to Training

Training may be defined as those activities that are designed to help an employee begin performing tasks for which he or she is hired or to help the employee improve performance in a job already assigned. The purpose of training is to enable an employee to begin an assigned job or to improve upon techniques already in use. In hotel or hospital housekeeping operations, there are three basic areas in which training activity should take place: skills, attitudes, and knowledge.

Skills Training: A sample list of skills in which a basic housekeeping employee must be trained follows:

— *Bed making:* Specific techniques; company policy

— *Vacuuming:* Techniques; use and care of equipment

— *Dusting:* Techniques; use of products

— *Window and mirror cleaning:* Techniques and products

— *Setup awareness:* Room setups; what a properly serviced room should look like

— *Bathroom cleaning:* Tub and toilet sanitation; appearance; methods of cleaning and results desired

— *Daily routine:* An orderly procedure for the conduct of the day's work; daily communications

— *Caring for and using equipment:* Housekeeper cart; loading

— *Industrial safety:* Product use; guest safety; fire and other emergencies The best reference for the skills that require training is the job description for which the person is being trained.

Attitude Guidance: Employees need guidance in their attitudes about the work that must be done. They need to be guided in their thinking about rooms that may present a unique problem in cleaning. Attitudes among section housekeepers need to be such that, occasionally, when rooms require extra effort to be brought back to standard, it is viewed as being a part of rendering service to the guest who paid to enjoy the room.

The rooms are there to be enjoyed. Positive relationships with various agencies and people also need to be developed. The following is a list of areas in which attitude guidance is important:

— The guest/patient

— The department manager and immediate supervisor

— A guestroom that is in a state of great disarray

— The hotel and company

— The uniform

— Appearance

— Personal hygiene

Meeting Standards: The most important task of the trainer is to prepare new employees to meet standards. With this aim in mind, sequence of performance in cleaning a guestroom is most important in order that efficiency in accomplishing day-to-day tasks may be developed. In addition, the best method of accomplishing a task should be presented to the new trainee. Once the task has been learned, the next thing is to meet standards, which may not necessarily mean doing the job the way the person has been trained.

Ongoing Training

There is a need to conduct ongoing training for all employees, regardless of how long they have been members of the department. There are two instances when additional training is needed:

— the purchase of new equipment, and

— change in or unusual employee behavior while on the job.

When new equipment is purchased, employees need to know how the new equipment differs from present equipment, what new skills or knowledge are required to operate the equipment, who will need this knowledge, and when. New equipment may also require new attitudes about work habits.

Employee behavior while on the job that is seen as an indicator for additional training may be divided into two categories: events that the manager witnesses and events that the manager is told about by the employees. Events that the manager witnesses that indicate a need for training are frequent employee absence, considerable spoilage of products, carelessness, a high rate of accidents, and resisting direction by supervisors.

Events that the manager might be told about that indicate a need for training are that something doesn't work right, something is dangerous to work with, something is making work harder. Although training is vital for any organization to function at top efficiency, it is expensive. The money and man-hours expended must therefore be worth the investment. There must be a balance between the dollars spent training employees and the benefits of productivity and high-efficiency performance.

A simple method of determining the need for training is to measure performance of workers: Find out what is going on at present on the job, and match this performance with what should be happening. The difference, if any, describes how much training is needed. If the employee could not do the job even if his or her life depended on the outcome, there is a deficiency of knowledge (DK). If the employee could have done the job if his or her life depended on the outcome, but did not, there is a deficiency of execution (DE).

If either deficiency of knowledge or deficiency of execution exists, training must be conducted. The approach or the method of training may differ, however. Deficiencies of knowledge can be corrected by training the employee to do the job, then observing and correcting as necessary until the task is proficiently performed. Deficiency of execution is usually corrected by searching for the underlying cause of lack of performance, not by teaching the actual task.

Training Methods

There are numerous methods or ways to conduct training. Each method has its own advantages and disadvantages, which must be weighed in the light of benefits to be gained. Some methods are more expensive than others but are also more effective in terms of time required for comprehension and proficiency that must be developed. Several useful methods of training housekeeping personnel are listed and discussed.

On-the-Job Training: Using on-the-job training (OJT), a technique in which "learning by doing" is the advantage, the instructor demonstrates the procedure and then watches the students perform it. With this technique, one instructor can handle several students. In housekeeping operations, the instructor is usually a GRA who is doing the instructing in the rooms that have been assigned for cleaning that day. The OJT method is not operationally productive until the student is proficient enough in the training tasks to absorb part of the operational load.

Simulation Training: With simulation training, a model room (unrented) is set up and used to train several employees. Whereas OJT requires progress toward daily production of ready rooms, simulation requires that the model room not be rented. In addition, the trainer is not productive in cleaning ready rooms. The advantages of simulation training are that it allows the training process to be stopped, discussed, and repeated if necessary. Simulation is an excellent method, provided the trainer's time is paid for out of training funds, and clean room production is not necessary during the workday.

Coach-Pupil Method: The coach-pupil method is similar to OJT except that each instructor has only one student (a one-to-one relationship). This method is desired, provided that there are enough qualified instructors to have several training units in progress at the same time.

Lectures: The lecture method reaches the largest number of students per instructor. Practically all training programs use this type of instruction for certain segments. Unfortunately, the lecture method can be the dullest training technique, and therefore requires instructors who are gifted in presentation capabilities. In addition, space for lectures may be difficult to obtain and may require special facilities.

Conferences: The conference method of instruction is often referred to as workshop training. This technique involves a group of students who formulate ideas, do problem solving, and report on projects. The conference or workshop technique is excellent for supervisory training.

Demonstrations: When new products or equipment are being introduced, demonstrations are excellent. Many demonstrations may be conducted by vendors and purveyors as a part of the sale of equipment and products. Difficulties may arise when language barriers exist. It is also important that no more information be presented than can be absorbed in a reasonable period of time; otherwise misunderstandings may arise.

Training Aids

Many hotels use training aids in a conference room, or post messages on an employee bulletin board. Aside from the usual training aids such as chalkboards, bulletin boards, charts, graphs, and diagrams, photographs can supply clear and accurate references for how rooms should be set up, maids' carts loaded, and routines accomplished. Most housekeeping operations have films on guest contact and courtesy that may also be used in training. Motion pictures speak directly to many people who may not understand proper procedures from reading about them. Many training techniques may be combined to develop a well-rounded training plan.

Improving Potential

It is possible to have two students sitting side by side in a classroom, with one being trained and the other being developed. Recall that the definition of training is preparing a person to do a job for which he or she is hired or to improve upon performance of a current job. Development is preparing a person for advancement or to assume greater responsibility.

The techniques are the same, but the end result is quite different. Whereas training begins after orientation of an employee who is hired to do a specific job, upon introduction of new equipment, or upon observation and communication with employees indicating a need for training, development begins with the identification of a specific employee who has shown potential for advancement. Training for promotion or to improve potential is in fact development and must always include a much neglected type of training -supervisory training. Many forms of developmental training may be given on the property; other forms might include sending candidates to schools and seminars. Developmental training is associated primarily with supervisors and managerial development and may encompass many types of experiences.

Development of individuals within the organization looks to future potential and promotion of employees. Specifically, those employees who demonstrate leadership potential should be developed through supervisory training for advancement to positions of greater responsibility. Unfortunately, many outstanding workers have their performance rewarded by promotion but are given no development training.

The excellent section housekeeper who is advanced to the position of senior housekeeper without the benefit of supervisory training is quickly seen to be unhappy and frustrated and may possibly become a loss to the department. It is therefore most essential that individual potential be developed in an orderly and systematic manner, or else this potential may never be recognized.

Even though there will be times that the trainee may be given specific responsibilities to oversee operations, clean guestrooms, or service public areas, advantage should not be taken of the trainee or the situation to the detriment of the development function. Development of new growth in the trainee becomes difficult when the training instructor or coordinator is not only developing a new manager but is also being held responsible for the production of some aspect of housekeeping operations.

Whether you are conducting a training or a development program, suitable records of training progress should be maintained both by the training supervisor and the student. Periodic evaluations of the student's progress should be conducted, and successful completion of the program should be recognized. Public recognition of achievement will inspire the newly trained or developed employee to achieve standards of performance and to strive for advancement.

Once an employee is trained or developed and his or her satisfactory performance has been recognized and recorded, the person should perform satisfactorily to standards. Future performance may be based on beginning performance after training. If an employee's performance begins to fall short of standards and expectations, there has to be a reason other than lack of skills.

The reason for unsatisfactory performance must then be sought out and addressed. This type of follow-up is not possible unless suitable records of training and development are maintained and used for comparison. Although evaluation and performance appraisal for employees will occur as work progresses, it is not uncommon to find the design of systems for appraisal as part of organization and staffing functions. This is true because first appraisal and evaluation occurs during training, which is an activity of staffing. Once trainees begin to have their performance appraised, the methods used will continue throughout employment. As a part of training, new employees should be told how, when, and by whom their performances will be evaluated, and should be advised that questions regarding their performance will be regularly answered.

Probationary Period

Initial employment should be probationary in nature, allowing the new employee to improve efficiency to where the designated number of rooms cleaned per day can be achieved in a probationary period (about three months). Should a large number of employees be unable to achieve the standard within that time, the standard should be investigated. Should only one or two employees be unable to meet the standard of rooms cleaned per day, an evaluation of the employee in training should either reveal the reason why or indicate the employee as unsuitable for further retention. An employee who, after suitable training, cannot meet a reasonable performance standard should not be allowed to continue employment. Similarly, an employee who has met required performance standards in the specified probationary period should be continued into regular employment status and thus achieve a reasonable degree of security in employment.

EVALUATION OF PERSONNEL

Evaluation of personnel is an attempt to measure selected traits, characteristics, and productivity. Unfortunately, evaluations are generally objective in nature, and raters are seldom trained in the art of subjective evaluation. Initiative, self-control, and leadership ability do not lend themselves to measurement; therefore such characteristics are estimated. How well they are estimated depends to a great extent on the person doing the estimating.

Certain policies on the use of evaluations should be established so that they are understood by both the person doing the evaluating and the person being evaluated. These policies must be established and disseminated by management. Evaluation should be used at the end of a probationary period, and the employee must understand at the beginning of the period that he or she will be observed and evaluated. Each item, as well as what impact the 'evaluation will have on future employment, should be explained to the employee. People undergoing periodic evaluations, such as at the end of one year's employment, should also know why evaluations are being conducted and what may result from the evaluation. In both situations, the evaluation should be used for counseling and guidance so that performance may be improved upon or corrected if necessary. Certainly, strong points should be pointed out.

In certain locales, such as isolated resorts, hotels are tempted to use contract labor because the local market does not support the necessary number of workers, particularly in housekeeping. Advocates of outsourcing are quick to point out the advantages of the practice. Scarce workers are provided to the property, and there is no need to provide expensive employee benefits.

The entire staffing function is assumed by the contractor. There are no worries regarding recruiting, selecting, hiring, orienting, or even training the employees. Merely issue them uniforms and send them off to clean rooms. Some employers may even be willing to relax their responsibilities regarding employment law such as immigration and naturalization requirements. Management should never forget that once a contracted employee dons a company uniform, the guest believes that person is an employee of the hotel. The guest also believes the hotel has made every reasonable effort to screen that person in the hiring process to ensure that he or she is of good moral character, who has the best interest of the guest at heart.

Unfortunately, there have been several incidents in which the outsourced employees did not quite have the best interest of the guest in their hearts. There have been more than a few cases in which outsourced workers were wanted felons who inflicted considerable bodily harm on guests during the performance of their duties. A number of these incidents have resulted in lawsuits, with awards against the hotel in the millions of dollars.

EFFECTIVE HOUSEKEEPING

The housekeeper must consider herself as the immediate representative of her mistress, and bring, to the management of the household, all those qualities of honesty, industry, and vigilance, in the same degree as if she were at the head of her own family. Constantly on the watch to detect any wrong-doing on the part of any of the domestics, she will overlook all that goes on in the house, and will see that every department is thoroughly attended to, and that the servants are comfortable, at the same time that their various duties are properly performed.

A necessary qualification for a housekeeper is, that she should thoroughly understand accounts. She will have to write in her books an accurate registry of all sums paid for any and every purpose, all the current expenses of the house, tradesmen's bills, and other extraneous matter. Under the head of the Mistress, a housekeeper's accounts should be periodically balanced, and examined by the head of the house. Nothing tends more to the satisfaction of both employer and employed, than this arrangement. "Short reckonings make long friends," stands good in this case, as in others.

It will be found an excellent plan to take an account of every article which comes into the house connected with housekeeping, and is not paid for at the time. The book containing these entries can then be compared with the bills sent in by the various tradesmen, so that any discrepancy can be inquired into and set right. An intelligent housekeeper will, by this means, too, be better able to judge of the average consumption of each article by the household; and if that quantity be, at any time, exceeded, the cause may be discovered and rectified, if it proceed from waste or carelessness.

Although in the department of the cook, the housekeeper does not generally much interfere, yet it is necessary that she should possess a good knowledge of the culinary art, as, in many instances, it may be requisite for her to take the superintendence of the kitchen. As a rule, it may be stated, that the housekeeper, in those establishments where there is no house steward or man cook, undertakes the preparation of the confectionary, attends to the preserving and pickling of fruits and vegetables; and, in a general way, to the more difficult branches of the art of cookery.

. Much of these arrangements will depend, however, on the qualifications of the cook; for instance, if she be an able artiste, there will be but little necessity for the housekeeper to interfere, except in the already noticed articles of confectionary, etc. On the contrary, if the cook be not so clever an adept in her art, then it will be requisite for the housekeeper to give more of her attention to the business of the kitchen, than in the former case. It will be one of the duties of the housekeeper to attend to the marketing, in the absence of either a house steward or man cook.

The daily duties of a housekeeper are regula.ed, in a great measure, by the extent of the establishment she superintends. She should, however, rise early, and see that all the domestics are duly performing their work, and that everything is progressing satisfactorily for the preparation of the breakfast for the household and family.

After breakfast, which, in large establishments, she will take in the "housekeeper's room" with the lady's-maid, butler, and valet, and where they will be waited on by the still-room maid, she will, on various days set apart for each purpose, carefully examine the household linen, with a view to its being repaired, or to a further quantity being put in hand to be made; she will also see that the furniture throughout the house is well rubbed and polished; and will, besides, attend to all the necessary details of marketing and ordering goods from the tradesmen.

The housekeeper's room is generally made use of by the lady's-maid, butler, and valet, who take there their breakfast, tea, and supper. The lady's-maid will also use this apartment as a sitting-room, when not engaged with her lady, or with some other duties, which would call her elsewhere. In different establishments, according to their size and the rank of the family, different rules of course prevail. For instance, in the mansions of those of very high rank, and where there is a house steward, there are two distinct tables kept, one in the steward's room for the principal members of the household, the other in the servants' hall, for the other domestics.

At the steward's dinner-table, the steward and housekeeper preside; and here, also, are present the lady's-maid, butler, valet, and head gardener. Should any visitors be staying with the family, their servants, generally the valet and lady's-maid, will be admitted to the steward's table. After dinner, the housekeeper, having seen that all the members of the establishment have regularly returned to their various duties, and that all the departments of the household are in proper working order, will have many important matters claiming her attention.

She will, possibly, have to give the finishing touch to some article of confectionary, or be occupied with some of the more elaborate processes of the still-room. There may also be the dessert to arrange, ice-creams to make; and all these employments call for no ordinary degree of care, taste, and attention. The still-room was formerly much more in vogue than at present; for in days of "auld lang syne," the still was in constant requisition for the supply of sweet-flavoured waters for the purposes of cookery, scents and aromatic substances used in the preparation of the toilet, and cordials in cases of accidents and illness.

There are some establishments, however, in which distillation is still carried on, and in these, the still-room maid has her old duties to perform. In a general way, however, this domestic is immediately concerned with the housekeeper. For the latter she lights the fire, dusts her room, prepares the breakfast-table, and waits at the different meals taken in the housekeeper's room. A still-room maid may learn a very great deal of useful knowledge from her intimate connection with the housekeeper, and if she be active and intelligent, may soon fit herself for a better position in the household.

In the evening, the housekeeper will often busy herself with the necessary preparations for the next day's duties. Numberless small, but still important arrangements, will have to be made, so that everything may move smoothly. At times, perhaps, attention will have to be paid to the breaking of lump-sugar, the stoning of raisins, the washing, cleansing, and drying of currants, &c.

The evening, too, is the best time for setting right her account of the expenditure, and duly writing a statement of moneys received and paid, and also for making memoranda of any articles she may require for her storeroom or other departments. Periodically, at some convenient time — for instance, quarterly or half-yearly, it is a good plan for the housekeeper to make an inventory of everything she has under her care, and compare this with the lists of a former period; she will then be able to furnish a statement, if necessary, of the articles which, on account of time, breakage, loss, or other causes, it has been necessary to replace or replenish.

Like "Caesar's wife," she should be "above suspicion," and her honesty and sobriety unquestionable; for there are many temptations to which she is exposed. In a physical point of view, a housekeeper should be healthy and strong, and be particularly clean in her person, and her hands, although they may show a degree of roughness, from the nature of some of her employments, yet should have a nice inviting appearance.

In her dealings with the various tradesmen, and in her behaviour to the domestics under her, the demeanour and conduct of the housekeeper should be such as, in neither case, to diminish, by an undue familiarity, her authority or influence. As, in the winter months, servants have much more to do, in consequence of the necessity there is to attend to the number of fires throughout the household, not much more than the ordinary every-day work can be attempted.

In the summer, and when the absence of fires gives the domestics more leisure, then any extra work that is required, can be more easily performed. The spring is the usual period set apart for house-cleaning, and removing all the dust and dirt, which will necessarily, with the best of housewives, accumulate during the winter months, from the smoke of the coal, oil, gas, &c. This season is also well adapted for washing and bleaching linen, &c., as, the weather, not being then too hot for the exertions necessary in washing counterpanes, blankets, and heavy things in general, the work is better and more easily done than in the intense heats of July, which month some recommend for these purposes.

Winter curtains should be taken down, and replaced by the summer white ones; and furs and woollen cloths also carefully laid by. The former should be well shaken and brushed, and then pinned upon paper or linen, with camphor to preserve them from the moths. Furs, &c., will be preserved in the same way. Included, under the general description of house-cleaning, must be understood, turning out all the nooks and corners of drawers, cupboards, lumber-rooms, lofts, &c., with a view of getting rid of all unnecessary articles, which only create dirt and attract vermin; sweeping of chimneys, taking up carpets, painting and whitewashing the kitchen and offices, papering rooms, when needed, and, generally speaking, the house putting on, with the approaching summer, a bright appearance, and a new face, in unison with nature.

Oranges now should be preserved, and orange wine made. The summer will be found, as mentioned above, in consequence of the diminution of labour for the domestics, the best period for examining and repairing household linen, and for "putting to rights" all those articles which have received a large share of wear and tear during the dark winter days. In direct reference to this matter, that sheets should be turned "sides to middle" before they are allowed to get very thin. Otherwise, patching, which is uneconomical from the time it consumes, and is unsightly in point of appearance, will have to be resorted to.

In June and July, gooseberries, currants, raspberries, strawberries, and other summer fruits, should be preserved, and jams and jellies made. In July, too, the making of walnut ketchup should be attended to, as the green walnuts will be approaching perfection for this purpose. Mixed pickles may also be now made, and it will be found a good plan to have ready a jar of pickle-juice, into which to put occasionally some young French beans, cauliflowers, etc.

In the early autumn, plums of various kinds are to be bottled and preserved, and jams and jellies made. A little later, tomato sauce, a most useful article to have by you, may be prepared; a supply of apples laid in, if you have a place to keep them, as also a few keeping pears and filberts. Endeavour to keep also a large vegetable marrow it will be found delicious in the winter.

In October and November, it will be necessary to prepare for the cold weather, and get ready the winter clothing for the various members of the family. The white summer curtains will now be carefully put away, the fireplaces, grates, and chimneys looked to, and the House put in a thorough state of repair, so that no "loose tile" may, at a future day, interfere with your comfort, and extract something considerable from your pocket.

Executive Housekeepers

Executive housekeepers (ex'e-cu-tive 'house-keep-ers) oversee staff who keep hotels, hospitals, educational institutions, and similar establishments clean, orderly, and attractive. High standards for cleanliness and efficient housekeeping are important for the success of these institutions. Hospital rooms must be clean for the health, safety, and well-being of the patients. Executive housekeepers hire, train, and supervise others to help them in this task. In small organizations, they may be in charge of a staff of two or three workers. In large institutions, they may supervise a hundred people or more.

They may work in motels, resorts, clubs, condominiums, hospitals, nursing homes, retirement homes, or residence halls in schools and colleges. Most often, they work in large hotels. In very large hotels executive housekeepers, also called directors of housekeeping, spend most of their time on administrative duties. They organize housekeeping departments, establish cleaning standards and procedures, and set up work schedules.

They meet with the directors of other departments in the hotel to coordinate activities and schedules. Executive housekeepers hire, train, and supervise their assistants, room attendants, hall cleaners, house persons, laundry workers, linen room workers, wall and window washers, seamstresses, upholsterers, painters, cabinetmakers, and other housekeeping workers skilled in repair and maintenance.

They organize and direct training programs for the staff. They resolve personnel issues and evaluate employee performance. Executive housekeepers inspect rooms for cleanliness and check on other housekeeping tasks to make sure that workers are following proper procedures. They make sure that the work of the housekeeping department falls within the established standards of quality for the hotel.

In some establishments executive housekeepers supervise the staff who set up rooms for conventions, banquets, exhibits, and other programs. Executive housekeepers may be in charge of ordering housekeeping supplies and equipment. They may help in the selection and purchase of new furniture. Some executive housekeepers work with interior decorators to develop new decorating schemes for rooms and public areas.

The housekeeping staff tells the executive housekeeper about damage and equipment that needs repair. Executive housekeepers conduct their own inspections and make recommendations on the relocation of equipment and the use of space. They also develop procedures on how to inform the engineering/maintenance department when its services are needed. They keep records on personnel, payroll, expenses, and housekeeping activities.

They keep management informed about repair work, improvements, personnel difficulties, and expenditures. They submit a yearly budget for review and approval. In small or medium-sized hotels and motels executive housekeepers may share cleaning chores with the staff. Executive housekeepers who work in small institutions may also be in charge of other operations such as maintenance and ordering food. Housekeepers in hospitals make sure that patients have safe, clean rooms.

They follow strict procedures for cleanliness and sanitation to prevent the spread of infection and disease. They develop education programs for the staff and teach them how to handle contaminated wastes safely. They teach them safety techniques and the correct way to use supplies and equipment. Staff development is important, and executive housekeepers make sure staff education programs are ongoing.

As a rule, working conditions are very good. Executive housekeepers work in clean, attractive, comfortable buildings. Although they usually have their own office, they spend a good part of their time in other parts of the establishment. They may be on their feet most of the day.

Hours and Earnings

Most executive housekeepers work forty to forty-eight hours a week. Housekeepers in resort hotels or motels may work longer hours during the tourist season.

Executive housekeepers who live in the hotel have regular hours, but they may be on call at any time. Executive housekeepers in hospitals, schools, and other institutions usually work forty hours a week.

Salaries depend on the experience and education of the housekeeper and the size and location of the establishment that employs them. According to the Bureau of Labor Statistics, in 2000, executive housekeepers averaged $27,830 a year. Salaries ranged from $7.80 to $20.60 an hour, or $16,220 to $42,850 a year. Some hotels may offer executive housekeepers and their families room and board and use of hotel services. Other benefits are paid vacations, sick leave, hospital insurance, and tuition assistance for continuing education.

Education and Training

At one time the job of executive housekeeper went to the person in the housekeeping department with the most experience or seniority. Today, many executive housekeepers have a college degree or have taken advanced courses in business and management. Executive housekeepers will have better employment opportunities if they have at least a two-year college degree or have taken some advanced courses in hospitality.

They should have a basic knowledge of accounting to keep records and to prepare budgets and reports. A knowledge of labor laws and safety regulations is important. Executive housekeepers may also find it helpful to study sociology, psychology, economics, personnel management and human relations, and communications. Purchasing, interior design, maintenance and inventory control, basic computer skills, and rules and procedures for sanitation and health may be beneficial.

Universities, community colleges, and vocational schools offer programs that prepare students for institutional housekeeping. These schools may also offer continuing education courses for those already in the field. The Educational Institute of the American Hotel & Lodging Association, and the International Executive Housekeepers Association, offer home-study courses and certification programs for executive housekeepers.

High school students should take business courses, along with courses in general science and chemistry. Many students get a head start in housekeeping careers by working part time for hospitals, hotels, motels, resorts, and summer camps.

Professional Societies

International Executive Housekeepers Association (IEHA) is a professional organization with over 6,000 members who work in commercial, institutional, or industrial settings. The International Executive Housekeepers Association has established educational standards for the profession and sponsors certificate and college degree programs. IEHA also offers numerous self-study courses. Executive housekeepers may also belong to the American Hotel & Lodging Association (AH&LA). AH&LA is a professional organization with over 13,000 property members who work in the hotel and lodging industry. AH&LA also offers educational services and a certification program for executive housekeepers.

Personal Qualifications

Executive housekeepers should be intelligent, poised, and friendly. They should be flexible, patient, and have a sense of humor. They should have good organizational skills and should be able to manage several tasks at once. Executive housekeepers should be able to communicate well with management, staff, the public, and suppliers. Occupations can be adapted for workers with disabilities.

Persons should contact their school or employment counselors, their state office of vocational rehabilitation, or their state department of labor to explore fully their individual needs and requirements as well as the requirements of the occupation. Executive housekeepers work in hotels, motels, condominiums, and clubs. Others work in hospitals, nursing homes, and health-care centers. Some work on college campuses or in schools. Many of the best jobs are in large cities and their suburbs. A growing number of resort hotels and motels in less populated places also offer excellent opportunities.

Some developers are building new hotels and resorts. These establishments may create opportunities for executive housekeepers who are new to the field. The demand may be offset by the limited number of positions available-since each hotel requires only one executive housekeeper. Economy hotel chains often hire one executive housekeeper to oversee several hotels in the chain. Most jobs will open as workers retire or find work in other occupations. Some large establishments require prospective executive housekeepers to have a college degree in hotel and restaurant management. Others may hire experienced workers who have taken courses in the field. Job seekers may start as floor supervisors, executive assistants, or assistant heads of housekeeping departments.

They learn housekeeping procedures and policies and gain experience managing a staff. In time they may take over the management of the housekeeping department during the late afternoon or evening shift. Smaller hotels and motels may hire executive housekeepers who lack a formal education in the hospitality field but have worked their way up through the ranks.

However, even in these small institutions, the trend has been to look for candidates who have taken some hospitality or business courses. Job seekers may find opportunities at newly built hotels, resorts, hospitals, nursing homes, or other establishments. The International Executive Housekeepers Association maintains a referral service for job seekers and for employers looking for candidates.

Since executive housekeepers already hold the top position in their profession, further advancement may be limited. In many small establishments executive housekeepers may become assistant managers. With more education and experience they may be promoted to become managers. Executive housekeepers in many institutions are considered part of the top management team.

CHAPTER 7

PRODUCT DEVELOPMENT

The Tourism Product Development Strategy has identified, amongst other issues, the need to focus on coastal destination product development and marketing, in order to widen access into relatively untapped foreign tourist- source markets. These markets' primary choice for leisure holidays are coastal destinations, but they also need to be offered unique additional activities associated with wildlife, heritage and culture, when viewed within the African context. Similarly, the largest sector of domestic tourists also seeks coastal destinations. It is for this reason of sustainability that the Tourism Product Development Strategy identified the need for a parallel and inter-related coastal tourism product development strategy.

SUSTAINABILLE PRODUCTION

Identification of Key Tourism Destinations, Nodes and Sites for Public Sector Funding: Each of the spatial destinations referred to above have been analysed with a view to identifying the key nodes and sites for inclusion with the Tourism Product Development Strategy. The following provides a summary of the findings and recommendations for each of the proposed destinations:

Maputaland / St Lucia (Umlalazi River Mouth to Kosi Bay): Linkage to Wildlife:

Product Description: Approximately 250 kilometres of mostly pristine beaches, including the Greater St. Lucia

Wetland Park World Heritage Site, and stretching up to Kosi Bay. Wildlife areas of Mkhuze, Phinda, Tembe, Ndumu, Pongola, Itala and Hluhluwe- Umfolozi are included within this destination. These all contribute to the potential of creating a world-class unique coastal and wildlife destination and tourism cluster within the Kingdom of the Zulu.

Potential Market: Due to the potential uniqueness and product clustering of this destination, it is proposed that the focus of tourism product should be on high quality / mid to high income / low-density tourism, offering exclusive individual beach and wildlife destinations with sensitive environmental management. This should be targeted at 'A' income domestic and foreign tourists arriving by scheduled flights and connecting local charters to airstrips in close proximity to the destinations. Spinal corridor routes need to be able to provide close road vehicle accessibility without spoiling the perception of the exclusiveness of the destination.

Public Funding

Due to the advanced stage of the Lubombo Spatial Development Initiative, and the knowledge that KZNTA have been involved in the processes to date, research into the individual projects and infrastructural needs of this destination has not been undertaken. However, it is recommended that this destination should continue to be considered as a key priority for tourism product development in the province by KZNTA.

Product Description: Approximately 50 to 70 kilometres of superb beaches and coastline, which has already been identified as probably having the best prospects for re-attracting higher-income domestic and international tourism, given careful environmental management. With this stretch of coastline acting as the Primary Attraction, it is proposed that the development of Secondary Attractions and Visitor Facilities that will complement the destination as a major domestic and international coastal resort be investigated. This is closely identified as being linked to the Kingdom of the Zulu through providing direct linkage and accessibility to the proposed Zulu Heritage and Cultural Trail.

Potential Market: It is proposed that the focus of tourism product should be on medium to higher quality / lower middle to higher middle income / medium to high-density tourism, offering a range of beach resort style individual destinations. These should be targeted at 'A'and 'B' income domestic and foreign tourists arriving either direct by road or air via Durban, with international scheduled and/or charter flights for the foreign market.

Durban

Product Description: At present Durban can probably best be described as a confusing tourism destination as it does not appear to have a single focused image or reputation as to what its Primary Attraction is to both the domestic and foreign tourist markets. This can probably be attributed to the transitionary phase that it finds itself emerging from and is therefore not suggested as being the fault of any institution, but rather as a result of its circumstances.

At present it appears to be marketing itself as offering everything to everyone, which is resulting in other more focused competitive destinations gaining market share of the available tourist-source markets. Due to the strategic importance of Durban within the context of tourism growth within KwaZulu-Natal, it would be arrogant to be able to suggest the complete solutions.

Therefore the focus has been on providing an indication as to the direction that could be taken. The key stakeholders should then be tasked with more fully developing an agreed vision, image and strategic agenda for its implementation. Some fundamentals that are recommended to be addressed are as follows:

— As the principal gateway into the Kingdom of the Zulu, surely it needs to conform more to this branding. It is suggested that Durban has the potential of being the most significant African City as a coastal tourism destination. Its key access points, such as the airport, harbour and main roads, need to project more of an image in keeping with the branding of the Kingdom of the Zulu.

— What is Durban's Primary Attraction, and what are its Secondary Attractions and Visitor Facilities that could differentiate it from its competition? Again, coastal tourism is the dominant tourist-source market; therefore it is recommended that focus be given on developing its beach product to be more in keeping with the needs of its primary tourist-source markets.

— What should the focus be in identifying the tourist-source markets? Having identified what and where its target markets are, Durban will then need to identify what it must offer to meet the needs of those tourists.

If Rio de Janeiro is used as a comparative example, its beaches have names such as Copacabana; Ipanema; and Flamenco, which have all created international brand images in their own right. Durban offers North, South and Battery as some of its names, none of which conjure up an exotic image in keeping with the Kingdom of the Zulu. Umhlanga is perhaps the one exception and has certainly been able to develop its own image.

Hotels along the beachfront should be able to provide a degree of exclusiveness for use of certain areas of the beach. The hotels could then start to build on an image linked to their particular beach areas. The proposed beach areas could be operated under a concessionary arrangement to local qualified and trained SMME's, who then contract with the 'linked'hotels, in order to provide beach, refreshment and entertainment facilities for exclusive use of the hotel residents and other paying guests.

The tourist and visitor want to use the beach to its fullest extent, Durban needs to provide facilities in keeping with these needs and not create barriers between what the customer wants and what is available, otherwise the customer will certainly go where his / her needs are being met. The development of the Point Waterfront will go along way to providing a significant Secondary Attraction and range of Visitor Facilities, which will boost the Primary Attraction of the beach. Hopefully attention will be paid to its 'Zuluness' being in keeping with the Kingdom of the Zulu.

Yachting, boating and cruise tourism, together with related water sports and other activities, are significant opportunities that appear to be underestimated within Durban. Significant similar facilities are being developed to the north and into Mozambique which, if not linked to Durban, could pose serious competitive threats to the Durban tourism market within the next 10-years. Durban has the potential to act as the 'southern anchor' marina for the East African Seaboard. Such a development needs to be encouraged and supported, if not driven, by the appropriate Durban authorities.

All of the above are fundamentals that can contribute towards Durban maximising its tourist numbers, as well as their length of stay. However, in addition to the above, attention needs to be given to adding significant Secondary Attraction and Visitor Facilities within the Heritage and Culture and Wildlife sectors. Next to the beach, theses two sectors are identified as being the next highest on the visitors' list of things they want to do. The nature of the majority of Durban's tourists, usually for reasons of time and/or cost, means that they cannot travel northwards to enjoy the Game Reserves and Zululand areas. The opportunity therefore exists to provide such facilities within closer proximity to the Durban Beachfront. In this regard, support is recommended to the following product development:

— Cato Manor

— Inanda 'Freedom Valley'Community Tourism

— Inanda Tourism Route

— Isithumba
— KwaMashu
— Mkhambathini Game Reserve
— Shongweni Community Tourism
— The Valley of 1000 Hills
— Township Tourism
— Zulu Heritage and Cultural Interpretive Centre

Potential Market: Durban offers a range of medium to high-density beach tourism facilities in the high, medium and lower income range for both domestic and foreign tourists. It is proposed that it has the spatial capacity to maintain such a range, provided this is done within a controlled masterplanning environment. It is recommended that Durban needs to consider spatial sub-groupings of mini- destinations that link certain hotel groupings with exclusive beach areas, which can then develop their own market image, which can then be marketed to targeted tourist-source markets.

Product Description: The South Coast, as it has been known historically, comprises approximately 100 kilometres of sandy beaches, bays and lagoons stretching from Scottburgh to the Wild Coast. A variety of activities exist and have potential for further development. These include amongst others, golfing; scuba diving; whale and dolphin watching; and the annual sardine run. This area has been the preferred playground of the South African domestic holiday tourist for many years and has developed according to those needs.

Inland are vast areas of relatively poor rural communities that have received little or no benefit from the coastal tourism corridor. It is proposed that the South Coast be maintained primarily as a domestic tourism destination, due primarily to the affordability of the existing products. The Primary Attraction remains its wide variety of beaches, however, attention needs to be given to the standard and type of visitor facilities in keeping with the need and demands of the targeted domestic tourists, particularly the newly emerging Gauteng tourist market.

Inland, the potential exists to develop adventure, eco and cultural tourism products that would add value to the coastal destinations and again provide a differentiation with other destinations in KwaZulu-Natal and elsewhere.

Potential Market: It is proposed that the focus of tourism product should be on lower to medium quality / lower to higher middle income / medium to high-density tourism, offering a range of beach resort style destinations. These should be targeted at 'B'and 'C'income domestic and foreign tourists arriving either direct by road or air via Durban, with international scheduled and/or charter flights for the foreign market.

Zulu Heritage and Cultural Trail

Two marina / resort developments are in the planning stages for Port Shepstone and Hibberdene, which are considered as having the potential to significantly contribute to re- generating the South Coast as a tourist destination for the domestic market, and in particular the higher-spend tourists from Gauteng. The re-development of the Mpenjati Resort has also been identified, for a number of reasons, including its proximity to the Wild Coast, as a product that could act as a catalyst for the southern part of the South Coast destination.

Product Description: The principal tourism products are sites of scenic, heritage and cultural interest, as well as tourism retail and short-stay accommodation. In addition, a number of dams / nature reserves are frequented by tourists. At present, the area benefits predominantly from domestic tourism, with a limited support from the foreign tourist sector. Pietermaritzburg, the Midlands Meander and Howick were the most popular places visited. Apart from a component of the domestic tourist sector, most visitors appear to use this area as a secondary attraction during their visit to KwaZulu-Natal. It is also proposed that the Southern Drakensberg be linked to this destination cluster, which would include the potential of a 'Lesotho Loop' using Sani Pass, Ramatselisao's Gate and Qachas Nek.

Potential Market: Due to the strategic location of this corridor straddling the N3 with its large number of vehicle-travelling tourists, and even more so, its close proximity to the main tourism destination of Durban, it is proposed that the focus of tourism product should continue to remain on the Secondary Attraction products that will primarily benefit from the 'flow-through' effect of domestic and foreign tourists visiting the provinces' Primary Attractions.

New product should focus on medium to higher quality / lower middle to upper middle income / low to medium density tourism, offering a range of scenic sites; wildlife; and culture and heritage destinations. These should be targeted at the 'A' and 'B' income domestic and foreign tourists travelling along the N3, or staying in Durban; the north-coast; or the south-coast, who would be looking for day-trips or short-stay added components to their holiday. Whilst this area is not considered as a Primary Attraction within the Province, it is very much this type of product that will contribute towards lengthening the stay of the tourist during their visit to KwaZulu-Natal.

The continued support of development of the Mkhambathini Game Reserve, with its linkage to the Valley of 1000 Hills, is considered as being the single most significant tourism development within this destination. The ability of providing an appropriate wildlife attraction in such close proximity to Durban would not only provide a strong differentiation for KZN's primary destination of Durban, it would also significantly enhance further tourism development opportunities within these rural areas between Durban and Pietermaritzburg.

Thukela Gateway

— linkage to the Ukhahlamba

— Drakensberg World Heritage Site;

— Wildlife;

— Heritage and Culture; and

— Battlefields

Product Description: Most of this area falls within the region of the province currently being marketed as the "Berg, Bush & Battlefields", an initiative jointly being undertaken by the Uthukela and Umzinyathi District Municipalities together with Tourism KwaZulu-Natal.

At present the main reason for domestic tourists visiting the area appears to be linked to the Drakensberg Mountains, for a variety of outdoor pursuits and activities. However, the total percentage of these visitors appears to be less than 10% of the domestic tourists visiting KwaZulu-Natal. The associated wildlife, heritage, cultural and battlefields attract even less visitors at present, according to available research.

With the foreign tourists, again the Drakensberg Mountains proves to be the most popular destination, primarily for the scenery, hiking, mountain climbing and other outdoor activities. The Battlefields were perhaps one of the least supported of the attractions in the area and limited in their contribution to tourism revenue. Demand for wildlife, heritage and culture attractions from foreign tourists is high and it can be assumed that the lack of product within these categories is inhibiting further growth of foreign tourists into the area at present.

One of the key tourism assets of this area is the fact that the N_3, as well as the N_{11}, pass through the northwestern region. As stated previously, these are some of the busiest tourism transit routes in the country. The ability, therefore, to tap into the 'flow- through' effect of these tourists is vitally important in order to grow market share. The proximity to the major KZN tourist- source markets of Gauteng and KZN is also a critical factor in this regard.

Potential Market: It is understood that the area already has an initiative underway for the creation of a "tourism triangle" that will link the Drakensberg Mountains to the province's coastal and wildlife attractions. It is considered that this concept is sound and warrants further consideration. However, it is suggested that a re-alignment of the "tourism triangle" be undertaken taking the following issues into account: It has already been established that the Primary Attraction for the Province is its coastline - this is the area that has the potential to attract the greatest number of tourists, both foreign and domestic.

It has been identified, through market research, that the Primary Attraction within the "Thukela Gateway" destination is the Drakensberg Mountains. It has also been identified through market research, that the next most popular visitor attractions relate to wildlife and Zulu heritage and culture. It is suggested that the main tourist-source markets for the "Thukela Gateway" for the future, will be foreign and domestic tourists that are already visiting the province's coastline, as well as a direct source from the Gauteng and KZN markets. The "Thukela Gateway" area needs to develop more Secondary Attractions and Visitor Facilities in order to strengthen its 'Tourism Clustering' within the area.

In terms of market demand, such attractions and facilities need to be focused on improving the Primary Attraction of the Drakensberg, as well as Wildlife and Zulu Heritage and Culture Secondary Attractions and Visitor Facilities. It is also suggested that the "Battlefields", whilst they may appeal to certain niche-market tourism, on their own they are not considered as a high-ranking secondary attraction in terms of visitor numbers, nor with the low tourism revenue they generate.

However, through the linkage of some of the sites to Zulu heritage and culture, and particularly the story they have to tell being told from a Zulu perspective, it is believed these products can be re-generated into more significant visitor attractions. Particular attention is recommended to the development of wildlife attractions due to the distinct advantage for the foreign tourists of the area being malaria free.

The focus of tourism product within the "Thukela Gateway" should be on medium to higher quality / lower middle to higher income / low to medium density tourism, offering a range of experiential tourism in the Drakensberg Mountains, as well as key secondary attractions in the Wwldlife and Zulu heritage and cultural sectors, initially in close proximity to the N_3. The Thukela Gateway. Linkage of the 'Battlefields' to the Zulu Heritage and Cultural Trail.

Continued support for community-based tourism product development within the Mnweni Valley, and in particular, the proposed Drakensberg Cableway. As well as the proposed Zulu Cultural Theme Park and associated Game Reserve.

INFRASTRUCTURE FOR PRODUCT DEVELOPMENT

Infrastructure has been identified as falling into two categories: Soft and Hard, which have been defined as follows:

Soft Infrastructure

This relates mainly to intellectual, managerial, administrative and technical support that KZNTA is recommended to provide on a variety of tourism initiatives that have been identified; as well as market research and other marketing related issues. The focused objective is on maximising tourist numbers into KZN and the resultant tourism revenue yield, in accordance with the goals and targets contained within the Tourism Strategy 2000. It is considered that the 'soft infrastructure' issues recommended below are a pre-requisite in bringing about sustainability for the recommended core product development issues. In certain cases they will be followed by hard infrastructure implementation.

Soft Infrastructure Required for Tourism Development- Management of Perceptions of Personal

Safety - Market Research of Tourist-source Markets & their 'Needs' - Management of the 'Supply Chain' - Accessibility - Destination Marketing - Accessibility - Ease of Access - Accessibility - Tourism Route / Access Development within each Destination - Product Development Monitoring Database & Prioritisation Model

Hard Infrastructure

Hard Infrastructure relates more to the physical built requirements that are necessary to facilitate 'ease- of- access' for tourists once they are in the province, as well as making it easier and simpler for the tourists to remain in the province for longer periods, due to the expanded range of tourism product in keeping with the tourists' needs. Hard Infrastructure also relates to physical built requirements that are necessary to be facilitated in order to make areas more attractive to potential investors looking at specific tourism product development.

Hard Infrastructure Required for Tourism Development: - Richards Bay Cruise Ship Passenger Terminal - Local Airstrip Upgrades at Dukuduku; Hluhluwe; & Manzangwenya - Coastal Marina Developments (Durban; Port Shepstone; Hibberdene) - Ukhahlamba-Drakensberg Access Road Upgrades - Continued Implementation of Infrastructure within the Lubombo SDI - Margate Airport Upgrade - South Coast Marinas

The following projects have been identified for prioritisation for Private Sector Investment within the context of the Tourism Product Development Strategy. In most cases these projects are seen as joint Public / Private sector initiatives due to their recommended strategic importance in achieving the goals and targets set with the Tourism Strategy 2000:

- Coastal Marina/Resort Developments - Dolphin Coast - Coastal Resort Development - King Shaka International Airport - Lubombo SDI / Greater St. Lucia Wetlands Park - various product developments - Margate Airport

Upgrade - Point Waterfront - Richards Bay Cruise Ship Passenger Terminal - South Coast - Mpenjati Resort

TOURISM DEVELOPMENT PROJECTS

The following have been identified and are recommended as the most significant development projects in terms of attaining the various goals and objectives as contained within the KZNTA Tourism Strategy 2000, as well as having been formulated within this Tourism Product Development Strategy. Detailed project sheets, containing preliminary proposals, budgets and timeframes for implementation, for each project are included as Annexure 2 of this document:

Zulu Heritage and Cultural Trail

On the basis that a single project will not provide the strategic intervention necessary to act as the catalyst for the formation of the Zulu Heritage and Cultural Trail, it is recommended that the minimum implementation should focus on 2 strategic components, namely -

— To enable 'ease-of-access' onto the trail from the major tourist-source markets - Durban and north and south coast in close proximity to Durban.

— To provide world-class attractions, which will draw the tourists 'through' the Zulu Heritage and Cultural Trail once they have been initially attracted to it.

LSDI / MAPUTALAND / ST. LUCIA

With the objective of focusing on 'accessibility' and increasing the number of tourists and tourism revenue, the development of the proposed Cruise Ship Passenger Terminal at Richards Bay is recommended as the key infrastructure project. Redirection of world tourism, as well as demand for new destinations in the Cruise Ship industry, support this initiative as a key strategic intervention for increasing tourists into the Greater St. Lucia Wetlands Park, Wildlife and Cultural attractions of this destination, as well as providing a 'word-of-mouth marketing tool for future tourism visits.

Dolphin Coast

With the objective of focusing on the need to develop world-class coastal resort developments along the KZN Coastline, the recommendation is for support for the development of the proposed Coastal Resort Complex on the Tongati River, as identified by the Ilembe District Municipality. The underlying logic for this selection revolves around the fact that this stretch of coastline has already been identified as being probably the most suitable for such a development. The recent favourable news regarding the development of the King Shaka International Airport also provides the motivation for resort development in close proximity to this key transportation hub. The development of such a resort is also considered as having the potential to act as a catalyst for further resort and similar development along this stretch of coastline.

Durban Beachfront

The preparation of a Strategic Tourism Development Plan for Durban Beachfront, including the Point Development and Marina's to the south and up to and including Blue Lagoon / Umgeni River Mouth to the north, in terms of the recommendations previously contained.

Valley of 1000 Hills

This spatial tourism attraction has the ability to provide accessibility for tourists into rural areas associated with eThekweni Unicity; uGungundlovu and King Skaka District Municipalities. It can provide a range of scenic, wildlife and cultural attractions in close proximity to the major tourist-source market of Durban, thereby adding to the value of Durban as tourism destination, with the potential of growing tourist numbers and their length of stay, but perhaps most importantly providing a strategic intervention for developing tourism into the previously disadvantaged areas around the periphery of Durban. The key projects are the continued development of Community / Cultural Tourism in Inanda with a linkage to, and including, the Valley of 1000 Hills Tourism Routes, plus the establishment of the Mkhambathini Game Reserve.

Ukhahlamba-Drakensberg

A number of Access Road Projects have been identified, which are proposed as being grouped together as a single project for implementation. The development of the Mnweni Valley is considered as the key development initiative that will act as a catalyst for further tourism related development within the area. In particular the development of the proposed Drakensberg Cableway is considered as being the most significant tourism draw-card and major attraction that could be developed within the area.

South Coast

Two principal aspects inform the recommendations for key development projects for the South Coast. The first is motivated as a strategic intervention to improve upon attracting (or rather re- attracting) the higher-spend category of domestic tourists, as well as foreign tourists. The concept of one or more coastal resort complexes, incorporating waterfront and/or marina facilities, are considered as being the type of primary attraction that could help rejuvenate the South Coast tourism industry.

Such developments could act as the necessary catalyst to increase tourist numbers, which in turn could leverage new investment for upgrading of existing private sector tourism assets, as well as new developments. It is understood that the Ugu District Municipality are presently engaged with two such development initiatives at Port Shepstone and Hibberdene. It is recommended that it may be necessary to initially step back from these 'project driven' initiatives and first re-evaluate two key components:

— What would the market demand be for such developments?

— What would be the best locations along the stretch of coastline between Port Edward and Scottburgh for such developments?

In this regard, it is recommended that investigations should include historical research as to why yacht owners previously relocated mooring of their boats to Cape Town from Durban. With the recent opening of new marinas at Richards Bay and Maputo, as well as the ability to sail / cruise further north along the East African coastline, plus the additional proposed marina facilities in Durban, whether, with additional mooring capacity along the South Coast, these boat owners would consider relocating back to KwaZulu-Natal.

The second is motivated by the recognised need to open up 'inland-tourism' into the rural areas of the South Coast hinterland. Whilst a number of individual projects within these areas have been identified during this assignment, it appears that 'individual' is just what they are. The recommendation is to develop some form collective framework whereby the variety of individual projects focusing on culture, heritage, wildlife and the scenic beauty of the area, is brought together with the objective of creating a single inland destination image.

CHAPTER 8

TOURISM MARKETING AND PLANNING

One of the most important steps a business or community can take to improve the effectiveness and efficiency of their marketing efforts is to develop a written marketing plan. This plan will guide their marketing decisions and assist them in allocating marketing resources such as money and personnel time. The plan should include:

— the overall business objectives-what you want to accomplish;

— an assessment of the market environment-what factors may affect your marketing efforts;

— a business/community profile-what resources are available,

— market identification (segmentation)--the specific groups or clientele most interested in your product;

— the marketing objectives for each segment;

— the marketing strategies (or mixes) for different markets you target-the best combination of the 4 Ps (product, price, place, promotion) for each segment;

— an implementation plan-how to "make it work;"

— the marketing budget-how much you have to spend; and

— a method for evaluation and change.

Businesses, agencies, and communities should develop overall objectives and regularly monitor their progress.

The objectives should provide guidance for all decisions including finances, personnel and marketing. They should be quantitative and measurable statements of what the business or community wants to accomplish over a specified period of time.

Business objectives are often stated in terms of sales, profits, market shares and/or occupancy rates. Communities frequently establish objectives relating to such things as increasing the number of tourists, developing or changing their image, facility and activity development, cooperation among tourism related businesses and increasing length of stay and local expenditures. It is important that the objectives be reasonable given the market conditions and the firm's or organization's resources. Establish a few reasonable objectives instead of a long, unrealistic "wish list." This is especially true for new businesses or communities which do not have much experience in tourism development and/or marketing.

MARKETING PLAN

The next step in developing a marketing plan is to assess the impact of environmental factors (such as economic, social and political) on present and future markets. Changes in these factors can create marketing opportunities as well as problems.

Demographics and Lifestyles

Changing demographics and lifestyles are having a major impact on R/T participation. An assessment of these trends is important to understand how they will likely affect your business or community. Some of the important trends that bear watching:

— population growth and movement;

— rural community growth compared to metropolitan areas;

— number of adult women employed outside the home;

— the number of households is growing, especially non family and single parent households, but family size is decreasing;

— the impact of two wage earner households on real family income;

— the number of retired persons with the financial ability to travel;

— better health to an older age; and

— continued aging of the population.

Economic Conditions .

Overall economic conditions can have significant impacts on recreation and tourism markets. A marketing strategy that is effective during periods of low unemployment rates may have to be significantly adjusted if unemployment increases. Businesses and communities should monitor and assess the likely impact of factors such as unemployment rates, real family income, rate of inflation, credit availability, terms and interest rates. Consideration should also be given to the prices of complementary products, such as lodging, gasoline and recreation equipment.

Laws and Government Actions

As a complex industry, tourism is significantly affected both positively and negatively by laws and by actions of governmental agencies. For instance, rulings on such things as liability issues or decisions regarding building and health codes may change or possibly prevent the construction of a proposed facility. If a public facility changes the prices of its services, this could affect the service offerings of associated private businesses. These actions may have both positive and negative effects on the marketing efforts of the business and community. To avoid wasting valuable resources it is important that R/ T businesses, agencies, and communities continually monitor and evaluate governmental actions.

Technological Developmentsgy

Technological developments are increasing rapidly. New recreation products, such as all-terrain vehicles and wind surfers, provide new ways for people to satisfy their recreational preferences. New production technologies and materials offer recreation and tourism businesses ways to reduce costs and improve the quality of their products/ services. Advances in telecommunications have and will continue to create new promotional opportunities. Technological innovations, in relation to jobs and the home, have resulted in increased leisure time for many people.

Competition

Businesses and communities must identify and analyze existing and potential competitors. The objective of the analysis is to determine the strengths and weaknesses of the competition's marketing strategies. The analysis should include the competition's:

— product/service features and quality;

— location relative to different geographic markets;

— promotional themes and messages;

— prices; and

— type of customer they are attracting.

Too many communities attempt to market themselves as tourist destinations without accurate information about their resources (facilities, services, staff), image, and how well their customers are satisfied. Without this information, it is difficult to make other decisions in the planning process. Included should be such things as recreational and entertainment facilities, cultural and historic sites, overnight accommodations, restaurants, shopping opportunities, special events and activities, staff size, and transportation. Each item of the "inventory" should also be assessed in terms of quality and availability.

MARKET SEGMENTATION

Recreation and tourism businesses and communities often make the mistake of attempting to be all things to all people. It is difficult, and risky, to develop marketing strategies for the mass market. Strategies designed for the "average" customer often result in unappealing products, prices, and promotional messages. For example, it would be difficult to develop a campground that would be equally attractive to recreational vehicle campers and backpackers or promote a property to serve both snowmobilers and nature oriented cross country skiers. Marketing is strongly based on market segmentation and target marketing. Market segmentation is the process of:

— taking existing and/or potential customers/visitors (market) and categorizing them into groups with similar preferences referred to as "market segments;"

— selecting the most promising segments as "target markets;" and

— designing "marketing mixes," or strategies (combination of the 4 Ps), which satisfy the special needs, desires and behavior of the target markets.

There is no unique or best way to segment markets, but ways in which customers can be grouped are:

— location of residence---instate, out-of-state, local;

— demographics---age, income, family status, education;

— equipment ownership/use---RV's, sailboats, canoes, tents, snowmobiles;

— important product attributes---price, quality, quantity; and

— lifestyle attributes---activities, interests, opinions.

To be useful, the segment identification process should result in segments that suggest marketing efforts that will be effective in attracting them and at least one segment large enough to justify specialized marketing efforts. After segments have been identified, the business or community must select the "target markets," those segments which offer them the greatest opportunity. When determining target markets, consideration should be given to:

— existing and future sales potential of each segment;

— the amount and strength of competition for each segment;

— the ability to offer a marketing mix which will be successful in attracting each segment;

— the cost of servicing each segment; and

— each segment's contribution to accomplishing overall business/community objectives.

It is often wiser to target smaller segments that are presently not being served, or served inadequately, than to go after larger segments for which there is a great deal of competition. Marketing objectives which contribute to the accomplishment of the overall business objectives should be established for each target market. Objectives serve a number of functions including:

— guidance for developing marketing mixes for different target markets;

— information for allocating the marketing budget between target markets;

— a basis for objectively evaluating the effectiveness of the marketing mixes (setting standards); and

— a framework for integrating the different marketing mixes into the overall marketing plan.

The target market objectives should:

— be expressed in quantitative terms;

— be measurable;

— specify the target market; and

— indicate the time period in which the objective is to be accomplished.

For example, increase the number of overnight stays by people from the Chicago market over the next two years by five percent. Remember, rank objectives by priority and carefully evaluate them to ensure that they are reasonable given the strength of the competition and resources available for marketing.

MARKETING STRATEGY

The marketing strategy, or mix, should be viewed as a package of offerings designed to attract and serve the customer or visitor. Recreation and tourism businesses and communities should develop both external and internal marketing mixes for different target markets.

External Mix

The external marketing mix includes product/service, price, place/location, and promotion.

Product: Earlier we said the principal products that recreation and tourism businesses provide are recreational experiences and hospitality. The factors that create a quality recreational experience often differ among people. A quality experience for one skier might include an uncrowded, steep slope. To another it might be a good restaurant and a chance to socialize.

Decisions on what facilities, programs and services to provide should be based on the needs and desires of the target market(s). They should not be based on the preferences of the owner/manager or necessarily on what the competition is providing. Recognize that a recreational/tourism experience includes five elements: trip planning and anticipation; travel to the site/area; the experience at the site; travel back home; and recollection. Businesses should look for ways to enhance the quality of the overall experience during all phases of the trip. This could be accomplished by providing trip planning packages which include maps, attractions en route and on site, and information regarding lodging, food and quality souvenirs and mementos.

Recreation and tourism businesses should also view their service/product in generic terms. Thinking of products/services in this manner helps focus more attention on the experiences desired by customers and also the facilities, programs and services that will produce those experiences. For example, campgrounds are the business of providing recreational "lodging" not just campsites to park an RV or set up a tent. Marinas should provide recreational "boating" experiences, not just slippage.

Location and Accessibility/Place: Too many tourism businesses and communities fail to recognize their role in improving travel to and from their areas. They focus instead on servicing the customer once they arrive at the site/community. A bad experience getting to or leaving an R/T site can adversely affect a person's travel experience. Ways to help prevent this include:

— providing directions and maps;

— providing estimates of travel time and distances from different market areas;

— recommending direct and scenic travel routes;

— identifying attractions and support facilities along different travel routes; and

— informing potential customers of alternative travel methods to the area such as airlines and railroads.

Potential businesses should also carefully assess alternative locations for:

— distance and accessibility to target markets;

— location of competitors with respect to target markets;

— modes of travel serving the area; and

— other attractions and activities that might induce travel to the area.

Pricing: Price is one of the most important and visible elements of the marketing mix. When setting prices it is important to take into consideration all of the following:

— business and target market objectives;

— the full cost of producing, delivering and promoting the product;

— the willingness of the target market to pay for the product or service you provide;

— prices charged by competitors offering a similar product/service to the same target market(s);

— the availability and prices of substitute products/ services (for example, campgrounds, motels, and bed and breakfast are all substitutes for lodging);

— the economic climate (local and national); and

— the possibility of stimulating high profit products/ services (such as boats) by offering related services (such as maintenance) at or below cost.

When establishing prices, R/T businesses should give attention to pricing strategies which may encourage off season and non-peak period sales, longer stays, group business, and the sale of package plans (combination of room, meals, and recreational facilities).

Promotion: Promotion provides target audiences with accurate and timely information to help them decide whether to visit your community or business. The information should be of importance and practical use to the potential or existing visitor and also accurate. Misrepresentation often leads to dissatisfied customers and poor recommendations. Don't make claims you cannot live up to.

Developing a promotional campaign is not a science with hard and fast rules. Making decisions regarding which type or combination of promotion types to use (personal selling, advertising, sales promotions, or publicity) is not always easy. If, however, you follow a logical process and do the necessary research, chances for success will be improved. It will be necessary to make decisions regarding:

— Target audience—the group you are aiming at;

— Image—that which your community or business wants to create or reinforce;

— Objectives–those of the promotional campaign;

— Budget—the amount of money available for your promotion;

— Timing—when and how often should your promotions appear;

— Media—which methods (television, radio, newspaper, magazine) will most effectively and efficiently communicate your message to the target audience; and

— Evaluation—how can the effectiveness of the promotional campaign be determined.

Internal Mix

As stated, marketing services such as recreation and tourism differ from marketing tangible products. Recreation and tourism businesses must direct as much attention at marketing to customers on site as they do to attracting them. In this respect, internal marketing is important because dissatisfied customers can effectively cancel out an otherwise effective marketing strategy.

The success of internal marketing is dependent on creating an atmosphere in which employees desire to give good service and sell the business/community to visitors. To create such an atmosphere requires the following four important elements:

— *Hospitality and Guest Relations*—An organization wide emphasis on hospitality and guest relations, including a customer oriented attitude on the part of the owners and managers as well as the employees. If the owner/manager is not customer sensitive, it is unlikely the lower paid employees will be.

— *Quality Control*—A program which focuses on improving both the technical quality (the standards associated with what the customer receives) and the functional quality (the standards associated with how the customer receives the service). All employees who come into contact with customers should receive hospitality training.

— *Personal Selling*—Training the staff in the selling aspects of the property (business) or community. This also includes rewarding them for their efforts. By being informed about the marketing objectives, and their role in accomplishing those objectives, they can help increase sales.

— *Employee Morale*—Programs and incentives aimed at maintaining employee morale. The incentives can be both monetary and non-monetary.

A customer oriented atmosphere usually results in customers that are more satisfied, do less complaining and are more pleasant to serve. This helps build employee morale, their desire to provide good service and their efficiency.

MARKETING BUDGET

Successful marketing requires that sufficient money and personnel time be made available to implement activities comprising the marketing strategy. A marketing budget is a financial plan which shows the total amount to be spent on marketing during different times of the year and how it is to be allocated among alternative activities. Separate marketing budgets should be developed for each marketing mix strategy. The separate budgets should then be aggregated to develop an overall marketing budget.

If the total amount is too great it will be necessary to modify the overall objectives and the target market objectives, narrow down or drop target markets, or adjust marketing mixes. The final budget should be realistic given your objectives. When deciding on a marketing budget, consideration should be given to the job that needs to be done as defined by the objectives.

Basing marketing budgets on some percent of sales or what the competition spends usually leads to over spending or under spending. Decisions should also be based on the costs, projected revenues, and desired profitability of different activities, not just costs alone.

Successful marketing activities will generate additional revenues which can be projected based on the marketing objectives (such as increase off season stay by 5%).

Although budgets should be viewed as flexible plans, every effort should be made to adhere to them. Revisions in the budget should only be made after careful consideration of the likely impact of the change on the marketing mix and accomplishment of your objectives.

TOURISM MARKETING PROGRAM

Step-by-step instructions describe how to inventory attractions, assess current marketing efforts, find existing market research, determine target markets, determine tourist motivators, develop promotional goals, determine campaign themes, find an advertising media, develop public relations and gather the correct data for an evaluation.

Inventory

The first step in developing effective marketing plans is to inventory the attractions a community has to offer tourists. A community must know what it has to offer or sell before plans can be laid for marketing the product. These can include natural, manmade, historical, cultural or ethnic, festivals, special events and recreational attractions.

Current Marketing Efforts

Listing current advertising efforts for all attractions is necessary to assess the present promotional campaign's successfulness, and to develop new campaigns.

Market Research

Market research is an important part of developing a market plan. Several important pieces of information are needed to develop a market plan. These include:

— An inventory of tourist attractions in the area, region, or destination

— Market trends

— Tourist motivations

— Tourist profiles, including expenditures

It helps to review other successful marketing plans, remembering that a marketing plan should meet the individual needs of the area, region or destination for which it was developed. Learning from previous mistakes is a key to developing better programs.

There are two types of research data that can provide this information. The first is primary research gathered through phone calls, surveys, or other interviewing techniques. Secondary data has been compiled by outside organizations. Be careful when using secondary data; confirm the reliability of the source.

Target Market

Trying to appeal to everyone is a common mistake made in marketing. Not everyone looks for the same thing in a destination, and every destination cannot be all things to all people. Target marketing, focusing on a particular segment or segments of the market,allows for a more effective marketing plan. Market research will define the market segments, which will find those tourists most interested in what a community has to offer. Data on past visitors can indicate the type of tourist or the geographic region on which to focus. A target market can be a geographic region, a type of tourist, a combination of the two or any grouping that makes sense.

Tourist Motivators

The fifth step is detemine tourist motivetors. Tourist motivators should be studied once a target market has been defined. Discovering where and why tourists travel is important when focusing advertising. Enticing the tourist to chose a historical destination because of its mystique, or choosing a full-service resort where every need can be catered to requires different motivational factors.

Promotional Goals

Establishing goals provides the basis to determine what a community wants its marketing and promotion program to accomplish. Goals should be well thought out and be measurable, and can also serve as controls. Writing down goals provides directional guidelines. It can be difficult to get feedback on promotional goals, but with specific goals set, an evaluation and feedback plan can be implemented. This will gather the necessary data for the evaluation process, which can determine the successfulness of a community's plans and program.

Campaign Theme

A campaign theme should emphasize the image aimed at tourists in a given area. Remember, always capitalize on the positive aspects in the area, region or destination. Campaign themes should be developed for a clearly defined target market. For example, New Mexico's promotion, "More to Explore... New Mexico USA," targets nonresidents, and capitalizes on the fact that New Mexico is a part of the United States, although many tourists think it is a part of Mexico.

A campaign focusing on New Mexico residents, on the other hand, would emphasize what their home state has to offer. It could incorporate a theme of "Travel Close to Home."

Advertising Media

Determining which advertising media to use should not be done until after the target market is identified. Once the market has been determined, the tourist profile of the target market can be matched to the audience profile of specific advertising media. Most advertising media can provide an accurate profile of their audience.

Public Relations

Public relations can be an excellent way to promote a

community or attraction. Public relations activities are uniquely different from advertising. Advertising is paid, but public relations uses free public exposure to ensure goodwill. Public relations can use radio,television or newspapers. Public relations efforts not only can be used to promote the destination to tourists, but also to promote the community itself. It can help create a feeling of pride in the community by educating the local community about what it has to offer tourists. This can develop a feeling of pride for the residents when they are asked to describe their community to tourists. Instead of seeing tourists as invaders, they will be seen as an economic boost to the local economy.

CREATING AN EVALUATION PLAN

This is the 10th step. An evaluation plan requires detailed planning during the initial stages of a marketing plan. Establishing measurable goals in a marketing plan is the first step in this evaluation. From this step, decide what information is needed to prove or disprove the accomplishment of the goal. If methods to gather the information are established at the beginning, all needed information for evaluation will be available at the end.

One of the most difficult parts of an evaluation is uncovering all the information that is needed, especially if an organized system is not included at the beginning. The second most difficult part is convincing everyone of the importance of such an evaluation. It is the key to the entire marketing plan that says, "Yes, it worked" or "No, it didn't work." An evaluation can show if the wrong audience was targeted or the plan conveyed the wrong message. Evaluation also provides the information needed to improve marketing. Great care should be taken to incorporate an evaluation plan into the marketing plan.

Another important part of an evaluation is the conversion study, which compares the number of inquiries to the number of people who actually visit. The conversion study is conducted by using the list of inquiries generated over the specified time frame, randomly choosing a sample, then performing a follow-up telephone or mail survey. Other information that can be collected along, with a conversion study, when it is determined that the inquiring person has actually visited, is:

— Place of residence

— What time of year visited

— Transportation

— Estimated expenditures during trip

— Purpose of trip

— Would you visit again

These questions help establish a tourist profile. Information that needs to be collected for a proper evaluation of a marketing plan is:

— Advertisement cost

— Advertisement dates

— Number of times an advertisement was run

— Advertisement agency costs (if any)

— Media in which advertisement was placed

— Number of inquiries received from each advertisement

— Request fulfillment costs (mailing costs, envelopes, mailing brochures)

— Follow up information

Gathering this kind of data provides information to determine the effectiveness of advertising. When follow-up information on actual visitation and expenditures is obtained, advertising effectiveness can be further evaluated.

— *Number of Inquiries*—The number of people who requested information through the advertisement.

— *Ad Costs*—The cost of placing an advertisement in the advertising media.

— *Ad Cost Per Inquiry*—Ad cost divided by number of inquiries.

— *Request Fulfillment Cost Per Inquiry*—Request fulfillment cost divided by number of inquiries: includes mailing, brochure, and envelope costs.

— *Ad Agency Fixed Cost Per Inquiry*—Ad agency fixed cost divided by number of inquiries.

— *Total Cost Per Inquiry*—Total costs divided by number of inquiries.

Data collection methods should be decided on and in place before any advertising is done. Thus, all needed information will be available when evaluation procedures start. Suggested advertisement monitoring methods include:

— A phone answering script that determines the caller's name, address, phone and type of information requested.

— Coding advertisements so inquiries received are easily tracked to a specific advertisement.

— Monitoring guest registrations for visitor's points of origin.

OBJECTIVES OF TOURISM MANAGEMENT

A historic town in the United States was practically deserted, raising the question of whether to let the cultural resource continue its natural decline or intervene to restore the site for more intensive tourism. Unfortunately, no old photographs remained from the town's heyday, and experts feared a misrepresentation of the past if restoration was carried out. The state historical society recommended managing the site to permit the town's natural deterioration. Major restorations were rejected in favour of simple shoring and bracing. To accommodate tourism needs, minimal construction activities were recommended including parking, footpaths and signage.

The local historical society, however, recommended that the town be completely restored. It favoured more intensive tourism and was not concerned with philosophical issues and the consequences of intervention. In the end, the town was restored but with doubts remaining over whether the quality, character and authenticity of the site was compromised. Practically, policy decisions are often heavily influenced by economic considerations. A decision on maintaining the values of ancient ruins in relation to the extent to which stabilisation and conservation is carried out may be a function of the funds and personnel available.

Allowing visitors to view a ruin from a distance may be more practical and preferable than the more expensive option of structurally stabilising the site to permit visitor access. In some cases all that may be needed is vegetation control to reduce deterioration. When developing tourism policies at World Heritage sites, the overriding priority is to maintain the form and fabric of the resource. The nomination dossier of a World Heritage site can give guidance to the process of balancing policy and management objectives against tourism needs. These dossiers usually describe a site's features and previous changes in detail and may set out necessary preservation actions. Dossiers are available through each country's State Party and/or through the World Heritage Centre.

Policy Goals

The general nature of policy goals is reflected in a policy statement from the Australia Wet Tropics Management Authority. It says the Authority's purpose is to "provide for the implementation of Australia's international duty for the protection, conservation, presentation, rehabilitation and transmission to future generations of the Wet Tropics of Queensland World Heritage Area, within the meaning of the World Heritage Convention."

While policy goals are general, management objectives set out in detail how a site will be managed. Within the framework of the general policy goals, the objectives spell out desired conditions, reflecting what management wants to maintain and the experiences a visitor would ideally encounter at a site. For example, if a policy goal is to provide local employment opportunities, then a management objective may be to encourage the use of local guides.

If a goal is to maintain a sacred site in a manner ensuring respect and tranquillity, then objectives may include limiting visitation and noise levels. Objectives should be subject to evaluation. They should therefore be specific, quantifiable, have time limits and be stated in clear language so that they can be understood by all those responsible for implementation.

They should be the basis for a standard by which to gauge the performance of site management. For example, at a historical monument, a policy goal may be to support local educational activities, while a management objective could be to increase the number of local schoolchildren who attend the site's educational programme. In this case a quantifiable measure could be the number of school groups that visit the site during the year.

Clearly stated policy goals and objectives provide direction in decision making and responding to change. Constructing a tramway through a wilderness park, building a high-rise modern hotel near a low-lying archaeological site, installing artificial lights at a monument, and increasing helicopter traffic in a national park are all examples of tourism initiatives that World Heritage site managers have had to face.

Clearly documented goals and objectives give direction and provide a historical context for addressing tourism initiatives in a consistent manner. Any new initiative can change a site. Examining initiatives within the context of policies and objectives can help managers determine whether they are within acceptable parameters. If goals and objectives are based on stakeholder needs, and fall within the law and the World Heritage Convention, they can form a solid basis for management decision making.

In addition, activities such as interpretation, promotion, carrying capacity control and monitoring all depend on the direction given by policy goals and objectives. A project in the Carpathian Mountains in Eastern Europe illustrates the need for clearly defined tourism policy goals. An international funding agency assigned a team of experts to write a regional tourism development plan to aid small businesses. Market research suggested a comparative advantage for small-scale accommodations, emphasising natural and cultural attractions.

Some members of the government and business community, however, favoured the rebuilding of large-scale tourism infrastructure from the Soviet era. At the time, no unified national or regional policies for tourism development existed to give direction to and clarify these efforts. The disparity of goals persisted throughout the life of the project.

When the time came to present a final report, the team found it impossible to present strategy and cost recommendations that met the needs of both groups. A forest reserve in Costa Rica whose operational budget is largely based on visitor fees had no clear-cut policies on tourism development until several years ago. A project to build a larger visitor centre met with opposition from some in the administration because they saw the site more as a nature reserve than as a tourist destination.

Others liked the idea and wanted to attract more tourists. While members of the community were against it, people in other nearby communities were in favour of increasing tourism because of the economic benefits it would bring. After months of controversy, the issue was resolved with a consultant's study and dialogue among the different stakeholder groups. With an established process within the reserve's administration to discuss policies and define goals, these conflicts would have been minimised and no doubt resolved without outside help.

Role of Stakeholders

Stakeholders' involvement in setting goals and objectives links a tourism strategy with those who will have an impact on a site now and in the future. Stakeholders can be consulted on a number of management concerns such as infrastructure development and monitoring programmes. Stakeholders usually include government officials, members of the environmental and conservation community, scientists, historic preservation organisations, hotel and tour agency owners, visitors, guides and residents.

Following is a list of stakeholders with suggestions on how they may contribute to developing tourism goals and objectives.

— Park, forestry or archaeological department officials may provide information on past management and visitor issues.

— Guides can offer information on the social and environmental conditions of the site, and their input can bring to light important interpretation issues.

— Guides working for tourist agencies can give advice on their employers' concerns and input on site monitoring needs.

— Community leaders often have concerns and ideas about how tourism will affect local social values and economic development. For example, local leaders may think it necessary to avoid tourism impacts on the main population centre.

— Hotel owners can have a direct influence on tourism development and community interactions. They may be concerned about potential crowding, or coordinating visitor arrivals between the hotel and site management personnel through a reservation system. Hotel owners can also help in the development of interpretation and promotional materials.

— Tour operators will have concerns about visitor comfort and security. They stay apprised of changes in the international travel market and usually have information on user preferences and demand. The value of contacting tour operators to discuss their concerns, potential demand for a site, and possible cooperation on activities such as marketing should not be underestimated.

— Scientists can spell out concerns about significant flora and fauna or historical or archaeological remains. They can suggest ways to protect resources from impacts and offer advice on attracting research grants. Field assistants working directly with scientists can share practical concerns and complementary information.

When developing goals and objectives, libraries and department archives are useful sources of valuable supplemental information, for example on endemic or endangered species of fauna or flora, or on visitor use and impacts on wildlife or archaeological ruins. National tourism and protected area laws and policies including the legal requirements for licensing and taxation can help in setting government policies and in understanding current conditions of tourism development.

Old master plans and the recommendations contained in them are also useful. At Copan, a Mayan World Heritage archaeological site in Honduras, a major international hotel was built even though many had suggested that smaller existing hotels in a nearby town would have been adequate with some minor upgrading. Many unattended ruins were destroyed just because they lay near a new access road to the Copan ruins.

Common interests with stakeholders:

Conflicts with the local community may prevent cooperation in tourism development: For this reason consultation with community members during planning is essential. They may voice concerns that development will bring increased pollution or crime; that tourist traffic may endanger their children; or that tourists will have a negative impact on social conditions, for example by wearing inappropriate dress. They also may fear that the development will not benefit local people, for example that jobs as guides will be given to outsiders.

Consultations may result in actions such as the creation of a tourism development committee or a system for training local guides. Tour operators may be asked to educate their clients to respect community values. A visitor centre may be built some distance away from the village to avoid encroaching on everyday village life.

Environmentalists and conservationists have important concerns over the potential negative impacts of tourism development on natural and cultural sites: Environmentalists involved in the protection of flora and fauna may fear that opening an area for tourism could also invite hunters, or they may voice concern over potential disturbances to nesting birds, for example. Archaeologists might warn against vandalism and other potential damage to ruins and monuments.

Both groups may complain about increased litter, particularly if existing funds are insufficient for garbage collection. Both are likely to press for conditions in which visitors do not feel rushed or crowded, or spend too much time waiting to enter a site. Members of this stakeholder group often complain of a lack of communication with the tourism sector, including both the ministry and private operators.

They may also complain that staff members value tourism development more than educational activities and scientific research. This stakeholder group might wish to persuade site managers to implement an efficient reservation system, to limit access to areas with pristine, fragile ecosystems or to vulnerable archaeological sites, and to mount an education campaign to minimise impacts. They might insist on strict supervision of visitors, especially student science groups. Researchers often advocate the appointment of a science adviser at the site who could promote and manage research.

Agreement could be reached on specific targets for tourism promotion and development.

Tour guides are a valuable source of information and advice concerning conditions affecting the environment as well as the visitor experience: They will point out unsafe trail sections and help ensure that trails are maintained for comfortable walking, as well as alert management to problems of crowding and noise. Guides can inform management when local people use the site for hunting and killing birds and other wildlife. Like the environmentalists and conservationists, guides are usually concerned about the quality of their clients' experience, and will insist that the time it takes to purchase a ticket be kept to a minimum, that congestion on the aecess road to the site be eliminated, and so on.

They may suggest maintaining limits on the numbers of visitors permitted at a site through use of an effective reservation system, and measures such as staggering visits by promoting afternoon tours. A direct telephone or radio connection between site management staff and guides would ensure consistent and effective communication.

Hotel owners and managers usually want a site to provide a broad base of opportunities for different types of visitors: They are also concerned about crowding and littering, the amount of parking at the site entrance, and the presence of persistent beggars and/or souvenir hawkers. As with independent guides, hotels appreciate consistent and reliable communication with site management, perhaps by a specially installed direct phone line. Members of this stakeholder group might ask staff management to develop a reservation system for tours. They would also advocate formation of a tourism advisory committee to meet with the local community about development issues and the needs and preferences of tourists.

Overseas tour operators and ground operators are especially concerned about logistical questions: Will their tour groups have to wait in line behind other tours scheduled at the same time? Will their groups meet up with noisy or inconsiderate groups? Is there enough parking? And, as with other shareholder groups, operators are anxious for a site to be well maintained and safe for visitors, and in the case of natural sites that the wildlife are adequately protected. These stakeholders often advocate efficient reservation systems, good communications and regular maintenance.

A stakeholder advisory group can facilitate the development of policy goals and management objectives: Such a panel provides a mechanism for exchanging ideas and information. The group should draft a written policy or vision statement that can be developed and publicly endorsed. The group could also help to set management objectives, including standards for desired conditions and actions. Practically, stakeholder groups can be engaged in the management process and serve as forums for exchanging views and reaching agreement on tourism issues. If an advisory group is not feasible, some mechanism for exchanging ideas is needed.

This can be as simple as a regular exchange of memos between site management staff and stakeholder groups, to solicit opinions and describe current activities. The process of developing goals and objectives should also take into account the site's uniqueness in relation to other sites with which it competes. Tour operators and other tourism professionals who may be members of the advisory group can be a valuable source of information about a site's comparative advantage over others in the area.

Demand and preferences:

Data about visitors' preferences and demand for a site is essential for establishing objectives: Information on the number of visitors and their likes, dislikes, motivations and expectations will help the planner divide visitors into subgroups of people with similar characteristics, needs and spending behaviours. This information is useful in setting objectives for infrastructure, personnel needs and education and interpretation programmes. Combined with data on tourism markets, the information can be used to develop objectives for attracting certain types of tourists to a site. For example, managers with a policy of boosting local community development might set a goal of attracting tour operators who use local guides.

Numbers of visitors also affect management objectives and infrastructure and facility design: The experience at Liffey Falls in Tasmania illustrates the usefulness of information about visitor preferences when setting management objectives. The Forestry Commission discovered that visitors wanted to see the falls and were not interested in the other available recreation facilities. Knowing this, officials were able to concentrate their efforts and save a considerable amount of money and staff time. At Uluru National Park in Australia, a survey found that most tourists mainly wanted to see and to climb Ayers Rock. Fewer cited experiencing the outback and seeing wildlife as prime reasons for visiting. This information helped park staff to focus their attention on Ayers Rock.

Existing sources can be used to start the process of assessing visitor preferences and demand: Information and statistics from the tourism ministry, protected area staff and tour operators can help provide an idea of current and future demand and the mix of market segments. National tourism officials have information on tourism development and studies or statistics on tourism markets. Statistics and reports from the site staff and tour operators can provide an idea of visitor preferences and demand.

Existing studies from national tourism officials can provide information on the kinds of tourists the government is attempting to attract and the type of tourist expected to visit a site in the future. Interviews with retired parks, forestry or archaeological survey officials may shed light on past management plans and visitation records. Records may include statistics on the number of park visitors, their country of origin and the number of days they spend in the area. Through discussions, officials can help managers identify changes in visitor interests, activities and travel patterns.

A look at tourism development in neighbouring communities can indicate a site's potential demand and show how tourism has affected the economies and social conditions of the community. Local guides and hotel and pen sion owners can provide information on visitor preferences and demand cycles. Also, because they are in constant touch with changes in the international travel markets, they can help in identifying and tracking user preferences and demand, for example, whether visitors travel in tours or organised groups or travel independently. They can provide helpful information for developing infrastructure and interpretation material. Scientists and archaeologists can also share information about visitor preferences and patterns.

Observations, surveys and interviews provide more detailed visitor profiles: Such information on visitors and their interests may be needed to fine-tune management objectives, for example, on crowding preferences or tourists' spending patterns. Observations are qualitative and less exact than surveys and interviews, but they are quick, inexpensive and useful for indicating trends or suggesting targets for an eventual survey or interview.

Observations may include: organisation (group size), forms of transportation, type and amount of equipment, uses of time, maps of where people go and behaviour including languages used and noise levels. Since most people have difficulty analysing their own behaviour and motivations, observations can be a quick and useful technique for monitoring what people actually do.

Surveys are less expensive than face-to-face interviews, can reach a broad range of visitors and can provide valuable quantitative data, which is useful for reinforcing management decisions. However, with surveys communication is only one-way, and they require skills in questionnaire design and data management. They are also less effective than interviews in educating visitors.

Ideally, a combination of methods should be used to determine preferences and construct accurate visitor profiles. Categorising tourists according to preferences and behaviours can contribute to the realisation of a site's goals and objectives. For example, if income generation is a key goal, information should be compiled on variations in spending by visitors. If education of schoolchildren is a priority, they should figure in a survey.

Sites offering multiple activities:

At large sites, whether cultural, natural or mixed, management objectives may vary from one area to another within the site: People visit attractions with different expectations. Serious bird-watchers may come to a site to see an endangered species in a seldom visited, quiet environment. At the same time, local tourists may come to the site to see an archaeological ruin and to picnic or socialise with family members, and they may be not be particularly bothered by noise levels.

The Recreation Opportunity Spectrum (ROS) has proven a useful tool for setting objectives for these different visitor experiences. The ROS is a means of describing how tourism and recreation will be managed for different areas within a site. It works under the assumption that certain activities fit best in certain physical areas, for example, wilderness trekking fits better in relatively untouched forests than in farming areas.

It also assumes that activities should provide visitors with certain experiences or opportunities, such as solitude or adventure. For example, on Tanzania's Mt. Kilimanjaro, planners created a hiking zone where numbers were restricted and visitors could expect infrequent contact with other walkers. An even more restricted wilderness zone allowed only very minimal use. All huts and other permanent facilities were removed, only tent camping was permitted and the highest degree of solitude was provided, the area being free of permanent human presence.

To separate different activities, the ROS system uses preestablished categories called opportunity classes that match the site's physical resources with the activities best suited to them. For example at a mixed site, one area may be managed for archaeological tourism and another for bird-watching. Opportunity classes set out the desired conditions for the different areas and provide guidelines for management objectives.

These include guidelines on tourism/recreation activities and infrastructure development. In the United States, parks and forest services use a set of predetermined opportunity classifications including primitive, semi-primitive non-motorised, semi-primitive motorised, rural and modern urban.

.   Other countries have designed their own categories to fit the physical realities of their particular region. Each. classification entails management standards and desired conditions that fall within a site's policy goals. The information needed to identify and establish opportunity class areas is drawn from background information on policy goals, existing legislation and stakeholder concerns. Each opportunity class encompasses a set of experiences and activities for the visitor.

Each has guidelines for ecological, social and management conditions. For example, an area classified as primitive might be maintained as a wild stretch of terrain where vehicles are not permitted and where visitors are highly likely to experience physical challenge and solitude. Because such areas appeal to tourists seeking a wilderness experience, appropriate activities may include sports such as backpacking and canoeing.

Moving across the spectrum, rural areas within a site, for example farmland, can have varying degrees of human impacts and contact with other people is to be expected. Here activities such as wilderness backpacking would probably not be appropriate. On the other hand, birdwatching along rural roads may be an appropriate tourist activity. Infrastructure development for different activities is closely related to an area's opportunity class.

The ROS system matches infrastructure objectives with the experiences on offer. For example, if an objective is to provide an isolated wilderness experience, only basic infrastructure would be needed. In populated rural areas, infrastructure may be more sophisticated, with accommodations that fit visitors' expectations.

BIBLIOGRAPHY

Mann, Mark for Tourism Concern, "The Good Alternative Travel Guide: Exciting Holidays for Responsible Travellers", Earthscan, London, 2002.

Mann, Mark, "The Community Tourism Guide: Exciting Holidays for Responsible Travellers", *Earthscan*, London, in association with Tourism Concern, 2000,

Mann, Mark with Ibrahim, Zainem, "The Good Alternative Travel Guide", *Earthscan*, London, for Tourism Concern, 2002.

Manning, T., "Indicators of tourism sustainability", *Tourism Management*, 1999.

McCarthy, John, "Are Sweet Dreams made of this *Tourism in Bali and East Indonesia*", IRIP, 1995.

Middleton, Victor T.C. & Hawkins, Rebecca, "Sustainable Tourism: a marketing perspective", Butterworth Heinemann, Oxford, 1998.

Neale, Greg, "The Green Travel Guide", *Second Edition*, Earthscan in association with The Sunday Telegraph, British Airways & WWF-UK, April, 1999.

Newson, Carey, "Tourism without traffic: a good practice guide", Transport 2000, London. Oversize G155, 2001.

Pendleton, Tom, "Young People and Bicycle Touring", Velo City '01 Conference, Edinburgh, Glasgow, September 2001.

Pizam, Abraham & Mansfield, Yoel, "Consumer Behavior in Travel and Tourism", The Haworth Hospitality Press, Binghampton, New York, 1999.

Prideaux, B., "The role of the transport system in destination development", (Elsevier) *Journal of Tourism Management* 21 (1), December, 1999.

Taylor, Gordon D, "Tourism and Sustainability - Impossible Dream or essential objective?", *Travel and Tourism Research Assocation*, Canada, 1991.

WTTC, World Tourism Organisation (WTO) & Earth Council, "Agenda 21 for the Travel and Tourism Industry: Towards environmentally sustainable tourism", *WTO*, Madrid, 1996.

INDEX

Adverse Tourism 149
Advertising media 298
American Hotel & Lodging
    Association (AH&LA) 266

Benefit Cost analysis (B/C) 42

Civil aviation industry 23
Coastal Tourism 160, 184
Community-based tourism 28
Computer Reservation
    Systems (CRSs) 15
Computer-based instruction
    26
Convention and Visitor
    Bureaus (CVBs) 151
Cooperation mechanisms 21
Crime-ridden environment, 28

Economic distortions 1
Economical objectives 2
Economist Intelligence Unit
    (EIU) 17
Environmental education 60
Environmental Management
    Systems (EMSs) 154
Environmental Tourism 149
E-ticket selling, 16
Evaluation Plan 299
External marketing mix 291

Fair Employment Practices
    Agencies (FEPA) 243

Formal orientation 246
Furniture, Fixtures, and
    Equipment (FFE) 226

Growth, Employment and
    Redistribution (GEAR) 10
General Agreement on Trade
    in Services (GATS) 163
Global Distribution Systems
    (GDSs) 15
Globalization, 238

Hospital housekeeping
    operations, 248
Hospitality Industries Training
    Board (HITB) 26

International Labour
    Organisation (ILO) 162
Information infrastructure 30
Input-output model 54
Internal Mix 294
International Civil Aviation
    Organisation (ICAO) 13
International consumer
    advocacy organisations
    156
International Environmental
    Education Programme
    (IEEP) 54
International Executive
    Housekeepers
    Association (IEHA) 268

International tourism 168
International travel markets 311

Judicial assistance agreements 173

Localisation 8
Lodging industry 232

Market Segmentation 289
Marketing budget 295
Multi-channel distribution networks 26

National Councils for Sustainable Development (NCS) 151
Non-governmental organisations 2

On-the-Job Training (OJT) 251

Performance evaluation 241
Preemployment procedures 244

Responsible Care programme 156
Rural tourism 6

South Tyrol agro-territorial system 35
Spatial Development Initiatives (SDIs) 22
Step-by-step instructions 296
Strength, Weakness, Opportunities and Threats (SWOT) 18

Tourism Information Centre (TIC) 5
Tourism information infrastructure 29
Transfrontier Conservation Areas (TFCA) 23
Transport infrastructure 13

Value-added qualit 7

Waste management infrastructure 147
World Tourism Organisation (WTO) 10